T. S. Eliot's Ascetic Ideal

# Costerus New Series

*Editors*

C. C. Barfoot (*Leiden University*)
Michael Boyden (*Uppsala University*)
Theo D'haen (*Leiden University,* and *Leuven University*)
Raphaël Ingelbien (*Leuven University*)
Birgit Neumann (*Heinrich-Heine-Universität Düsseldorf*)

VOLUME 225

The titles published in this series are listed at *brill.com/cos*

# T. S. Eliot's Ascetic Ideal

*By*

Joshua Richards

BRILL
RODOPI

LEIDEN | BOSTON

Cover illustration: Wendeltreppe - Stock image. Credit: alexander_h_schulz. Photo ID: 489345630.

Library of Congress Cataloging-in-Publication Data

Names: Richards, Joshua, author.
Title: T. S. Eliot's ascetic ideal / by Joshua Richards.
Description: Leiden ; Boston : Brill Rodopi, 2020. | Series: Costerus new series, 01659618 ; volume 225 | Includes bibliographical references and index.
Identifiers: LCCN 2019026528 | ISBN 9789004372580 (hardback) | ISBN 9789004375826 (ebook)
Subjects: LCSH: Eliot, T. S. (Thomas Stearns), 1888-1965--Knowledge--Asceticism. | Eliot, T. S. (Thomas Stearns), 1888-1965--Knowledge--Mysticism. | Asceticism in literature. | Mysticism in literature.
Classification: LCC PS3509.L43 Z82457 2020 | DDC 821/.912--dc23
LC record available at https://lccn.loc.gov/2019026528

Typeface for the Latin, Greek, and Cyrillic scripts: "Brill". See and download: brill.com/brill-typeface.

ISSN 0165-9618
ISBN 978-90-04-37258-0 (hardback)
ISBN 978-90-04-37582-6 (e-book)

Copyright 2020 by Koninklijke Brill NV, Leiden, The Netherlands.
Koninklijke Brill NV incorporates the imprints Brill, Brill Hes & De Graaf, Brill Nijhoff, Brill Rodopi, Brill Sense, Hotei Publishing, mentis Verlag, Verlag Ferdinand Schöningh and Wilhelm Fink Verlag.
All rights reserved. No part of this publication may be reproduced, translated, stored in a retrieval system, or transmitted in any form or by any means, electronic, mechanical, photocopying, recording or otherwise, without prior written permission from the publisher.
Requests for re-use and/or translations must be addressed to Koninklijke Brill NV via brill.com or copyright.com.

This book is printed on acid-free paper and produced in a sustainable manner.

# Contents

Introduction: The Ideal    1

1   Grounding    8

2   Interrogating    20

3   Integrating    40

4   Bridging    61

5   Pining    86

6   Dramatizing    113

7   Embracing    134

Conclusion: Summing    168

Bibliography    171
Index    180

INTRODUCTION

# The Ideal

"[S]ome of us feel intensely the charm of the ascetic ideal," so writes T. S. Eliot's professor J. H. Woods (Woods *Practice and Science* 31). From his earliest poems and book reviews until his masterwork in *Four Quartets*, T. S. Eliot was enthralled by an ideal of asceticism, with, in his own words, "ardor, selflessness, and self-surrender" ("The Dry Salvages" v.22). Eliot acquired this ideal primarily from his readings on mysticism, religious philosophy, and psychology in graduate school at Harvard. Whether in early parodies or a whole-hearted embrace later in life, the ascetic ideal forms a consistent undercurrent throughout Eliot's work.

As might be expected, the origin of the ascetic ideal in Eliot's work is not simple to delineate. Eliot does not often speak of "asceticism" in his poetry—the word appears only twice in his final *Collected Poems*, and one of those occurrences is in French,[1] but ideas of self-renouncement and an interest in mysticism are obvious enough even to casual observation. However, this is not a lurking and murky theme for psychoanalytic criticism to investigate; Eliot thought systematically about asceticism which was also integrated into his personal spiritual practices. In his 1933 essay "The Modern Dilemma," Eliot asserts, while defending a supernatural religion, that

> As the sense of sin depends upon the supernatural, so from the sense of sin issues the ascetic life. The ascetic ideal is essential to Christianity. [...] The benefit of monasticism is not only for those individuals who have the vocation for that life; it is also in the ideal of life that it sets before those whose lives are in the world. For Christian asceticism is a matter of degree; and every life, in so far as it is Christian, is ascetic: in self-abnegation, self-discipline, and the love of God. Exceptional austerities are for exceptional men; for ordinary men, the practice of prayer and meditation and the daily battle against the distractions which the world offers to the mind and the spirit. The ascetic ideal—and asceticism is of course far more than a mere *doing without*—seems to me implied in the Summary of the Law.
>
> *Prose* IV.813.

---

1  "*Lune de Miel*" 16 and the note to *The Waste Land* 309. All poetry citations are to *The Poems of T. S. Eliot* but are referenced by line number.

© KONINKLIJKE BRILL NV, LEIDEN, 2020 | DOI:10.1163/9789004375826_002

The conclusion is startling. Eliot asserts that the ascetic ideal is implicit in the "golden rule" of Matthew 7:12, which is the core of all Christian morality. As central as this idea appears to have been, Eliot's expositions of the ascetic ideal are almost never so direct. The primary reason, as the above quotation suggests, is that he consistently believes that the word "asceticism" would not, to his readers, convey the fullness of meaning that he intends. Generally, Eliot seems to prefer some combination of words such as "discipline" and "purgation." Consider his comment in "Religion without Humanism" (1930): "For the modern world [mysticism] means some spattering of indulgence of emotion, instead of the most terrible concentration and *askesis*. But it takes perhaps a lifetime to realize that [the great mystics] really *mean what they say*. Only those have the right to talk of discipline who have looked into the Abyss" (*Prose* IV.39). *Askesis* is the transliterated Greek word at the root of English's asceticism. While it is complex, this ascetic ideal, as absorbed from Eliot's personal background and education, is present in various forms through his work in a way that is surprisingly consistent.

Since Eliot tends to define the ascetic ideal by multiple words, it is reasonable to ask whether there is a single concept of asceticism in Eliot's work or multiple ones. Many of the authors whom Eliot read, such as Woods, suggest there is a unified one. However, even in Eliot's early prose, several very disparate definitions are quoted in his own words: Paul Elmer More defines "askesis, [as] a *formula* to be imposed upon him from above" (*Prose* I.407). While in "Durkheim," asceticism is described parenthetically as the "gain of power through suffering" (*Prose* I.422). Even in the works of the same author, the ascetic ideal may possess seemingly divergent definitions. Within the space of half a page, Evelyn Underhill, one of the most enduring influences on Eliot, defines asceticism as "the slow and painful completion of conversion" and, by a quotation from Richard of St. Victor, "self-simplification" (Underhill 246). Yet, Underhill would insist that the concept is a single entity and expands the scope of asceticism to include the dark night of the soul. I will not bury the reader at the outset with a theological excursus to prove the inherence of all these definitions; rather, I will treat these various aspects of the ascetic ideal with the understanding that to Eliot they ultimately did cohere, even if he struggled to express how. Additionally, more detailed delineations will be provided in Chapters 1 and 4.

Although Eliot's Unitarian upbringing provided fertile soil for philosophies of self-denial, the ascetic ideal began taking root in recognizable form when he studied mysticism during his Harvard years. The ideas of discipline and purgation encountered there lasted through his life, even if they were not always embraced. I will, as such, examine Eliot's involvement with his ascetic ideal

THE IDEAL                                                                                    3

chronologically and focus on how it was derived from his education on mysticism. Since many of these works on mystical philosophy are arcane in every sense, I do quote more expansively than usual to provide the reader with the proper context. While such an approach could risk anthologizing, these are important sources for Eliot's thought, and it seemed better to err on the side of excess than leave the reader hunting for a rare tome. In addition, I have avoided biographical and psychoanalytic speculation as a rule; it is not my purpose to peep into the confessional. I have, also, not treated the Eastern sources as they have already been studied extensively, most fully by Cleo McNelly Kearns.

The first chapter is a detailed exposition of Eliot's encounter with mystical philosophy. A set of note cards extant in Harvard's Houghton library details an extensive reading list on an array of subjects including mysticism. It appears that the bulk of the cards date from 1909; Eliot likely utilized this prior study during his research for his paper on primitive religions. These works, referred to as his mystical readings throughout, formed the foundation of his knowledge on the subject, and Eliot would return to not only the ideas within the books but the authors themselves throughout his life.

The second chapter is an examination of Eliot's earliest poetry in light of this recent education, often with references to works, such as psychological studies, which would not be enduring influences. Eliot employs the trope of the ascetic saint, which he distorts to caricature, as a means of interrogating the ascetic ideal. In "Prufrock," the psychological profile of the convert and the suffering saint are merged into an ironic character modeled on the characters of Jules Laforgue. In the two saint poems, "Sebastian" and "Narcissus," Eliot explores the pathological excesses of ascetic practices as he portrays the failure of the ideal of sainthood.

In the ten years before his conversion, Eliot's engagement with the ascetic ideal splits. There is a public engagement through his prose and a private one through his poetry. Each interacts with different aspects of the ascetic ideal found in his readings in mysticism.

The third chapter shows how the ascetic ideal manifests in his early prose. As his interests in impersonality, the literary tradition, Classicism as well as Royalism and Anglo-Catholicism deepen, a distinct undertone of asceticism to these ideas gradually interlinks them as his thought proceeds organically toward his famous Classicist, Royalist, Anglo-Catholic pronouncement in the "Preface to *For Lancelot Andrewes*" (Prose III.513). The essays "Tradition and the Individual Talent" and "The Function of Criticism" form the core of this analysis.

The fourth chapter is a theoretical exposition of the most complex aspects of Eliot's ascetic ideal. Triangulating between Eliot's readings on mysticism, his dissertation on F. H. Bradley, and his 1926 Clark Lectures, I explore the interconnection between sin, isolation, and an absent λόγος; one of the purposes of ascetic purgation in Eliot's mystical readings is to allow the self to expand to a larger, communal existence from sin-induced isolation. This forms the theoretical background for the examination of the poetry in the following chapter.

The fifth chapter examines "Gerontion," *The Waste Land*, and "The Hollow Men" in light of this triad of sin, isolation, and an absent λόγος. As in the third chapter where disparate themes slowly coalesce, so too do these three aspects of ascetic failure become more intimately connected until, in "The Hollow Men," they are so unified as to be indistinguishable.

The lack of an extended discussion of *Ash-Wednesday* or the *Ariel* poems may seem an odd omission from this study. While performing the preliminary research for this study, I had a similar expectation. On detailed examination though, *Ash-Wednesday* and the early *Ariel* poems showed very little engagement with the ascetic ideal and very few connections with the mystical readings. There are promising passages in the poem: the entire concept of turning, the dismemberment of the bodies in *Ash-Wednesday* ii, and the suggestion of some kind of ladder of spiritual experience in *Ash-Wednesday* iii. However, with a few exceptions, these surface appearances of the ascetic ideal are the totality of *Ash Wednesday*'s 's involvement. The concept of turning is an image of conversion and not asceticism, the ideas of dismemberment are purely an elaboration on Ezekiel, and, shockingly, the stairs in *Ash-Wednesday* iii are *not* an allusion to some particular paradigm in the mystical readings except as a gesture to the standard imagery of a mystical experience.[2] Upon further consideration, the relative absence of the ascetic ideal should not be a surprise; asceticism is, as Evelyn Underhill says "the long completion of conversion," and so it makes sense that a poem discussing the first stage, conversion, would not be overly involved in the second, purgation (Underhill 246). The most detailed and theologically orthodox of the authors on mysticism tend to take conversion for granted. Underhill, for instance, only devotes only one of her book's seventeen chapters to the topic, which she elides with the awakening of the

---

2  "The mystic, as we have seen, makes it his life's aim to be transformed into the likeness of Him in whose image he was created. He loves to figure his path as a ladder reaching from earth to heaven, which must be climbed step by step. This *scala perfectionis* is generally divided into three stages. The first is called the purgative life, the second the illuminative, while the third, which is really the goal rather than a part of the journey, is called the unitive life, or state of perfect contemplation. We find, as we should expect, some differences in the classification, but this tripartite scheme is generally accepted" (Inge *Christian Mysticism* 9). Cf. Underhill 130–2.

THE IDEAL

mystical consciousness.[3] In short, though they are very religious poems, the ascetic ideal is not strongly present in *Ash-Wednesday* or the *Ariel* poems.

The sixth chapter focuses upon how Aristophanic structures derived from Francis Cornford are used to dramatize the ascetic ideal in Eliot's earliest plays. Plays by Aristophanes are, according to Eliot's reading, really debates between philosophical principles; both *Sweeney Agonistes* and *Murder in the Cathedral* follow this formal, Aristophanic structure and so exhibit this philosophical debate structure. In both instances, the victorious principle in the debate is the ascetic ideal. While *Sweeney Agonistes* is incomplete, the evidence from the epigraph suggested that Eliot considered a world-denying theme in opposition to the crude materialism presented by the title character. In *Murder in the Cathedral*, Eliot dramatizes not only Thomas's ascetic refusal of the worldly tempters but the dark night of the soul, the purification of the will. The later plays, written at the same time as the *Four Quartets*, are not considered in this chapter as they reflect that stage of his interest in asceticism rather than these earlier dramatic texts.

The final chapter establishes how Eliot, having slowly espoused the ascetic ideal up through his conversion, wholeheartedly portrayed, particularly in the last three of the *Four Quartets*, the doctrines and dogmas of the most orthodox and Anglo-Catholic authors from the mystical readings, particularly those of Evelyn Underhill and W. R. Inge. Although there are only a few direct quotations from these authors which he read so many years before, Eliot recasts their ideas in his own words, which shows how deeply integrated his ascetic ideal had become.

There are some prior works of Eliot criticism whose approach might seem similar, and it is necessary to contrast them from the present analysis.[4] The most obvious is the book by Eloise Knapp Hay. This work, *T. S. Eliot's Negative Way*, though, is over thirty years old and was written without access to Eliot's letters, juvenilia, or any collected prose. These would be enough reasons for a reconsideration by itself, but Hay's "negativity" is by no means the same as the ascetic ideal presented here. Her definition fluctuates depending on the period studied, a fact that Hay herself alludes to rather awkwardly at the start of her chapter on *Four Quartets* (Hay 153). For instance, in her discussion of the *1920* poems, Hay's "negativity" seems to mean a Baudelaire-like contemplation of

---

3  Cf. Underhill 213–38.

4  A doctoral thesis by Manish Popat on a similar topic to mine was submitted to the University of Warwick in 1996; however, this work has yet to be digitized, and the University of Warwick library has proven unwilling to lend the item. Dr. Popat was personally contacted, but she was unable to provide a digital or hard copy.

the sordid aspects of life; while in "East Coker," it refers to the *via negativa*. The single term hides a variety of disparate meanings and creates a false air of continuity. Hay's vague conception of apophasis stands contrary to the nuanced, technical portrayal of asceticism and purgation found in Eliot's own reading and writing.

Yet, there are more technical and recent studies on Eliot's mysticism. Donald Childs' monograph *T. S. Eliot: Mystic, Son and Lover* is perhaps the closest to my own; however, there are a number of important differences in our approaches. Childs' monograph is focused strongly on the biographical and philosophical implications of mysticism, of which asceticism is only a portion, and he does not always consult the works that Eliot read personally. So though our work may seem similar, there is little overlap between Childs' study and this one.

Generally, works examining mysticism and asceticism in Eliot have focused primarily on *Four Quartets*. Paul Murray in his impressive 1991 work *T. S. Eliot & Mysticism* considers only those poems and, again, does not generally use the sources that Eliot himself read. Additionally, his work is thematically organized, and so the ascetic ideal is only discussed in "East Coker," although it is clearly present in the other Quartets as well. Nonetheless, his ideas on mysticism in *Four Quartets* are still very relevant and will be considered in the final chapter. In her 1995 study *Language Mysticism*, Shira Wolosky devotes a chapter to what she calls the "linguistic asceticism" found in Eliot. Like Murray, Wolosky only examines *Four Quartets* and, indeed, seems far more interested in Beckett and Romanian-born poet Paul Celan to whom she devotes the next four chapters. Nonetheless, her consideration of asceticism in terms of aphasia and apophasis is intriguing, if, perhaps, anachronistic in terms of Eliot's own conceptions.

There have been authors interested in tracing mysticism and asceticism in Eliot's early works. In her article "'New Mysticism' in the Writings of May Sinclair and T. S. Eliot," Rebeccah Neff charts the evolution these themes in Eliot's work as, perhaps, deriving from May Sinclair's. While containing some interesting sources for possible allusions, the article is forced to admit that "[b]y the time Eliot read Sinclair's *Dark Night* in 1924, the [antagonistic dualism between the spiritual and bodily self] was already a consistent element of his own poetry" (Neff 91). Neff's article is not able to provide concrete evidence that Eliot encountered Sinclair or her work before 1917 after the ascetic ideal is clearly present in Eliot's poetry. Thus, it seems more likely that Eliot acquired his taste for mysticism elsewhere and simply liked Sinclair's employment of the theme. Additionally, Neff overstates the similarities between Sinclair's mysticism of immanence which embraces of sensual pleasures as a component of the mystical experience and the distinctly apophatic mysticism of *Four Quartets*.

THE IDEAL

Her description of Sinclair's *Dark Night* has more in common with D. H. Lawrence than T. S. Eliot. Michael Malm's article analyzes Eliot's use of mysticism in his prose works, although this article was written before the advent of the *Collected Prose*. Malm does briefly treat asceticism but only in its incarnation as intellectual discipline (Malm 117–8). This is, though, a fascinating application, and his argument will be taken up again in the chapter on Eliot's early prose. Henry Michael Gott in his recent work *Ascetic Modernism in the Work of T. S. Eliot and Gustave Flaubert* provides a deeply theoretical discussion of asceticism in Eliot's early poetry, although his focus is largely on *The Waste Land*. His definition of asceticism is emphatically nonreligious in nature, and he insists that asceticism is "a quality of the text itself" (Gott 6). Obviously, his work has little intersection with the line of argumentation pursued here.

The fullest treatment of Eliot's engagement with the mystical tradition is Barry Spurr's 2010 study of Eliot's Anglo-Catholicism in *Anglo-Catholic in Religion*—a well-researched, though largely historically-focused, monograph. Primarily geared to understanding the works written after his conversion, Spurr's study devotes little attention to Eliot's earlier poems. Eliot's education in mysticism receives only a brief treatment (Spurr 22–25). Spurr recognizes the interest in the "expressions of orthodox Christian mysticism" and correctly differentiates this from the occult but concludes that this had no lasting influence, even while quoting Eliot's discussions of mysticism into the 1950's (Spurr 23). Nonetheless, Spurr's work is useful for charting the larger zone of the Anglo-Catholic faith during the latter part of Eliot's life and showing the historical context of the poems written after his conversion.

CHAPTER 1

# Grounding

The origin of Eliot's interest in and conception of the ascetic ideal stems from two sources: his mother and his education in mystical theology at Harvard. While I focus primarily on the latter's more tangible sources for the ascetic ideal, it would be imprudent to ignore completely his mother's on his ideas of self-renunciation, despite the temptation of biographical speculation. Charlotte Eliot was deeply religious and wrote numerous poems for newspapers and publications like *The Christian Register*.[1] Several dozen are preserved in a scrapbook now held in Harvard's Houghton Library, but it is difficult to know which ones, if any, date from Eliot's formative years. However, a handwritten note by Henry Ware Eliot beneath her poem "Theodosius and St Ambrose" states that "an engraving of this episode hung in my mother's bedroom ever since I can remember.[2] I believe it was from a well-known painting" (note to "Theodosius and St Ambrose").[3] The most germane stanza of that particular poem reads:

> The Heaven's peace descending fell
> Upon his heart and all was well.
> Though the old wound might throb again,
> In memory of former pain,
> 'Twas as a goad that spurs the soul
> To nobler deeds, to self-control.
> Like him, through suffering alone
> May we for evil wrought atone.
> "Theodosius and St Ambrose" 65–72.

The ascetic moral of this stanza is obvious, and this is not an isolated incident.[4] Unfortunately, the most that can be said is that an ascetic ideal was

---

1  Cf. Skaff 20–1.

2  Cf. Srivastava 3.

3  There are quite a number of possibilities for the painting. While Alessandro Magnasco's would be the most interesting option, it could as easily be the rendering by Pierre Subleyras, Anthonis van Dyck, Camillo Procaccini, or a more obscure artist. Attempts to identify the painting in existing pictures of his mother's room have, as yet, been unsuccessful.

4  Cf. her poems "The Vision of St Francis" and "The Present Hour." The latter is notable for its statement: "Purge from thy heart all sensual desire; / [l]et low ambitions perish in the

GROUNDING

9

important to his mother, though to what degree this transferred to Eliot himself is unclear.

The evidence for this primal influence does exist in one of Eliot's early poems, "A Fable for Feasters." The poem ends jokingly with the monks turning to asceticism after the ghostly disappearance of the abbot:

> But after this the monks grew most devout,
>> And lived on milk and breakfast food entirely;
> Each morn from four to five one took a knout
>> And flogged his mates 'till they grew good and friarly
>>> "A Fable for Feasters" 89–92.

Obviously, this is an early work which seems saturated with irony, and thus, there are clear limits to what can be judiciously concluded from the appearance of the ascetic ideal in "A Fable for Feasters." However, I believe the following can be safely maintained. First, Eliot encountered the ascetic ideal before his education in Eastern mysticism. This poem was, according to Hayward's notes, written in 1905—seven years before his education in Eastern religions in 1912 (*Poems* I.1070–1). Thus, it is not exclusively an idea that Eliot acquired from his reading in Eastern religions. Second, that Eliot associated asceticism with being devout or at least thought others would, if the poem is taken sarcastically. Third, that Eliot was not attempting merely to please his devout family as, according to Valerie Eliot's introduction, he never mentioned the poems to his family until long after their publication (Valerie Eliot qtd. in *Poems* I.1067). Fourth, and perhaps most tenuously, the poem presents a movement from riotous physical excess to an ascetic spirituality by means of a supernatural revelation, and given the title, it appears that Eliot is presenting, even if it is rather tongue-in-cheek, a warning against bodily excess as it is a "Fable *for* Feasters" and the lack of definite article may indicate a wider applicability. *Aesop's Fables* is mentioned by name, and so the didactic implication of fable in the title seems likely ("A Fable for Feasters" 46). Given the poem's humorous tone, how seriously the moral is to be taken is unclear; however, it is sufficient for my purposes here that Eliot would think to posit such an ascetic ideal as a moral, even in jest.

---

fire / [o]f Higher aims. Then, as the transient dies, / [t]he eternal shall unfold before thine eyes" ("The Present Hour" 42–8).

An early association of the evil in human nature and particularly in the physical body can also be seen in an anecdote that Eliot relates to Mary Trevelyan:[5]

> When I was a very small boy, I was given a tricycle or velocipede: a beautiful shiny japanned and nickelplated affair, with brake, bell etc., and was riding it proudly up and down the pavement, under the eye of my nursemaid, when an odious small boy who lived a few doors away, who wore a kind of frilly blouse, sidled up and said ingratiatingly: "Mother says I may ride your velocipede if I let you blow my whistle." That aroused my first disgust with human nature.
> "Letters to Mary Trevelyan" 19th December 1944.

Obviously, Eliot is telling this story nearly fifty years after the fact; however, it must have made an impact on him to have recalled it so late in life. In the postscript to the letter, Eliot added that "I would as soon have used his toothbrush as blown his whistle. But I know a man who thinks nothing of using somebody else's sponge" ("Letters to Mary Trevelyan" 19th December, 1944). The intriguing part of this little story is Eliot's final comment on "disgust with human nature." It is not clear if the disgust was with the little boy's behavior or revulsion at bodily contact. The postscript hints at the latter. This is emphasized by Eliot in the next letter to Mary Trevelyan, dated 2nd January 1945, where he asserts that "No, I didn't blow the whistle, and he didn't ride the velocipede. I never spoke to him again" ("Letters to Mary Trevelyan" 2nd January 1945). Nonetheless, this implies at least some association of fallen human nature with the human body. This connection is highlighted by another, earlier letter to Mary Trevelyan where, on an entirely different topic, he writes "but there is something else which I can't get to the bottom of, disgust, horror, physical nausea, the <u>nightmare</u> of evil" ("Letters to Mary Trevelyan" 24th June 1944). Again, there is the conflation of human nature with both physical disgust and disgust with the physical. It appears that the bodily had some association with moral evil in Eliot's mind when he was young.

Whatever inclination to ascetic thought Eliot had early in life, these influences seem to have primed him for a deeper involvement with the ascetic ideal. This was not a simple thing, though. Eliot was interested in a more formal, philosophical idea of asceticism than these earliest reflections display. In the passage from "Religion without Humanism" quoted in the introduction, Eliot references a more formal definition of mysticism than what he takes others to

---

5  I am grateful to the Eliot estate for access to these letters, and I will not speculate on why Eliot decided to tell these stories to Mary Trevelyan.

GROUNDING                                                                    11

mean. His comments in his 1926 Clark Lectures indicates that he thought systematically about mysticism and asceticismeven before his conversion:

> I wish to linger a little over this twelfth-century mysticism, not because we are interested in mysticism, but because we cannot get away from it. There is always some type of mysticism about, whether that of Mr. Russell, or Mr. Lawrence, or Mr. Murry; the number of types is limited, and it is possible and useful to distinguish them.
>
> *Prose* 11.651–2.

This implies that Eliot thought systematically about mysticism and suggests that a cavalier approach to the ascetic ideal would be ill-advised. Now, I have mentioned that asceticism was related to mysticism; however, this is not precise. Asceticism was, according to Eliot's reading, a *component* of mystical experience. There is a classical, three-step mystical journey seen in works like the *Cloud of Unknowing* and the more historically influential *Theologia Germanica*, an anonymous work of 14th century German mysticism. Evelyn Underhill posited an idiosyncratic five-step process. In both of these schemes, purgation is the second step. As will be proven, Underhill becomes one of the most enduring influences on Eliot's ascetic ideal as well as a personal friend, and her definition, complex as it is, will be the one employed in this study generally.

For Underhill, *askesis* is the soul's "attempts to eliminate by discipline and mortification all that stands in the way of its progress towards union with God [...] [; it is] a state of pain and effort"; it is a result of the soul's awareness "for the first time of Divine Beauty" and "by contrast its own finiteness and imperfection, the manifold illusions in which it is immersed, the immense distance which separates it from the One" (Underhill 205). She divides this further into two aspects:

> "No one," says another authority in this matter,[6] "can be enlightened unless he be first cleansed or purified and stripped." Purgation, which is the remaking of character in conformity with perceived reality, consists in these two essential acts: the cleansing of that which is to remain, the stripping of that which is to be done away. It may best be studied, therefore, in two parts: and I think that it will be in the reader's interest if we reverse the order which the *Theologia Germanica* adopts, and first consider Negative Purification, or self-stripping, and next Positive Purification, or character-adjustment. These, then, are the branches into which

---

6  *Theologia Germanica* xiv [Underhill's Note].

this subject will here be split. (1) The Negative aspect, the stripping or purging away of those superfluous, unreal, and harmful things which dissipate the precious energies of the self. This is the business of Poverty, or Detachment. (2) The Positive aspect: a raising to their highest term, their purest state, of all that remains—the permanent elements of character. This is brought about by Mortification, the gymnastic of the soul: a deliberate recourse to painful experiences and difficult tasks.

UNDERHILL 247.

This two-fold definition of self-purification and self-simplification forms is the functional core of the ascetic ideal evinced throughout Eliot's work.

Yet, ascetic purification, though a component of mysticism, does have two additional implications which were gleaned from elsewhere in Eliot's studies in mystical theology. The first implication is that without ascetic preparation, mysticism is likely to end in pathological behavior rather than spiritual insight. This can be seen, for instance, in Eliot's portrayal of failed saints. The second implication is more abstruse as it is rooted in the Christian Neoplatonism seen in Eliot's education in mysticism. The purpose of asceticism, *i.e.* purgation, is the dissolution of the selfish aspects of the character, and this is necessary not only to communion with the Divine but with other souls. Without ascetic preparation, humans are incapable of having any substantial interaction with other beings. Eliot's reference to the ascetic ideal underlying the golden rule in "The Modern Dilemma" suggests his absorption of this communal aspect of the ascetic ideal (*Prose* IV.813). This idea stems from combining the belief that sin severs the link between the soul and the Divine λόγος with the Stoic understanding that mankind's collective participation in the λόγος allows meaningful communication with others. Together with Underhill's composite definition, these ideas collocate to form the ascetic ideal that Eliot acquired through his education in mysticism and theology, which influenced him throughout his life. While that is the core of the ascetic ideal for Eliot, the origins of it in his reading need to be detailed.

Eliot's education in mystical theology is recorded in the archive at Harvard's Houghton Library on sixty index cards. While a partial list of the books from these cards has been published for over thirty years, these have been all but ignored by scholars.[7] Childs' *Mystic, Son and Lover* represents the most thorough employment, and he discusses only three of the over thirty works on the list.[8]

---

7  Gordon's 1977 biography *Eliot's Early Years* has an appendix dedicated to the cards.
8  William Skaff briefly discusses the readings, but some of his conclusions are unconvincing (Skaff 39, 42).

GROUNDING

13

Since this education is the foundation for the ascetic ideal, an understanding of this archival source is key to this study. To ease the dry exposition of minutiae, I have avoided burdening this summary with hosts of bibliographic derivation.

The notecards comprise sixty-nine three-by-five-inch index cards, of which the last nine are blank. While most of Eliot's notes from his coursework are contained in ledgers labeled by course and date, no such identification accompanies the cards. The notes are written primarily in pencil and are uneven in nature as some seem to record content, others bibliography, and still others seem to synthesize ideas. For an example of the latter, Eliot refers to Romantic and Classical mysticism with regards to W. R. Inge's *Christian Mysticism*, terms the author does not employ ("Notecards" 1). The notes on the cards are also distinctly macaronic; Eliot read works in French and also took notes on some of these works in French as well. Additionally, there is some record of process: the final notecard has what appears to be a book list with check marks ("Notecards" 60). Even compared to the other items held among the restricted material in Eliot's archive in Harvard's Houghton library, these notecards are rarely accessed, according to the librarians I encountered, and are not included in the *Collected Prose*, and this study will not have exhausted the interpretive and historical opportunities offered by this neglected archival store.

Since the contents of these cards which record of Eliot's education on mysticism, asceticism, and theology, represent a significant part of this study, let me briefly introduce the various works and provide some terminology for how they will be referenced. The books discussed on the cards can be roughly divided into five categories—these divisions are my own as Eliot's notes do not categorize them. The bulk of the books are roughly concerned with mysticism, theology, and religious philosophy. For ease, I refer to these as the mystical readings. Additionally, I have subdivided these into two further categories: the orthodox mystical readings and the skeptical mystical readings based on whether they tend to treat mysticism as a genuine religious experience or, for the skeptical, as a psychological illness or at least a symptom of spiritual morbidity. Interestingly, there are no books focusing on Eastern mysticism among the notecards. The third category is his reading on primitive religions; the fourth on pre-Socratic Greek Philosophy; the fifth focused squarely on abnormal psychology with little discussion of mysticism.

The orthodox mystical readings come to exert the most influence on Eliot, if not so initially, and include Evelyn Underhill's *Mysticism*, three books by W. R. Inge, Rufus Jones's *Studies in Mystical Religion,* A. A. Caldecott's *Philosophy of Religion*, Augustin Poulan's *Des grâces d'oraison*, and the Blessed Henry Suso's autobiography. The saints and mystics that Eliot read later in life are the ones these books introduced to him, and many of the theological positions in these books eventually become his own. It may seem dubious initially that works he read as a graduate student in Harvard would have such a lasting impact, and yet, he knew several of the authors personally, and there are direct, linguistic echoes of Inge in *The Waste Land* and Underhill in *Four Quartets*. Additionally, when Eliot chose a confessor upon his conversion, he chose none other than Evelyn Underhill's cousin, Father Francis Underhill. Given the enduring nature of these authors, let me further introduce the three most prominent.

Evelyn Underhill's *Mysticism* was first published in 1911, although the 1912 date in Eliot's notes suggests that he likely read the revised third edition of the work, and it is this third edition that has been cited in this study ("Notecards" 45). Underhill's work is both a systematic treatment and *apologia* for mysticism containing extensive quotations from a wide array of mystics from many faith traditions including Dante whose *Divine Comedy* Underhill treats as being close to genuine revelation. Unlike Inge and Jones respectively, she does not seem particularly interested in technical theology nor in church history but instead focuses on a vigorous defense of mysticism as journey to the Absolute. Underhill is unique in her emphatic assertion that artists, poets, and philosophers are capable of a partial mystical revelation and are, for a time, fellow travelers down the mystic's road (Underhill 56). She herself is presented as a novelist in the edition Eliot likely read; the title page of the third edition refers to her as "Author of 'The Grey World,' 'The Column of Dust,' *etc*" (Underhill 1). After the success of *Mysticism*, which is, a century later, still one of the definitive works on the subject, she turns her focus to writing religious works (and was the first female lecturer in theology at Oxford), but she began her career as a mildly successful and critically underrated novelist, and her fantasy writing had enough influence that Charles Williams edited her collected letters after her death.

Three books by W. R. Inge are found in Eliot's notes: *Christian Mysticism*, *Studies in English Mystics*, and *Personal Idealism and Mysticism*. His works have the most technical theology of all the readings and are also avowedly Neo-Platonic in nature. *Christian Mysticism* is both a historical discussion of the great mystics and a theological exposition of their doctrines, though the latter is emphasized. *Studies in English Mystics* is of similar nature but focuses on English figures, particularly Julian of Norwich, Wordsworth, and Browning. *Personal Idealism and Mysticism* is the most technical of all three, focusing on the exposition of λόγος-Christology both before and after the first Nicaean council and the interrelation between this and Christian Neo-Platonic mysticism. Inge expresses a pronounced dislike of the occult, Roman Catholicism, and Eastern religion consistently through his works. Inge seems to have made enough of an impression that Eliot wrote to his mother about meeting him in

GROUNDING 15

two letters about ten years after reading his books at Harvard (*Letters* 1.522–4). In the second, Eliot expresses disappointment that "the gloomy dean's speech consisted almost wholly of quotations" (*Letters* 1.524). "The Gloomy Dean" was a nickname Inge acquired after becoming Dean of St. Paul's in 1912, a title which was bolstered by his caustic columns in the *Evening Standard*. Eliot's use of this later nickname shows his continued interest in Inge's work after his schooling. Additionally, Eliot waged a war of words with Inge, both personally and via Bonamy Dobrée, in the mid-1920's (Harding *Criterion* 131–2). Notably, Eliot seems to have criticized Inge for positions that contradicted the ones previously held by Inge in the works which Eliot read.

Despite its title, *Studies in Mystical Religion* by Rufus Jones, a prominent Quaker author of the time, is actually a work of church history, although one focused on mysticism.[9] Unsurprisingly, the book presents an anti-authoritarian view of church history with mysticism being the means and evidence of spiritual infusion into a church in perpetual descent to empty ritual. His work focuses on various pneumatic movements such as the Montanists and the Beghards as well as theologians such as Johannes Scotus Eriugena and Meister Eckhart. Like Inge, Jones favors Christian Neo-Platonism and displays a bias against Roman Catholicism, though on account of Jones' liberal Quaker beliefs rather than Inge's more socio-political reasons.

In contrast to the more orthodox mystical authors, the skeptical mystical readings tended to regard the great mystics as suffering from mental illness and also represent a greater percentage of the works that Eliot studied. While these books are more prominent early in Eliot's poetry than the orthodox ones, their influence begins to wane after 1918, and they are predictably absent in Eliot's post-conversion poems. In this group are such works as William James' *Varieties of Religious Experience*, E. D. Starbuck's *Psychology of Religion*, Max Nordau's *Degeneration*, G. T. Ladd's *Philosophy of Religion,* G. B. Cutten's *Psychological Phenomena of Christianity*, E. Récéjac's *Fondements de la connaissance mystique*, and two books by J. H. Woods. While varying in their sympathy, most of these readings are interested in scientific and psychological analysis of religious activity. Of these, James, Starbuck, and Nordau have the most influential and are especially visible in the poems written around 1912. These will be discussed at length in Chapter 2.

The third set of readings in Eliot's note cards are the works on primitive religions, and these include F. B. Jevons' *Introduction to the History of Religions,*

---

9 Despite the relative obscurity of Jones' work today, Claus Bernet published a biography in 2003. This indicates the relative prominence of his work in its day. The copy of his work referenced in this study is a 1919 reprint of the 1909 edition referenced in Eliot's notecards.

R. R. Marett's *Threshold of Religion*, and some assorted articles. These particular works have little or nothing to say on either mysticism or asceticism, so a detailed treatment of them is outside the scope of this study. They have also been discussed more extensively by others, notably Robert Crawford and Laurie MacDiarmid.

The fourth set of readings are works of Pre-Socratic philosophy which include G. T. W. Patrick's translation and commentary on Heraclitus, John Burnett's *Early Greek Philosophy*, and the Empedocles chapter of Theodore Gomperz' *Greek Thinkers Vol. 1*. These books, especially Heraclitus, represent the foundational education in Greek Philosophy that Eliot went on to expand during his doctoral study at Oxford. Additionally, Patrick's work on Heraclitus, especially when coupled with Inge, is a key to understanding the intricate λόγος-Christology seen as early as "Gerontion" and continuing throughout Eliot's later work.

The final set of readings are the works of technical psychology, sometimes with a religious focus, like Pierre Janet's *Néuroses et idées fixes*, J. B. Pratt's *Psychology of Religious Belief*, Ernest Murisier's *Maladies du sentiment religieux*, and several articles by J. H. Leuba. Discussion of these works, even more than the skeptical readings, is usually outside the scope of this study, and so they will only be referenced occasionally.

Because this study is an intellectual history, it is important to establish when the note cards were produced, and when Eliot read the works in question. While it cannot be known for certain, I believe that the orthodox and skeptical mystical readings, with the exception of Underhill, date to 1909. In the fall of 1909, Eliot took a course entitled "Philosophy of History—Ideals of Society, Religion, Art and Science" with George Santayana, and I believe most of the material recorded in the cards was accomplished for this seminar. (*Letters Vol 1*. xxiv).[10] The relationship between mystical religion, art, and society would already have been suggested to the young Eliot by *The Symbolist Movement in Literature* which seems to have inspired him greatly the year before.[11] The Greek philosophy is, I believe, from a different course altogether.[12] While it has been proposed that the mystical readings represented an outside interest

---

10    Contra Hay 74. She argues, based on the dating of Underhill's edition alone, that it must have been done for Royce's 1913 seminar.

11    The title and content of this course helps explain the inclusion of Max Nordau's *Degeneration* amongst the mystical material.

12    While later dates for Gomperz and Burnet seem likely, it is possible that Patrick's work on Heraclitus is from 1909. According Lyndall Gordon, Eliot studied pre-Socratic philosophy that year under George Palmer, who introduced him to Heraclitus, one of the two pre-Socratics that Eliot studied individually (Gordon *Early Years* 22). Patrick's book could date

GROUNDING                                                                    17

accomplished after his return from Paris, this seems unlikely.[13] Pursuing a master's degree, travelling, writing poetry, and teaching undergraduates would likely have left little time for so extensive and esoteric a side-project as the readings in the cards. However, Eliot's reading of Underhill and the books on development of early religions likely date from Josiah Royce's seminar which produced Eliot's preserved graduate paper on primitive religion, and it seems that Burnet and Gomperz may date to 1913 as well. Admittedly, the case for this is circumstantial.

First, given the diversity of the material, it seems likely that the notecards are not a part of a single, eclectic work but an accumulation of material from a variety of projects. With the single exception of Evelyn Underhill's *Mysticism* (1912), every book can be dated to 1909 or earlier. The sole book from 1909, Jones' *Studies in Mystical Religion* dates to April—well before Santayana's seminar would have begun. A rapid acquisition of Jones' book would not be unlikely as he had finished his M. A. at Harvard a few years earlier and taught locally. Everything else can be dated earlier, and there is no material dating from 1910–11. The lack of current books and articles suggests that Eliot was researching. before his year in Paris and not in 1913–14. The best evidence for the early date is card (60) which seems to be a checklist. The list contains most of the mystical material but excludes the pre-Socratic philosophy, the primitive religions books, and, notably, Underhill's *Mysticism*.[14] This supports, not only the segregation of these books into distinct categories, but also the separation of Underhill's book from the other mystical material. Based on the evidence, the books listed on card 60 seem to be the early readings for Santayana's seminar which would mean that the other material is from a later time.[15]

There are three reasons why all of the material should not be dated to Josiah Royce's seminar. Firstly, the mystical readings do not seem particularly related to the topic of Royce's seminar, "A Comparative Study of Various Types of Scientific Method" (Jain 113). While Royce was certainly interested in religious

---

      from this seminar; however, a precise dating of that particular work is irrelevant to this study.

13    Cf. Childs *Mystic* 34, Skaff 22—the latter vacillates but leaves it implied.

14    Childs also observes that the notes on Underhill are of a different character than those of the other authors, though he attributes this to another reason (Childs *Mystic* 34).

15    Additionally, Childs' assertion that Eliot used Underhill's bibliography as the basis for selecting the other mystical readings seems tenuous (Childs *Mystic* 34–5). The bibliographies of James, Jones, or Inge would have produced similar results, and given that Inge's *Christian Mysticism* is on the first card, his work may be the point of departure. The odd inclusion of Jevons, Nordau, and Caldecott in the bibliography of Inge's *Christian Mysticism* also speaks to the incipiency of this work. However, most of the conclusions of Childs, Gordon, and Hay are in no way invalidated by my chronology.

questions, his course focused more on questions of epistemology rather than the historical studies which compose most of the religious readings in Eliot's notes. Secondly, Eliot's Primitive Religions paper for that seminar contains almost no discussion of mysticism—certainly not in proportion justifiable to the readings on the cards. Given the large amount of reading involved, it seems odd that he would not utilize it. Thirdly, there are no Indic readings in the notes on mysticism as mentioned before. As Eliot was studying Sanskrit with Lanman from 1912 onward, it seems particularly strange that he would not have employed this unusual skill if he were indeed studying mysticism under Royce. Additionally, it seems that Gomperz and Burnet were read for a 1913 course "Philosophy 10." In the margins of the preserved notes for this course, Eliot scrawled "Burnett's [sic] Early Gk. Philosophers / T. Gomperz: Greek Thinkers" ("[Notes on] Philosophy 10" 20). It seems then that these works may have been mentioned as outside readings during the lecture. The following few pages of notes (21 and 23) contain onionskin inserts summarizing Gomperz ("[Notes on] Philosophy 10" 20). These notes likely date to 1913 as Eliot's handwriting at the start shows the distinctive "spiky" characteristics that his handwriting acquired during his time in Paris, but there is a distinct shift away from this on approximately page 39. Additionally, there are Sanskrit characters doodled in the margins on page 43 of this ledger ("[Notes on] Philosophy 10" 39, 43). This suggests that Burnet and Gomperz date from this later time period. Thus, their exclusion from card 60 suggests that this card is a list for an earlier project. On the whole, this lends credence to a diphasic dating of Eliot's notecards. Taking all this into account, it seems more reasonable that most of the mystical readings (excluding Underhill) were read for Santayana in 1909 rather than for Royce in 1913.

The importance of such a dating scheme is that most of Eliot's earliest poetry is written after his 1909 study in mysticism, including, importantly, "Prufrock." Thus, he had already encountered and absorbed this material when writing his earliest poetry which helps explain the presence of spiritual material in a fairly secular period of Eliot's life. As an aside, I do not see why "Silence," one of the poems of this time, need be a depiction of Eliot's own mystical experience.[16] If most of the mystical readings were read in 1909, he could as easily be writing an exercise or simply expounding on a topic from his reading, as in the poem "Appearances, Appearances" with F. H. Bradley's philosophy. Regardless of whether "Silence" describes an actual experience or is merely an exercise influenced by his readings, the poem shows that these ideas were on his mind outside of the classroom.

---

16    *Pace* Gordon *Early Years* 34–5, Murray 2, Schuchard 121, Skaff 22.

With the nature and date of these mystical readings explained, I will clarify how they will be used in this study. The ideas of asceticism and mysticism in Eliot's work will be explained using passages from the texts which Eliot actually read. In his later works, there are rarely direct citations of these authors, but these texts are the foundations of his theological education. The ideas espoused by the orthodox mystical readings that he read but often doubts and subverts in the early poems come to be affirmed in the later ones. I will also identify where, intentionally or not, Eliot seems to be directly borrowing phrasing and images from the works found in the notecards. Again, this is more prominent shortly after Eliot encounters the mystical readings; however, even as late as *Four Quartets*, there are still verbal echoes of these texts. These discoveries open new interpretive possibilities in the poems not only to the ascetic ideal but in other fields of Eliot's work as well.

CHAPTER 2

# Interrogating

In Eliot's earliest works, such as "The Love Song of J. Alfred Prufrock," "The Love Song of St. Sebastian," and "The Death of St. Narcissus," he synthesizes descriptions of historical saints and extreme religious behavior from his mystical readings into negative, composite portraits. The poems display a morbid fascination with asceticism and sainthood gone awry—a fact that Eliot himself even acknowledges (*Letters* 1.48–51). As a procedural matter, I will examine these three works in the order of writing rather than publishing. In "Prufrock," Eliot infuses features of converts and mystics from the systematic studies in his education into the eponymous character. There are, as might be expected, more direct quotations of works in "Prufrock" and not always from the most lasting portions of his education in religious mysticism. In "Sebastian," the titular saint is an exploration of sainthood with an improper object of worship; in "Narcissus," the spiral of self-destroying reincarnation is seen as part of a failure to express love for something beyond the self. In all of these, Eliot is directly relying on information from his education as he interrogates the ascetic ideal.

Much ink has been spilled on the nature of J. Alfred Prufrock as a character, the relation of him to the reader, and the interaction of these with the epigraph.[1] For my purposes, these are immaterial; whether a fully-formed character or not, Prufrock has characteristics, many of which derive from Eliot's mystical readings. Particularly, Eliot seems especially fascinated by the portraits of converts from E. D. Starbuck's *The Psychology of Religion* and the "mystical degenerates" of Max Nordau's *Degeneration*. These are the primary places where Eliot's early interest in the ascetic ideal appears in this poem with the exception of the passages where Prufrock compares himself to biblical characters. I am not asserting that these should or could be used to create a profile or history of Prufrock as they are, again, simply ingredients that Eliot used to create the character. These three influences seem to account for most interactions with the ascetic ideal in "The Love Song of J. Alfred Prufrock."

The detailed descriptions of the conversion experience in Eliot's reading seems to have influenced Eliot's portrayal of "Prufrock." Starbuck's *Psychology*

---

1  For a sampling of the sheer diversity of opinions on the matter, cf. Eliot qtd. in Bush 33, 144, Donoghue 6, Ellmann 69, George 105, Hay 18, 22, Kenner 34, Manganiello 18–19, Schneider 27, Smith 49, 151–2.

© KONINKLIJKE BRILL NV, LEIDEN, 2020 | DOI:10.1163/9789004375826_004

INTERROGATING

*of Religion* is a systematic and statistical treatment of the experience of conversion brimming with quoted testimonials. As such, this book provided ample material for a dramatized portrait like those common in Eliot's early poetry. Starbuck's description of the preliminary phase of religious conversion "as if two lives [...] were pressed together in intense opposition, and were both struggling for possession of consciousness" seems an accurate portrayal of Prufrock's vacillation (Starbuck 82). Starbuck describes how "[t]he person is principally an observer in the struggle, but suffers from it, and is often torn between the contending forces until he is held between life and death" (Starbuck 82). I am not asserting that Prufrock is himself a convert, but that Starbuck's ideas of how, particularly, adolescents behave in personal crisis influenced how Eliot portrays Prufrock. The true evidence for the influence of Starbuck, though, is an echo in one of the quoted testimonials. A young man of 19, undergoing the aforementioned aspects of conversion, states that "I mourned and wept and prayed, and stood trembling with tears in my eyes" (Starbuck 83). The resemblance to line 81, "[b]ut though I have wept and fasted, wept and prayed," is striking[2] and suggests that Eliot may be, at least unconsciously, echoing this passage ("Prufrock" 81).[3] This single quotation, while the most shining example, is not the only resemblance of the convert's action to Prufrock; elsewhere, Starbuck lists the afflictions associated with individuals undergoing conversion. Those most common in young men were: depression, sadness, pensiveness; restlessness, anxiety, uncertainty; prayer, calling on God; tendency to resist conviction; loss of sleep and appetite (Starbuck 67). The resemblance of these symptoms to Prufrock is obvious. Neither the poem nor its speaker, however, should be reduced to a conversion narrative; it seems that Eliot either drew upon the patterns of behavior presented in Starbuck to create the indistinct behavior of a man before a moment of crisis, or else his reading formed his own interests in the actions and affects of individuals undergoing conversion, which he portrayed in "Prufrock."[4]

Starbuck overtly ties the behavior of his quoted conversion narratives to the person of Hamlet. While discussing the behavior of individuals vacillating between moral knowledge and sexual desires, Starbuck states that

> [t]he ability to forecast experience, together with this complexity of impulses, complicates the situation still more. The will is paralyzed, in

---

2  Cp. Brooker 133.

3  This allusion was provided to the editors of *The Poems of T. S. Eliot* during the drafting phase of this study.

4  Cf. George 105, Starbuck 159–60.

the presence of many possibilities of action. The something-to-be-said-on-both-sides, of Will Wimble, whose dilemma is not serious enough to check the flow of his vitality, may grow into the perplexity of a Hamlet when the conflicting possibilities of action are vital and momentous.[5] This is one aspect that may come with growth. Each impulse to action is inhibited by others which have equal right to express themselves.

STARBUCK 155.

This may underlie Prufrock's assertion that he is not Prince Hamlet. Although he displays the effects of profound strain upon the will, the questions concerning him, admittedly, "are no great matter" ("Prufrock" 84). Additionally, every impulse of his action is countermanded by "decisions and revisions which a minute will reverse" ("Prufrock" 48). In his own discussion of *Hamlet* a few years later, Eliot describes much of Prufrock's behavior while attempting to describe Hamlet's, stating that

[t]he intense feeling, ecstatic or terrible, without an object or exceeding an object,[6] is something which every person of sensibility has known [...]. It often occurs in adolescence: the ordinary person puts these feelings to sleep or trims them to fit the business world; the artist keeps them alive by his ability to intensify the world to his emotions. The Hamlet of Laforgue is an adolescent; the Hamlet of Shakespeare is not, he has not that explanation and excuse.

*Prose* II.126

The sudden introduction of Laforgue's Hamlet may seem a strange non-sequitur; however, in light of Starbuck's concepts of conversion, it is much clearer.[7] One of the chief arguments of his book is that *"conversion is a distinctively adolescent phenomenon"* [italics his] (Starbuck 28). In short, the behavior associated with conversion in both Hamlet and Prufrock would be linked to adolescence.[8] In the passage of Laforgue's Hamlet quoted by Symons—Eliot's first introduction to this reimagining—asks, "Perhaps I have still twenty or thirty years to live, and I shall pass that way like the other. Like the others?

---

5  Cf. Laforgue *"mes grandes angoisses métaphysiques / [s]ont passées à l'état de chagrins domestiques"* (*"Complainte d'une Convalescence en Mai"* 29–30). Trans: "my metaphysical anxieties / [h]ave reached the level of domestic quandaries" (Dale 177).
6  This particular theme is especially prominent in Prufrock's Pervigilium. Cp. Menand 138.
7  For details on Eliot's later interaction with Laforgue's Hamlet, Cf. Habib 82–3.
8  *Contra* Donoghue 13 Cp. Smith 54, 58.

INTERROGATING 23

O Totality, the misery of being there no longer! Ah! I would like to set out to-morrow, and search all the world for the most adamantine processes of embalming" (Laforgue qtd. in Symons 105).[9] Despite the dates given for his remaining lifespan, Eliot seems to have associated Laforgue's Hamlet with adolescence, possibly due to the resemblance of his behavior to the adolescent converts that he read in Starbuck. Thus, Prufrock is not Prince Hamlet because he is fundamentally different in nature, but merely in scope; the former is distinguished from the latter only by the smallness of his aspirations.[10] Eliot seems to have drawn on this collocation of images of individuals wavering before self-renunciation in Starbuck and Laforgue when composing "Prufrock."

Max Nordau's *Degeneration*[11] also seems to have influenced the portrayal of "Prufrock" in a similar fashion. Nordau files the degenerates, associated with *Fin-de-siècle* decadence, into several categories, one of which is mystical.[12] This particular type is distinguished by his "disinclination to action of any kind, attaining possibly to abhorrence of activity and powerlessness to will (*aboulia*)" (Nordau 20). This affliction is something to which Eliot felt some kinship. In a letter to Richard Aldington whilst writing *The Waste Land*, Eliot mentions that he suffers from "an *aboulie* and emotional derangement which has been a lifelong affliction. Nothing wrong with my mind—which should account, *mon cher*, for the fact that you like my prose and dislike my verse" (*Letters* I.603). That Eliot believed later in life that he himself suffered from such an illness—even if he would likely disagree with how he would be classed as a degenerate by Nordau[13]—hints at the possible influence. Additionally, one of the hallmarks of this degeneracy, according to an expert quoted approvingly by Nordau, is that sufferers "are perpetually tormented by a multitude of questions which invade their minds, and to which they can give no answer; inexpressible moral sufferings result from this incapacity. Doubt envelops every

---

9    Laforgue's fascination with Hamlet is not limited to this mention. A large number of his later poems, especially in *Des Fleurs de Bonne Volonté*, are affixed with epigraphs from *Hamlet*. The "get thee to a nunnery" exchange seems to have been Laforgue's favorite as it is quoted numerous times.

10    Cp. Ellmann 80.

11    Childs discusses the broader notions of degeneration in his work *Modernism and Eugenics*, and I will not repeat his argumentation; however, he does not employ Nordau in his discussion of Eliot.

12    Eliot occasionally categorized mystics as degenerates according to Nordau, so he certainly was in the habit of utilizing Nordau's schematic at the time he wrote "Prufrock" (*Notecard* 12).

13    Nordau asserts that degeneracy is a mental problem of which an emotional problem, like an *aboulie*, is a symptom (Nordau 22). Cp. Donoghue's comments on Eliot's mental state (Donoghue 16–7).

possible subject:—metaphysics, theology, etc." (Legrain qtd. in Nordau 21). The applicability of these descriptors to Prufrock requires no exposition.[14]

According to Nordau, mystical degenerates have a defect in their brain in which the non-sexual centers of the brain are stimulated in a method equivalent to sexual ecstasy (Nordau 61–3). Thus, like piano keys sticking together, striking one emotion will trigger other unrelated emotions in the degenerate mind—especially morbid and sexual sensations. Thus, asceticism, for Nordau, is a kind of auto-erotic behavior. In his discussion of Tolstoism [sic], Nordau states that such a person "sees in woman an uncanny, overpowering force of nature, bestowing supernatural delights or dealing destruction, and he trembles before this power, to which he is defenselessly exposed" (Nordau 168–9). For the case of Eliot's use of this idea of degeneracy, what is pertinent is the sense of exposure that Nordau lists. Prufrock bestows the women with the ability to "fix him in a formulated phrase" and penetrate his every attempt at defense with a trite rebuttal of "[b]ut how his arms and legs are thin!" or "[t]hat is not it at all" ("Prufrock" 56, 44, 109). Laforgue associates such an attitude with mental disease in his poem *"Maniaque"* when he mentions, *"[l]a peur d'examens sans merci"*[15] (*"Maniaque"* 15). This seems to be something specific to women, as in another poem, Laforgue describes *"[E]lles, des Regards incarnés"*[16] (*"Complainte des Cloches"* 28). There is, of course, no actuality in the speaker's statements; Prufrock imagines what the women will say[17] and bestows this power upon them.[18] Nordau continues to highlight this view of women in what he considers the most quintessential of mystical degenerates, Richard Wagner.[19] According to Nordau, "Wagner's imagination is perpetually occupied with woman" but

> [t]he woman that he knows is the gruesome Astarté[20] of the Semites, the frightful man-eating Kali Bhagawati of the Hindoos,[sic] an apocalyptic vision of smiling blood-thirstiness, of eternal perdition and infernal torment, in demoniacally beautiful embodiment. No poetical problem has so profoundly moved him as the relation between man and this his ensnaring destroyer.
>
> NORDAU 188–9.

---

14 Cp. George 109, Kim 62.

15 Trans: "The fear of merciless scrutiny" (Dale 271).

16 Trans: "They[female]of the incarnate Glance" (Dale 135).

17 Cf. Ellmann 69.

18 Contra George 107.

19 The relationship between Eliot and Wagner is beyond the scope of this study. For biographical details on what Eliot may have seen whilst in Paris, Cf. Hargrove 198–207.

20 Cf. Laforgue referring to a female companion as Astarté in *"L'île"* 2.

INTERROGATING 25

While this theme is more prominent in Eliot's later poetry, nonetheless, there is an undercurrent of the femme fatale[21] within "Prufrock." Aside from the violent imagery used to describe the gaze of the women in lines 55–61, the speaker also imagines them as the Salomé to his John the Baptist, the seductive woman who destroys the saint ("Prufrock" 82). Prufrock intimates something ineffably, ominously seductive in the question

> Is it perfume from a dress
> That makes me so digress?
> Arms that lie along a table, or wrap about a shawl.
> > "Prufrock" 65–7.

the lines contain an implicit suggestion that it is *not* the perfume, but something more intangible. This hanging, unspoken sentiment implies something like the creeping horror seen in "Prufrock's Pervigilium," which Eliot, perhaps wisely, left unstated in the final poem. The anacoluthon in line 67 quoted above, again, suggests but does not state that the women possess some seductive power to compel "the timid voluptuary," to use Nordau's phrase (Nordau 191). While Nordau's cynical view of the ascetic ideal, as arising from a mental defect, may not have had a lasting influence, it seems to have informed the characterization of Prufrock.

Nordau's idea of degeneracy is carried over in the most overt engagement with the ascetic ideal in "Prufrock" when the speaker posits himself to be John the Baptist.[22] Aside from the obvious biblical allusion, some have proposed that this is based on Laforgue's or Wilde's portrayals or derived from Eliot seeing paintings of this scene while in Paris—particularly Solario's which models the decapitated saint on the painter (Hargrove 129).[23] All of these are likely; however, they are, to some degree, beside the point: a saint dies for the caprice of a sensual girl. By positing himself as a saint and the women as a composite Salome, Prufrock is, once again, imbuing the women with the seductive power to martyr him. In addition to his own retelling in *Moralités Légendaires,* Laforgue invokes the figure of Salome, in "*XLVIII Dimanches*" stating

> *Et vous donc, filles d'Ève,*
> *Sœurs de lait, sœurs de sève,*

---

21  Cf. Crawford 29, MacDiarmid 29 Cp. Habib 84.

22  Habib's assertion that there is a duality of registers seems to ignore the indistinction in Laforgue (Habib 79).

23  Cf. Manganiello 25, Moody 34–35, Sultan 253.

26

CHAPTER 2

*Des destines qu'in se rêve!*

*Salomé, Salomé!*
*Sarcophage embaumé*
*Où dort maint Bien-Aimé*[24]
    *"XLVIII Dimanches"* 16–21.

The descriptions in Laforgue express sensuality with a deathly undercurrent. Eliot seems to retain this within the figurative gaze of the women, so that their eyes

> fix you in a formulated phrase,
> And when I am formulated, sprawling on a pin,
> When I am pinned and wriggling on the wall,
> Then how should I begin
> To spit out all the butt-ends of my days and ways?
>     "Prufrock" 56–60.

In addition to the lepidopterological implications,[25] this description bears remarkable resemblance to an incident in the life of the blessed Henry Suso, an ascetic mystic who caught Eliot's interest at Harvard. In his chapter on saintliness in *Varieties of Religious Experience*, William James recounts a long passage where Suso, on hot summer nights and having fitted himself with all manner of mortifications,

> Would sometimes, as he lay thus in bonds, and oppressed with toil, and tormented also by noxious insects, cry aloud and give way to fretfulness, and twist round and round in agony, as a worm does when run through with a pointed needle.
>     SUSO qtd. in JAMES 307.

Prufrock compares himself under the imagined gaze of the women to a Suso-like figure under his ascetic tortures. For Prufrock, like Suso, these torments are self-inflicted;[26] however, they lack the higher purpose of the mystic's. This

---

24    Trans: "Eve's daughters, next: sisters / Fostered, and vimful trysters, / Dream-destinies to misters! / Salomé, Salomé deep / Embalmed tomb-keep / Where many Loved Ones sleep..." (Dale 369).

25    Cf. Schneider 29, Williamson 62.

26    Cp. Ellmann 85, Kim relates this to line to the stifling effects of the industrial city as compared to the deserts of the ascetic fathers, which, given the influence of Suso, seems somewhat contradictory. Contra Kim 76, Bush 10.

INTERROGATING

27

resonates with another mask that Prufrock wears—curiously, that of Aeneas. In line 69, Prufrock simply asks "And how should I begin?" ("Prufrock" 69). This is an allusion to the *Aeneid* where deciding how to broach the news of his departure to Dido, Aeneas asks, "*quae prima exordia sumat?*" (*Aeneid* IV:284).[27] Dryden translates this line simply "And how should he begin?" (Dryden IV:408).[28] I believe the primary focus of this allusion is Aeneas's handwringing vacillation as he decides how to tell Dido of his departure. Unlike the Trojan Prince, however, Prufrock is not so assured of divine assistance when he begins his speech (*Aeneid* IV:294–5). Ultimately, all of these particular masks, often derived from his reading, only exhibit Prufrock's inadequacy. He is no more Aeneas, Lazarus, Suso, or John the Baptist than he is Hamlet. Thus, the readings that will form his ascetic ideal are marshaled to the creation of an indistinct character; in this, his earliest major work, Eliot employs his education on mystical theology and the characters referenced in a loose pastiche.

In 1914, the year before his marriage, Eliot returned to poetry after a nightwo-year hiatus. During this period, he produced two poems featuring ascetic saints: "The Love Song of St. Sebastian" and "The Death of St. Narcissus."[29] While the poems are generally read as self-revealingly erotic and violent, this oversimplifies Eliot's understanding of mysticism and asceticism.[30] Simply put, Eliot understood the ascetic ideal and how saints should behave, and the figures of "Narcissus" and "Sebastian" do not behave as such. It seems more likely that these poems depict a deliberate inversion rather than some kind of subversive Freudian slip. Eliot is interrogating the ascetic ideal by examining its failures. Eliot states in a letter to Conrad Aiken that "Sebastian" is "morbid and forced" and later as "labored and conscious" (*Letters* I.48–51). He repeats this appellation in another letter to Aiken calling his latest material "not good, [...] very forced in execution" (*Letters* I.63). This indicates the presence of some schema at least.

While the choice of name for "Narcissus" is obvious, the reasons behind "Sebastian" are a good deal murkier. That Eliot was fascinated by the various

---

27  All passages from the *Aeneid* are marked to the original Latin text unless noted to be from Dryden's translation.

28  I provided this reference to the editors of *The Complete Poems* during an earlier stage of this study.

29  "The Love Song of St. Sebastian" was enclosed in a letter to Conrad Aiken on July 25th 1914 (*Letters* I.48–51). "The Death of St. Narcissus" is harder to date, Cf. the discussion in *Poems* I.1154–6. I have somewhat arbitrarily placed "Sebastian" before "Narcissus" in this chapter; it is not assertion of chronology. For some critical debate on the matter, Cf. Rainey 198–201, Gordon *Early Years* 58, 142, Childs *Mystic, Son, and Lover* 89–90. MacDiarmid's assertion that "Sebastian" was "revised" into "Narcissus" seems unfounded (MacDiarmid 11).

30  Cf. Ellmann 64–5, Gordon *Imperfect Life* 50, MacDiarmid 9–11.

portrayals of the saint in art is certain; however, the applicability for the poem is less obvious.[31] The reasons for why the name should imply a juxtaposition of grim sensuality with spirituality, I think, lies in the production of *Le Martyre de Saint Sébastien* that took place during Eliot's year in Paris.[32] In this production, Italian poet Gabriele D'Annunzio "was defying tradition and deliberately provoking scandal by casting a woman in the role [of Sebastian], and, by choosing [Russian ballerina Ida Rubenstein] with her reputation for sensuality, he created a sensation" (Hargrove 117). Thus, in Eliot's 1914 letter Aiken where he asks "[b]ut no one ever painted a female Sebastian, did they?" the emphasis should probably not be placed on the word "female" but rather on "painted" (*Letters* 1.49).[33] This may imply that Eliot at least knew *of* the play. Given the differences in action, the influence must have been at a more thematic level, but the idea of turning a religious drama into a violent and sensual rite may have lingered with Eliot. It is part of his fascination with ascetic failures.

The two Saint poems explore the failure to reach the ascetic ideal but in different ways: Where Narcissus lacks proper ascetic preparation, Sebastian goes the correct course for a saint but with an improper object: a created woman.[34] Eliot implies both are doomed enterprises. The critical difficulties of "Sebastian" are at a more fundamental level than those of "Narcissus," and so, due to the variance in interpretations, a closer reading of "Sebastian" is necessary.[35] Many of the themes are similar to "Narcissus" and so will be cross-applicable.

The experiences of a lover and an ascetic saint may initially seem irreconcilable, but Eliot's reading repeatedly stressed the similarities between the two. For example, in G. B. Cutten, one of the skeptical mystical readings, "the experience of newness" found in religion is likened to "that felt by 'the youth who has sung for the first time his love-tale to his lady and receives the assurance of requited love'" (Cutten 248).[36] However, there are two perspectives on this relationship offered in Eliot's readings. The first that earthly love is a path, when rightly walked, to the Divine, an idea with Plato's *Symposium* as its fountainhead. The second that mysticism and asceticism are the grim fruits

---

31    Cf. His letter to Conrad Aiken on July 25th 1914 (*Letters* 1.49).

32    I am indebted to Hargrove's *T. S. Eliot's Parisian Year* in this matter.

33    Cf. Hargrove 121. There are many interpretations of this letter. Cf. MacDiarmid 11–2.

34    It is possible that "Sebastian" is a satire in the vein of the "Hippopotamus" and "Mr. Eliot's Sunday Morning Service" with a focus on morbid sexuality in saints and the woman representing a cruel and capricious god. However, this would require the woman to be not merely a symbol for higher things but in some ways, God himself. While Eliot had certainly read of such, the theme is not otherwise present in his poetry until years later. Thus, I find it unlikely but possible.

35    Compare the disparity in readings between Hay 80, Ellmann 64–5, Hargrove 120–1, Childs *Mystic, Son, and Lover* 84–9, MacDiarmid 14–7 *et al.*

36    Cutten is partially quoting J. H. Leuba whom Eliot also read.

INTERROGATING 29

of thwarted sexual desire. I believe that the ambivalence and ambiguity in "Sebastian"—and, with some important differences, "Narcissus"—result from this divergence in his reading. Both psychological and theological authors express the view of the feminine as path to the divine. Starbuck, for instance, asserts that "[t]he sexual life, although it has left its impress on fully-developed religion, seems to have originally given the psychic impulse which called out the latent possibilities of development, rather than to have furnished the raw material out of which religion was constructed [his excessive italics removed]" (Starbuck 402). From a more committed theological stance, Inge states, when speaking of Plotinus, that[37]

> it is a great mistake to shut our eyes to the world around us, "and all beautiful things." The love of beauty will lead us up a long way—up to the point when the love of the Good is ready to receive us. Only we must not let ourselves be entangled by sensuous beauty. Those who do not quickly rise beyond this first stage, to contemplate [the] "ideal form, the universal mold," share the fate of Hylas; they are engulfed in a swamp, from which they never emerge.
>
> INGE *Christian Mysticism* 93.

Thus, Eliot's poem does portray the fact that "all mystical exercises are exercises of *love* rather than exercises of *thought*" (Jones 307).[38] However, the love seen in "Sebastian" is, to use Inge's terms, "distinctly sexual love, not Christian charity—ἔρος, not ἀγάπη" (Inge *English Mystics* 219).[39] Eliot portrays Sebastian and Narcissus falling into this trap.

In contrast to the lofty idealizations of the more orthodox Inge and Underhill, many authors considered the ascetic ideal the repugnant result of repressed sexual desires and degeneracy. Nordau states that "no difference exists between [mystical] tendencies and the religious manias observed in nearly all degenerates and sufferers from hereditary mental taint" (Nordau 22). Nordau associates this with sexuality blatantly: "[m]ystical reverie never fails to be accompanied by sensuality" (Nordau 89). While Eliot's exact

---

37 Underhill makes similar claims. Cf. Underhill 87. Nordau, unsurprisingly, scoffs at the use of a female figure as a vehicle for redemption (Nordau 184). Inge returns to this topic again with a slightly different emphasis (Inge *Christian Mysticism* 327). However, a discussion of this passage must wait till the Hyacinth Garden scene in *The Waste Land*.

38 Cf. "The mystic soul loves, and all its efforts for knowledge are in view of this single need" (Récéjac 49).

39 Inge says that this conflation is a facet of Browning's mysticism. Similarly, Cutten notes that "Christian love is not a pure emotion, as many mystics and others have supposed, but contains other elements, especially of will" (Cutten 382).

opinion of Nordau's views is unclear, he does in his notes, seem to favor his definition of mysticism in favor of Inge's technical theological one, for example (*Notecards* 12). While there is no way to know if he is stating his own views or someone else's, Eliot does reproduce the following line in his notecards on mystical readings: "Religion [...] thrives best in hypersensitive and neurotic soils" (*Notecards* 13). He also read, in Cutten: "[i]f the soul is baffled in its first desires, and defeated, not subdued, it may suddenly meet a new excitement of a different order, and combining with a novel element, rush on ungovernable" (Cutten 455). In other words, souls whose sexual desires are thwarted may find religious feelings as an outlet. In this light, "[t]he business of a saint was to eradicate a natural appetite and to become abnormal. Morbid introspection and hallucinations resulted" (Cutten 455). Ultimately, I suspect that Eliot was unable to commit to either view at this point in his life. Even a few years later, Eliot's autobiographically-flavored "Eeldrop and Appleplex" included the description of "a skeptic with a taste for mysticism" who was "learned in theology" (*Prose* I.525–6). With such divided interests and loyalties, Eliot produced flawed poems of murky ambivalence.

A detailed close-reading of "Sebastian" will demonstrate this ambivalence. The first lines of "Sebastian" have detailed allusions, though, that require examination. First, the poem itself:

> I would come in a shirt of hair
> I would come with a lamp in the night
> And sit at the foot of your stair;
> I would flog myself until I bled
> And after hour on hour of prayer
> And torture and delight
> Until my blood should ring the lamp
> And glisten in the light.
>> "Sebastian" 1–8.

The best example of this sort of asceticism in Eliot's reading was Henry Suso.[40] Inge in *Christian Mysticism*, James, Jones, and Underhill are the only authors who cite him, and even then, only James writes of him as more than a misguided footnote to the history of mysticism with Jones essentially reiterating Williams James' contentions. Nonetheless, he is the only of the mystics whom

---

40  Gordon assumes that Eliot read the 1913 edition of T. F. Knox's translation of Suso with an introduction by Inge. This is, however, a reissue of an 1865 edition and Eliot only specifies Knox's name. Harvard's particular copy of this older edition is from William James' estate (acquired in 1923); regardless of which edition, Eliot would certainly have read Suso by the time of the writing of "Sebastian."

INTERROGATING

the notecards state that Eliot read in the original text at Harvard. The passage that seems to inspire the early part of this poem is one that is quoted by William James:

> "He[41] was in his youth of a temperament full of fire and life; and when this began to make itself felt, it was very grievous to him; and he sought by many devices how he might bring his body into subjection. He wore for a long time a hair shirt and an iron chain, until the blood ran from him, so that he was obliged to leave them off. He secretly caused an undergarment to be made for him; and in the undergarment he had strips of leather fixed, into which a hundred and fifty brass nails, pointed and filed sharp, were driven, and the points of the nails were always turned towards the flesh"
>
> SUSO qtd. in JAMES 307.[42]

The details of the hair shirt and the blood running off are identical to Eliot's poem. All of the mystical authors, though, considered this type of behavior to be unusual. A footnote to Inge's discussion of Suso states that "[t]he extreme asceticism which was practiced by Suso, and (though to a less degree) by Tauler, is not enjoined by them as a necessary part of a holy life. 'We are to kill our passions, not our flesh and blood'" (Inge *Christian Mysticism* 173–4). Thus, it seems likely that Eliot is intentionally portraying something eccentric and repellent. Additionally, there are two probative differences between the poem and its source. The first is the presence of an audience. As the passage that James quotes states, Suso did these things "in secret," something that Suso's own biography reiterates repeatedly. As Inge notes, "[t]he story of his terrible penances which he inflicted on himself for part of his life is painful and almost repulsive to read; but they have nothing in common with the ostentatious self-torture of the fakir" (Inge *Christian Mysticism* 172). However, "ostentatious self-torture" is *exactly* what Sebastian does. He brings a lamp and goes to the foot of the stair of his beloved to be seen. The injunction against such displays of any religious act is, of course, Biblical (Matthew 6:5–7). The second difference is the ecstasy felt in the suffering. While Eliot certainly read of such things among the mystical saints, this is not included in Suso's account as James notes, "[h]is case is distinctly pathological, but he does not seem to have had the alleviation, which some ascetics have enjoyed, of an alteration of sensibility capable of actually

---

41    One of the (many) eccentricities of Suso's autobiography is his programmatic reference to himself in the third person as "The Servitor of Eternal Wisdom."

42    Jones also quotes this passage, meaning that Eliot encountered it on three separate occasions (Jones 284–5).

turning torment into a perverse kind of pleasure" (James 308). Feeling pleasure in the place of pain is, of course, entirely self-defeating for an ascetic exercise, as Eliot read. Underhill asserts that the mystics found pain to be "the grave but kindly teacher of immortal secrets," which "plunges like a sword through creation, leaving on one side cringing and degraded animals and on the other side heroes and saints" (Underhill 23). Sebastian revels in sadomasochistic, animal pleasure instead of learning to suffer which is "the gymnastic of eternity" (Underhill 196). Thus, he is perverting the ascetic ideal on two different fronts: The first by performing his asceticism for an audience and the second by enjoying rather than enduring his purgative affliction. Eliot appears to be intentionally combining the two most repulsive aspects of the medieval ascetics in his reading. He is, as such, constructing an artificial "saint" designed both to disgust and to display *none* of the qualities of genuine religious impulses. Sebastian, and indeed Narcissus, as will be seen, are then, not a portrait of eroticized sainthood, but rather inversions and failures of the genuine ascetic ideal.

Through the poem, Eliot is creating an asceticism-privileging contrast between Sebastian's object of worship, an ordinary woman and the incarnate Eternal Wisdom from Suso. The quotations and echoes in the poem contrast this very earthly person who inspires Sebastian's self-torture with the heavenly figure who inspires Suso's.[43] Now, aside from the initial report of his tortures, the passage where Suso espouses the Eternal Wisdom is the most frequently quoted,[44] so Eliot would certainly have encountered it. In Suso,

> the Eternal Wisdom is represented in Holy Scripture under a lovely guise, as a gracious loving mistress, who displays her charms with the intent to please every one; discoursing the while tenderly, in female form, of the desire she has to win all hearts to herself, and saying how deceitful all other mistresses are, and how truly loving and constant she is.
>
> SUSO IV[45]

By contrast, the imagery in the latter half of the first strophe of "St. Sebastian" is relatively conventional to sensuality and also quite Romantic in many

---

43    While Eliot's attitudes towards women are beyond the scope of this study, even a cursory glance at his letters about the time he wrote "Sebastian" will show this to be plausible—for instance, the ones to Conrad Aiken on September 30th and December 31st 1914 (*Letters* 1.48–51, 62–4, 74–6, 80–2).

44    Cf. Inge *Christian Mysticism* 174, Jones 287, Underhill 267.

45    As with many of the other primary sources on mysticism, I have cited the chapter number, due to the rarity of the editions in which Eliot first read their work.

INTERROGATING                                                                          33

ways,[46] which may account for Eliot's dislike of this poem on reflection. For
instance, the "white feet" are reminiscent, though without the striking detail,
of the bare and blue-veined feet of the eldritch Geraldine in *Christabel* or the
fairy-child in *"La Belle Dame sans Merci"* (*Christabel* 63, *"La Belle Dame sans
Merci"* 15). The white gown is a similarly romantic element.[47] Nonetheless, Eliot returns to such imagery many years later in *Ash-Wednesday*. Many of the
details are the same: the stairs, the white gown, and the long hair, and yet, the
effect is utterly opposite. The difference must be in the identities of the figures
as the details of the passage will reveal.

This dichotomy is clarified by a reference at the end of this first part of
"St Sebastian." The ending of the strophe introduces a reference to the Song
of Solomon: "when the morning came / [b]etween your breasts should lie my
head" ("Sebastian" 20–1). This is a curiously rich detail. Firstly, reading Song of
Solomon in a mystical context as a metaphor for spiritual marriage has "a well-
known and heartily abused" history as Underhill wryly notes (Underhill 509).
Underhill, always attempting to portray mysticism in the best light, states that
the pure-minded mystics "mean by [such a union] no rapturous satisfactions,
no dubious spiritualizing of earthly ecstasies, but a life-long bond 'that shall
never be lost or broken,' a close personal union of will and of heart between the
free self and that 'Fairest in Beauty' Whom it has known in the act of contemplation" (Underhill 512). Inge, also, dedicates an entire appendix in *Christian
Mysticism* to detailing the history of dubious interpretations of "Song of Solomon" (Inge *Christian Mysticism* 369–72). In his brief notes on Inge, Eliot does
highlight St. Bernard's meditations on the Song of Solomon.[48] He notes that
he espoused the "Romantic side of mysticism" and "founded the worship of
the saviour as the 'Bridegroom of the Soul,'" so he was clearly aware of this discussion (*Notecards* 1). I strongly suspect that these comments are Eliot's own
generalization as I cannot recall Inge ever being concerned with Romanticism
in *Christian Mysticism*. This discussion from his education seems to affirm the
details in the first strophe. Additionally, the image of lying with the head on
the chest was rather common in the mystical literature, but it generally had
maternal rather than sensual overtones.[49] Eliot may have drawn inspiration
from a curious juxtaposition of two disparate stories in Jones' recounting of
Suso, which I will quote in full:

---

46    I am generally convinced by Smith's assertion of Poe's "For Annie" hovering specter-like
      above the poem (Smith 37–50).
47    Cp. *Christabel* 49.
48    The page numbers are, unfortunately, not given.
49    For a not dissimilar example from Dante, Cf. *Inferno* XXIII:37–51.

34                                                                        CHAPTER 2

> In one of these visions he was granted a sight of "how God dwells in the soul."
>
> "He was told to look into himself and there he saw through a crystal in the midst of his heart the Eternal Wisdom in lovely form, and beside Him his own soul leaning lovingly to God's side, and embraced in His arms, and pressed to His Divine heart, and lying entranced and drowned in the arms of the God he loved."
>
> One of his most striking visions was the one granted to him at another spiritual crisis of his life when he gave himself in spiritual espousal to Eternal Wisdom as his heavenly bride.
>
> "It happened to him often," he tells us, "as when a mother has her sucking child pressed in her arms lying on her bosom, and the child lifts itself with its head and with the movement of its body towards its tender mother, and by its lovely bearing shows forth its joy of heart, so often did his heart within his body, turning towards the presence of the Eternal Wisdom, overflow with tenderness."
>
> JONES 287.

Again, these are very disparate passages in Suso's own work, but Eliot may have elided the two as they appear on the same page in Jones. However, Eliot, in the vein of Poe's "For Annie," seems to apply this language as crudely sensual and literal rather than the metaphorical uses that the mystical authors like Suso employ.[50] Eliot then is suggesting that Sebastian is a crude parody of sainthood.

However, the interpretive difficulties in "Sebastian" truly begin with the second strophe. The change in tone and content between the first and second has confounded critical interpretations thus far. One solution lies, I believe, in assuming that the break signals a change in speaker. This is a device that Eliot has used before; in "Portrait of a Lady," Eliot changes speaker with only a paragraph break as well ("Portrait of a Lady" 113–4). The woman, not the fraudulent saint, may speak the second strophe. I realize this to be a radical departure from current critical conversation; however, I feel that it offers the best explanation for the poem's difficulties.

> I would come with a towel in my hand
> And bend your head beneath my knees;
> Your ears curl back in a certain way
> Like no one's else in all the world.
> When all the world shall melt in the sun,

---

50    Cf. Smith *Ghost of Poe* 154.

INTERROGATING

Melt or freeze,
I shall remember how your ears were curled.
I should for a moment linger
And follow the curve with my finger
And your head beneath my knees—
I think that at last you would understand.
There would be nothing more to say.
You would love me because I should have strangled you
And because of my infamy;
And I should love you the more because I had mangled you
And because you were no longer beautiful
To anyone but me.

      "Sebastian" 22–38.

The opening of the second strophe parallels the first to signal that a change in perspective has occurred. This portion of the poem is equally as sensuous as the ending of the previous one. The internal logic of the poem would support the woman coming with a towel to mop the blood, a strangely mundane contrast to God's divine comfort. A towel would not heal, only clean, which could be interpreted as a crude parody of ascetic purification. The phrase "[a]nd bend your head beneath my knees" is a strange detail and is without a truly satisfactory explanation.[51] The wording implies both a perversion of Hamlet laying his head in Ophelia's lap and the subjection inherent in the word "beneath" (*Hamlet* III.ii.108–120). The phrase "your ears curl back in a certain way" is perhaps even more difficult to explain.[52] I can only speculate that Eliot is prefiguring Bertrand Russell in his role as the fecund satyr in "Mr. Apollinax," which was written about six months later. Perhaps, Eliot is casting him or at least using physical traits as the flagellant anti-saint.[53] Russell's pointed ears were one of his most definitive features which Eliot mentioned not only in "Mr. Apollinax" 19, but Vivien reports Eliot stating in 1921 on the birth of Russell's son that "he is quite sure the baby *will* have pointed ears, so you need not be anxious. Even if not pointed at birth, they will sharpen in time" (*Letters* 1.599). Nonetheless,

---

51    MacDiarmid suggests that it is "a hint at oral copulation" (Macdiarmid 16). If the woman is the speaker and, as such, the roles reversed from her argument, then the detail is far more anatomically plausible. While the crudity would certainly not be out of place within the poem, the exact referent of the phrase is irrelevant to my argument.

52    I am unconvinced by Macdiarmid's explanation (Macdiarmid 16).

53    Rainey dates the poem to April 1915 (Rainey 198). In a Feb. 25th 1915 letter to Conrad Aiken, Eliot mentions "[t]he idea of a submarine world of clear green light"—an image reincarnated in "Mr. Apollinax" 10 (*Letters* 1.96).

the woman's speech is as sensual as his, again, showing that she is in sharp contrast to Suso's Eternal Wisdom. One of the most telling points of contrast is the phrase "because of my infamy" ("Sebastian 35). In his chapter on espousing the Eternal Wisdom, Suso states that "[a]ll other mistresses have sweet words, but a bitter recompense. Their hearts are deadly nets, their hands are manacles, their discourse honied [sic] poison, and their pastime infamy" (Suso IV). This is a rough paraphrase of Ecclesiastes 7:25 with the sole exception of the final phrase "and their pastime infamy" which seems to be purely Suso's insertion. This signals Eliot's drawing, probably unconscious, on Suso's narrative. Additionally, Sebastian suffers the fate of the sinner in the Ecclesiastes passage as he is entrapped by her. This is highlighted by the end of the poem where she states "I should love you the more because I had mangled you / [a]nd because you were no longer beautiful / [t]o anyone but me" ("Sebastian" 36–8). With her as the speaker, the woman is sinisterly taking possession of his self-mutilation as her own action and rejoicing in the destruction. This is the fear of women evinced in many of the earlier poems with the darker tone expected of this time in Eliot's life. "Sebastian" in such a light is a grim and acerbic inversion of the ascetic ideal.

"Narcissus" is involved in many of the same themes as "Sebastian," and, so, I will only highlight the differences. Like Sebastian, Narcissus is the name of a genuine saint. The name, a common one in the first century, is mentioned in Romans 16:11; though no definite details are known, later lists, including an apocryphal work by Hippolytus of Rome, associate this Narcissus as the bishop of Athens and one of the seventy of Luke 10. In fact, there are no less than four patristic-era saints are named Narcissus; however, none is known to have been shot with arrows—a detail likely drawn from portraits of St. Sebastian. Yet, no St. Narcissus is ever mentioned in any of the mystical readings, and neither is there any mention of one in the poetry by Eliot's mother. Thus, I think it most likely that the name was chosen to parallel the story of Narcissus and Echo in Ovid rather than echo any particular religious tradition.

There is also a profound theological difference in the poems. Love in "Sebastian" fails to pass beyond itself and become anything more than animal sensuality. In "Narcissus", love fails to exit the sphere of the self and in so doing fails to be love at all. However, the explication of this requires explanation of Narcissus' transformations. The passage is quoted here:

> First he was sure that he had been a tree,
> Twisting its branches among each other
> And tangling its roots among each other.
> Then he knew that he had been a fish
> With slippery white belly held tight in his own fingers

Writhing in his own clutch, his ancient beauty
Caught fast in the pink tips of his new beauty.
Then he had been a young girl
Caught in the woods by a drunken old man
Knowing at the end the taste of his own whiteness
The horror of his own smoothness,
And he felt drunken and old.

"Narcissus" 21–33.

Critics have identified this as a metaphor for the instability of identity,[54] ontogeny recapitulating phylogeny,[55] or Buddhist reincarnation;[56] however, I think the primary referent is Pythagorean transmigration. During his years at Harvard, Eliot read the pre-Socratic philosophers in Burnet's *Early Greek Philosophy*. He also studied two of these authors on their own: Heraclitus and Empedokles.[57] Empedokles' belief in Pythagorean transmigration[58] provides the source for the transformations in Narcissus." In fragment 117,[59] the Empedokles says "For I have been ere now a boy and a girl, a bush and a bird, and a dumb fish in the sea" (Empedokles qtd. in Burnet 257). While certainly telling, this fragment does not seem to be what Eliot is remembering. In his own commentary, Burnet summarizes Empedokles views stating:

He himself is such an exiled divinity, and has fallen from his high estate because he put his trust in raving Strife. The four elements toss him from one to the other with loathing; and so he has not only been a human being and a plant, but even a fish. The only way to purify oneself from the taint of original sin was by the cultivation of ceremonial holiness, by purifications, and abstinence from animal flesh. For the animals are our kinsmen (fr. 137), and it is parricide to lay hands on them.

BURNET 289.

---

54  Childs *Mystic* 90–1, *Philosophy* 110, Ellmann 65.

55  Crawford 66. Eliot certainly was exposed to the idea in a theological context in Inge *Personal Idealism* 2–3.

56  Hay 94, Medcalf 76.

57  I follow Burnet's less-anglicized spelling of his name.

58  Eliot also read of Empedokles from Theodor Gomperz' *Greek Thinkers Vol. 1*. Only the chapter on Empedokles was consulted. His discussion emphasizes the same features as Burnet's. Cf. Gomperz 247–8. In his notes on Gomperz, unlike those on Burnet, Eliot specifically mentions the transmigration and purification of souls (*Notecards* 34–5).

59  Comley refers to Empedokles but to the philosopher's works directly, which is not what Eliot seems to have recalled specifically (Comley 283).

38                                                                                           CHAPTER 2

Burnet's recapitulation of Empedokles previous reincarnations removes the bird, which is the only one on the list that Eliot does *not* include in the poem. Not only that, the poem contains the ideas of two different fragments (117 and 137) that Burnet quotes in this excerpt, which encapsulates all of the themes of "Narcissus": sin, reincarnation, and the cure for these, which is ascetic purgation that Narcissus cannot accomplish.

That Narcissus' sin is onanistic hardly requires comment.[60] This is, however, not a mere foible, a blot on an otherwise saintly record. As Eliot read, "'the disease of sin,' 'the blindness of sin,' [Meister Eckhart] says, comes from 'self-love.' Sin is not merely an affair of the *flesh*; it is an attitude of the will" (Jones 234). In "Narcissus," Eliot takes the general conception of self-love, "the attempt, on the part of the creature, to be a particular This or That outside of God," and literalize it as onanistic self-absorption (Eckhart qtd. in Inge *Christian Mysticism* 155).[61]

Eliot is portraying a failure of a mystic and a saint, and the cause seems to be that Narcissus lacked ascetic preparation. As Inge notes, "[t]he danger to which mystics have often fallen victims is to clutch the fruits of spiritual union before they have gone through the toilsome preparation and the discipline of the will and intellect" (Inge *English Mystics* 30).[62] Narcissus' actions begin wellenough: realizing his own beauty and the desire thereof, he is "struck down by this knowledge / [h]e could not live men's ways, but became a dancer before God" ("St Narcissus" 16–7).[63] While Eliot certainly read that "'[t]he way to ascend to God [...] is to descend into oneself,'" Inge follows this with another quotation stating that "'[t]he ascent is through self above self,' [...] we are to rise on stepping-stones of our dead selves to higher things" (Inge *Christian Mysticism* 141).[64] This is what Eliot does *not* portray Narcissus doing. In other words, Narcissus does not discard his love-of-self but rather continually repeats the same action in each of his various incarnations. Simply put, "[i]t is easier to forsake worldly goods than the love of them" (Inge *English Mystics* 95). Narcissus, like Sebastian, is a failure because of his lack of detachment.

---

60    Cf. Crawford 66, Ellmann 67, Hay 78, MacDiarmid 7 Cp. Gordon *Early Years* 92.
61    While Jones translates this phrase of Eckhart's as "self-love," Inge translates the phrase as self-will. Both are to be expunged, according to mystics.
62    As Eliot read elsewhere in Inge's work, the word for discipline in Greek is ἀσκησις, the etymon for asceticism (Inge *Christian Mysticism* 87). Eliot makes this distinction himself in "Religion without Humanism" (1930).
63    To the best of my knowledge, the resemblance of this line to "Gerontion" 33 has never been properly explored.
64    This seems to be an unattributed quotation of *In Memoriam* I:4–5.

INTERROGATING

39

However, there is a distinct difference between Narcissus and Sebastian as failed saints. Sebastian worships a female figure; however, Narcissus only loves himself. For, as Eliot read, "there must be a real "Other" for love to be real" (Jones 227). While written years later, Eliot, in "The Function of Criticism" commented that "the Catholic practitioners [of the meditation of self-knowledge] were, I believe, with the possible exception of certain heretics, not palpitating Narcissi; the Catholic did not believe that God and himself were identical" (*Prose* II.461). Thus, at least later in life, Eliot associates Narcissus with heresy implying, as has been suggested, that this is a deliberate inversion. This comment also suggests a radical, pantheistic lack of exteriority in Narcissus' actions. This lack of an Other is shown by the manuscript variations in lines 31–2: [k]nowing at the end the taste of *her* own whiteness, / [t]he horror of *her* own smoothness" [emphasis mine] ("St Narcissus" qtd. in *The Waste Land Manuscript* 97). The fact that Eliot originally wrote "her" for "his" indicates a deliberate change to emphasize the lack of an other. The situation is identical to the fish earlier: "his ancient beauty / [c]aught in the pink tips of his new beauty" ("St Narcissus" 26–7). Each reincarnation visits violence on a previous one in direct contradiction of Empedokles' edicts.[65] Narcissus enacts a cycle of self-destruction and self-punishment. Eliot appears to be portraying how Narcissus' sin of self-love, his failure to purify himself, is the cause of his own destruction.

On the whole, these early experiments with the ascetic ideal acquired in his education show a very ambivalent and skeptical Eliot toying with the concept, as he did with other parts of his education such as Bradley's philosophy in "Appearances, Appearances." These poems show Eliot creating character studies in which he explores the ascetic ideal, but as the 1910s advanced, he will begin reconsidering the ascetic ideal in earnest.

---

65    Empedokles Fr.137 qtd. in Burnet 289.

CHAPTER 3

# Integrating

At the outset of his prose-writing career in early 1916, Eliot was primarily a reviewer of academic books. Yet, as his star ascended, he not only developed his famed impersonality theory but increasingly propounded his own positions. These showed an increasing conservatism in orthodox, Catholic religion, Classicist aesthetics, Royalist politics, and the literary Tradition. All of these ideas, as time progressed, become increasingly interdependent. Yet, his position in each of these, when not directly rooted in the ascetic ideal, quickly develops a distinctly ascetic cast.[1] Yet, this process is organic, and it is not for at least ten years into his career that these various strands of thought became fused in his famous Classicist, Royalist, and Anglo-Catholic pronouncement in *For Lancelot Andrewes* (*Prose* III.513). There is, though, an early hint at the interrelated nature of these ideas. In "An American Critic," one of his earliest reviews, Eliot explains the views of Paul Elmer More, with whom Eliot would come to be close.

> The fundamental beliefs of an intellectual conservatism, that man requires an askesis, a *formula* to be imposed upon him from above; that society must develop out of itself a class of leaders who shall discipline it; distrust of the promises of the future and conviction that the future, if there is to be any, must be built upon the wisdom of the past.
>
> *Prose* I.407.

Many of the features of Eliot's later thought are presaged in this quotation including not only the connection of an external formula—an idea that More insists is fundamentally ascetic—but also that the "wisdom of the past" is key to the development. This seems very similar to the idea of Tradition and the historical sense. Much of this review is devoted to expositing More's multifoliate conception of Romanticism. Eliot summarizes More's position that "[i]n art, these two tendencies [materialism and sentimentalism] find their expression in realism and romanticism; in refusing to refine upon Nature, or in refusing to handle it at all. In politics, the complementary tendencies are despotism and democracy" (*Prose* I.407). While it will be several years before Eliot himself

---

1 *Pace* Schuchard who argues that the turn to the religious and moral in Eliot's criticism is sudden at his conversion rather than the more gradual transition presented here (Schuchard 52).

© KONINKLIJKE BRILL NV, LEIDEN, 2020 | DOI:10.1163/9789004375826_005

INTEGRATING

41

opposes Romanticism, More's idea of a singular Romantic worldview expressing itself in multiple arenas seems to have impressed itself upon him. Eliot repeatedly quotes passages emphasizing the necessity of discipline "in order to be good, in order to be human" (*Prose* I.407). While Eliot is, as typical for these early reviews, reserved in his evaluations, he concludes by stating that "[w]hatever our reaction upon Mr. More's book, it must be admitted that his philosophy is much more akin to intellectual revolution than is most of what passes current for liberal thought in America" (*Prose* I.408). Compare these statements summarizing More to Eliot's own comments in "Mr. Read and M. Fernandez" in 1926: "The issue is really between those who, like M. Fernandez, and (if I understand right) Mr. Middleton Murry (otherwise very different from M. Fernandez) make *man the measure of all things*, and those who would find an extra-human measure" (*Prose* II.838). What was discussed dispassionately in 1916 has ten years later been adopted. This chapter charts this process.

The analysis of how Eliot's ascetic ideal slowly suffuses and unites his diverse thoughts on religion, culture, and aesthetics in his early prose, will proceed in three phases. The first will be to examine to what extent impersonality, Tradition, Classicism, and, finally, religion and politics have their roots in the ascetic ideal. The second will be where and when the boundaries among these concepts begin to blur. The third will be a detailed reading of Eliot's most thorough engagement with these concepts: "Tradition and the Individual Talent" and "The Function of Criticism." The primary evidence will be from his early prose (1916–1925). As such I will be summoning a panoply of disparate quotations; this is after all an undercurrent. Nonetheless, I have made no attempt to cite *every* instance of this ascetic underpinning.

Even early in Eliot's career, the idea of impersonality in art was framed in terms of the ascetic ideal, an escape from and a denial of the personality which is also, counterintuitively, an expansion. As an artistic ideal, this was common enough in the mystical readings, and it is worth exploring what some of these authors state on the matter.[2] Inge, for instance, comments that "Wordsworth was an ascetic of an unfamiliar type" (Inge *English Mystics* 188). Elaborating on a passage by William James, Cutten states in his chapter on monasticism and asceticism that "[t]here is needed the asceticism of art, of business, of sport, as well of religion for unless a man is willing to deny himself he cannot see the Kingdom of God in religion, nor his ideal in any branch of life" (Cutten 122). The athletic metaphor of ascetic training, likely derived from 1st Timothy 4:8, will be one that Eliot employs himself in other contexts. In fact, Inge devotes an entire chapter in *Personal Idealism and Mysticism* to what he calls

---

2  Underhill repeatedly invokes the artist in her chapter on asceticism, Cf. Underhill 275.

42                                                                          CHAPTER 3

"The Problem of Personality," wherein he fulminates against the "modern conception of a rigid impenetrable personality" and "the 'will-worship' which is
now treated with so much respect by philosophers" (Inge *Personal Idealism*
97, 107). Inge insists that "[w]e are to throw ourselves heartily into great and
worthy interests, to forget ourselves and lose ourselves in them"[3] insisting that
"[t]here is no self-expenditure without self-enrichment, no self-enrichment
without self-expenditure" (Inge *Personal Idealism* 104–5). In the end, Inge
scoffs at "[a]ny one who tries to attain complete self-expression—to build his
pyramid of existence, as Goethe put it, as an isolated individual, is certain to
fail ignominiously" (Inge *Personal Idealism* 105). When Eliot's early aesthetic
statements are examined, his approval of this ascetic escape from personality[4]
reflects these opinions. Much of the praise that Eliot heaps on authors employ
words associated with the ascetic ideal such as disinterested, austere, and self-
sacrifice. These are often concomitantly associated with impersonality as well.
For instance, in an early book review, he states that

> De Bosschère's austerity is terrifying. A poet is not a pure intellectual by
> virtue of any amount of meditation or abstractness or moralizing; the ab-
> stract thought of nearly all poets is mediocre enough, and often second-
> hand. [...] A poet like M. de Bosschère is an intellectual by his obstinate
> refusal to adulterate his poetic emotions with human emotions. Instead
> of refining ordinary human emotion (and I do not mean tepid human
> emotion, but human however intense–in the crude living state), he aims
> direct at emotions of art.
>
> *Prose* I.595–6.

Here, the associated ascetic term "austerity" is used as a form of praise and
associated with intellectuality. Additionally, there is a disassociation between
"poetic" and "human" emotions which hints at the escape from personality in
later works like "Tradition and the Individual Talent." Eliot praises de Boss-
chère for "his obstinate refusal to adulterate" the two kinds of emotion. The
idea of a refusal and the moral overtones in the word adulterate suggests the
ascetic ideal may lie behind an escape from "human emotions" which produces "an intense frigidity" that Eliot confesses to "find altogether admirable"
(*Prose* I.596). There are examples of similar statements elsewhere in Eliot's

---

3  Gott reaches, perhaps, a similar conclusion, although through a very different line of reasoning (Gott 67–8). Cf. Schuchard 74.
4  *Contra* Gott 46–7.

# INTEGRATING

other early prose.[5] He also expresses this opinion in his letters, including the adjectival reference to coldness, as his own in 1917: "I like to feel that a writer is perfectly cool and detached, regarding other people's feelings or his own, like a God who has got beyond them"[6] (*Letters* I.220). Although Eliot backs off on this opinion a few lines later, he is, even as early as 1917, was repeatedly stating a need for the writer to have detachment.

Additionally, scientific metaphors like Eliot employed most famously in "Tradition and the Individual Talent," appear simultaneously in passages that evoke both the ascetic ideal and impersonality. In his eulogy for Henry James, Eliot comments that "James's critical genius comes out most tellingly in his mastery over, his baffling escape from, Ideas; a mastery and an escape which are perhaps the last test of a superior intelligence. He had a mind so fine that no idea could violate it" (*Prose* I.650). An important emphasis[7] here is the combination of the ascetic idea of dominating emotions coupled with the impersonal aspect of a flight from it—suggestive of the two aspects of ascetic purification in Underhill. What Eliot means by "Ideas" in this passage is not perfectly clear; I take it to mean something akin to *idée fixe*, an idiosyncrasy to be expunged. On the prior page appears one of the earlier scientific metaphors in Eliot's prose: "It is in the chemistry of these subtle substances, these curious precipitates and explosive gases which are suddenly formed by the contact of mind with mind, that James is unequalled" (*Prose* I.649). This seems an inchoate version of the celebrated platinum catalysis metaphor in "Tradition and the Individual Talent" with an interesting distinction. Here the emphasis is on "the contact of mind with mind" (*Prose* I.649). Discussion of the ascetic ideal's curious corollaries about the contact between souls must wait

---

5 Eliot, summarizing Clutton-Brock's book on education, states: "the aesthetic activity, is no less important. For the boy whose childhood has been empty of beauty, the boy who has never learned the *detached* curiosity for beauty, the sexual instinct when it is aroused may mean the only possible escape from a prosaic world" before Eliot concludes that "its thought is not daring, but its commonsense is sound." (*Prose* I.436–7). Also, in his evaluation of Turgenev, Eliot concludes that "I am not sure that the method of Turgenev–this perfect proportion, this vigilant but never theoretic intelligence, this austere art of omission–is not that which in the end proves most satisfying to the civilized mind" (*Prose* I.617). In his discussion of technique, he praises James among other authors, saying "it may be harder and more orderly; but throbbing at a higher rate of vibration with the agony of spiritual life." (*Prose* II.517).

6 This may be a reference to the famed passage in Aristotle, whom Eliot studied under Harold Joachim, where the man who lives detached from society is "ὥστε ἢ θηρίον ἢ θεός," as such either a beast or a god (*Politics* I.1253a).

7 Obviously, this passage is a touchstone for Jewel Spears Brooker's well-regarded monograph. I will, however, not recapitulate her arguments here.

for the following chapter; however, here the idea of impersonality is expressed through the broadening of the self as a necessary part of artistic creation.

As the various strands of this conception become increasingly interwoven through the 1920s, the connection between impersonality and the ascetic ideal becomes more overt. In his reply to a letter by William Pollack in the *Athenaeum*, Eliot insists that "I do not believe that a work of art is *any* 'complete and precise expression of personality'" (*Prose* II.260). He goes on to object that Pollack has misquoted him, that personalities are not to be expressed but transformed: "Transformation is what I meant: the creation of a work of art is like some other forms of creation, a painful and unpleasant business; it is a sacrifice of the man to the work, it is a kind of death" (*Prose* II.260). Here, Eliot is stating very clearly a movement against the Romantic ideal of art as an expression of personality and for a classical, ascetic ideal of impersonality in creativity. The emphasis is on the extinguishing or flight from personality, which Eliot describes in ascetic terms like "painful," "a sacrifice," "a kind of death." Even as Eliot moves toward more overtly religious criticism near his conversion, the connection between ascetic ideals and impersonality remain. In a comparison between Donne's sermons and those of Lancelot Andrewes, Eliot asserts that Donne's sermons evince:

> his cunning knowledge of the weaknesses of the human heart, his understanding of human sin, his skill in coaxing and persuading the attention of the variable human mind to Divine objects, and [...] a kind of smiling tolerance among his menaces of damnation. He is dangerous only for those who find in his sermons an indulgence of their sensibility, or for those who, fascinated by "personality" in the romantic sense of the word—for those who find in "personality" an ultimate value—forget that in the spiritual hierarchy there are places higher than that of Donne.
> *Prose* II.826.

This shows the growing agreement with what he encountered in Inge, that a focus on individual personality is a sign of spiritual weakness. Eliot, then, is merging into his aesthetic judgment of Donne's sermons, an assessment rooted in their being overly expressive of Donne's own idiosyncrasies. This appears to be Eliot reflecting the religious component in which the impersonality theory was rooted.

When Eliot begins to speak of Tradition, it is not immediately connected to the ascetic ideal before "Tradition and the Individual Talent," but it is aligned with the concept of the earlier-developed impersonality theory. In one of the earliest passages of his critical prose, Eliot lays out "[*l*]'esprit historique, c'est le

# INTEGRATING                                                                45

*fondement de la culture*," an apparent early version of the historical sense[8] of "Tradition and the Individual Talent," but his focus is primarily on "*la solidarité entre les morts, les vivants, et ceux qui vivront après nous*" (*Prose* I.499). This emphasis on the "*la vie commune de nous et de nos ancêtres*" seems to relate directly to the personality-expanding ideas discussed previously.

Yet, as Eliot's ideas in this matter develop through the early 1920's, the influences of the ascetic ideal become directly integrated into the concepts of Tradition, particularly in his discussions on the role of criticism. Eliot, in a critique of more Romantically-inclined critics, concludes that "[i]n all of these attitudes the English critic is the victim of his temperament. He may acquire great erudition, but erudition easily becomes a hobby; it is useless unless it enables us to see literature all round, to detach it from ourselves, to reach a state of pure contemplation" (*Prose* II.287). The term "pure contemplation" is used technically by Underhill as a type of mystical vision, a state of "indifference, liberty, and peace" beyond subject-object consciousness (Delacroix qtd. in Underhill 394). It seems unlikely that Eliot, who wrote so scathingly against confuting religion and literature as will be discussed later, means this in the exact same way as Underhill. The idea of a critic achieving a mystical vision of the literary canon is, frankly, ludicrous. If Eliot is using "pure contemplation" as a metaphor, it supports the integration of the ascetic ideal into the concept of Tradition. The erudition discussed in the quotation seems analogous to the laborious acquisition of the historical sense in "Tradition and the Individual Talent." It becomes ascetic when Eliot insists that this effort must be supplemented by detachment. As Underhill states, "[r]eal detachment means the death of preferences of all kinds: even of those which seem to other men the very proofs of virtue and fine taste" (Underhill 269). Eliot, thus, seems to be implying that a critic must deny his or her personal preferences when studying literature to achieve a "purity" in examination. While this is similar to the impersonality theory, Eliot casts it in the language of the mystical readings from which his ascetic ideal derives. Later, when Eliot comes to discuss the role of a literary review, he uses ascetic language for both *The Criterion* and *The New Criterion*:

> To maintain the autonomy, and the disinterestedness, of every human activity, and to perceive it in relation to every other, require a considerable discipline. It is the function of a literary review to maintain the autonomy and disinterestedness of literature"
>
> *Prose* II.446.

---

8  Gott aligns this with F. H. Bradley's Absolute in line with his non-religious interpretation of asceticism, but I am uncertain of the helpfulness of this correspondence (Gott 42).

Again, Eliot is emphasizing disinterestedness in activity[9] and broadening the self in opposition to how "[i]n the common mind all interests are confused, and each degraded by the confusion" (*Prose* II.446). Yet, this is a mission statement for a literary magazine, but it does not sound so dissimilar from Underhill's discussion on the completion of the mystic's ascetic training, which she describes as "that ordering of disordered loves, that transvaluation [*sic*] of values, which the Way of Purgation began. The ascending self must leave these childish satisfactions; make its love absolutely disinterested" (Underhill 473). Thus, by the time that Eliot had transitioned from talking about Tradition to playing a part in its maintenance through *The Criterion*, the concept appears to have taken on clear, ascetic overtones in his mind.

Like with Tradition, the concept of Classicism may not stem directly from the ascetic ideal,[10] but as Eliot's thought develops, the ascetic ideal or language associated with it begin to creep into Eliot's discussions of Classicism. Often, the ascetic ideal expressed in Classicism seems largely independent of impersonality and Tradition. While "*Ulysses*, Order, and Myth" is one of Eliot's most frequently cited essays, its conclusion has rarely been studied in detail. Eliot insists that the mythical method of *Ulysses* with its backing of psychology and ethnology,

> is, I seriously believe, a step toward making the modern world possible for art, toward that order and form which Mr. Aldington[11] so earnestly desires. And only those who have won their own discipline in secret and without aid, in a world which offers very little assistance to that end, can be of any use in furthering this advance.
>
> *Prose* II.479.

In context, the "order and form" that will result from the application of the mythical method is clearly a reference to Classicism; interestingly, Eliot insists that only practitioners "who have won their discipline in secret" can help bring it about. In other words, some sort of asceticism on the part of the practitioner,

---

9    Eliot repeats this with *The New Criterion* that "[a]bove all the literary review [...] must protect its disinterestedness" (*Prose* II.764).

10   Although it is equally clear that the idea of emotional restraint was one of early importance to Eliot. He bemoans, even at the beginning of his prose career, how "[i]n England ideas run wild and pasture on the emotions; instead of thinking with our feelings (a very different thing), we corrupt our feelings with ideas; we produce the public, the political, the emotional idea, evading sensation and thought" (*Prose* I.650).

11   Earlier in this same essay, Eliot was clear that "I think that Mr. Aldington and I are more or less agreed as to what we want in principle, and agreed to call it classicism" (*Prose* II.477).

INTEGRATING

in the face of a hostile world, is necessary for Classicism. Later, when propounding the ideals of *The New Criterion*, Eliot is explicit on this point which had previously been only suggested. He states,

> I believe that the modern tendency is toward something which, for want of a better name, we may call classicism. [...] Yet there is a tendency— discernable even in art—toward a higher and clearer conception of Reason, and a more severe and serene control of the emotions by Reason.
> *Prose* 11.764–5.

Eliot, then, highlights this in opposition to his favorite representatives of Romanticism such as John Middleton Murry and George Bernard Shaw. This is still an ascetic ideal without direct religious overtones at this phase of Eliot's career. Nonetheless, a certain kind of ascetic practice, in the form of self-control by the higher intellect over the emotions, is now intrinsic to Classicism itself instead of merely a requirement of the practitioner.

As Eliot approaches the years of his conversion, an explicitly religious dimension becomes evident when he is contrasting Classical and Romantic art pieces. Eliot contrasts the more formal, orderly, Classical sermons of Lancelot Andrewes with those of John Donne. In a striking passage, he comments that

> About Donne there hangs the shadow of the impure motive; and impure motives lend their aid to a facile success. He is a little of the religious spellbinder, the Reverend Billy Sunday of his time, the flesh-creeper, the sorcerer of emotional orgy. We emphasize this aspect to the point of the grotesque. Donne had a trained mind; but without belittling the intensity or the profundity of his experience, we can suggest that this experience was not perfectly controlled, and that he lacked spiritual discipline.
> *Prose* 11.820.

This shows the complete integration of the ascetic ideal into Classicism. Instead of insisting that an ascetic approach is needed to be Classical, Eliot draws the conclusion from the absence of a Classical approach that Donne "lacked spiritual discipline" (*Prose* 11.820). This does not remain restricted to religious authors. Reviewing two books by Ramon Fernandez and Herbert Read, Eliot contrasts the prior more Romantic

> generation for whom the dissolution of value had in itself a positive value, and the generation for which the recognition of value is of utmost importance, a generation which is beginning to turn its attention to an

athleticism, a *training*, of the soul as severe and ascetic as the training of the body of a runner.

Prose II.835–6.

This seems a fairly clear reference to the aforementioned athletic metaphor for spiritual development in 1st Timothy 4:8. Thus, even before his formal conversion, Eliot had fully, explicitly integrated the ideal of asceticism into his conception of Classicism.

During this early phase of his prose writing, the ascetic ideal was not a large part of his thinking on religion and monarchism, even when Eliot considers such things at all. However, they still find their expression occasionally. In his most secular phase between 1915 and 1920, Eliot would review books on religion, using his expertise in anthropology. These reviews, within their limited scope, do show an interest in asceticism associated with religion. For instance, in the first of his reviews, Eliot states that:

> In Australian religion M. Durkheim finds the essential elements of all religion. For M. Durkheim *communion*, not worship, is the fundamental sentiment. He goes on to trace the origin of the idea of the soul, the beginnings of sacrifice, asceticism (gain of power through suffering).
>
> Prose I.422.

There are two matters of importance here. The first is that Eliot does highlight the early and essential place of asceticism in religious practice. The second is the highlighted importance of the concept of communion in association with asceticism. This will become absorbed into the ideas of Tradition and impersonality as Eliot's thought develops. Although he is only reviewing books, Eliot does show a distinct bias against the liberal Christianity of his upbringing and a preference for the concepts in his mystical readings. In his review of Rashdall's *Conscience and Christ*, Eliot sarcastically comments that:

> Thus we learn that Christ was not ascetic, that he did not consider celibacy superior to marriage, that monasticism was not improbably an imitation of paganism, [...] All that is anarchic, or unsafe or disconcerting in what Jesus said and did is either denied, or boiled away by the "principle of development".
>
> Prose I.428–9.

Eliot concludes his review with the similarly snide remark that "[c]ertain saints found the following of Christ very hard, but modern methods have

INTEGRATING 49

facilitated everything" (*Prose* I.429). These comments, while off-hand, display a number of important features. The first is, as with the Durkheim review, that Eliot not only emphasizes asceticism and monasticism but considers them a key and desirable feature of Christianity. The mention of saints' lives and their struggles—a core feature of many of the mystical readings—evinces Eliot's retention of their content. Similarly, Eliot chastises Wundt, in both of his reviews, saying "[w]e find nothing of the influence of the sexual instinct, for instance, upon religion and myth. Mysticism is not even included in the index. The treatment of primitive art quite neglects its aesthetic value" (*Prose* I.508).[12] This shows three things. First, that Eliot had a continued interest in mysticism (for which he checked the index). Second, Eliot retained some allegiance even to works like Cutten and Starbuck who wrote about the adolescent sexual impulse as a key facet in religious awakening. Third, both of these, without any apparent transition, are connected to aesthetics. Even early on in his prose career, asceticism had connections to both religion and art in Eliot's mind.

While Royalist politics are not a key focus of Eliot's thoughts in his early prose writings, they begin to appear during the early years of editing *The Criterion*. In his inaugural commentary, Eliot concludes his discussion of *King Lear* by condemning

> the modern democracy of culture. We say democracy advisedly: that meanness of spirit, that egotism of motive, that incapacity for surrender or allegiance to something outside of oneself, which is a frequent symptom of the soul of man under democracy. (II.525)

Eliot is beginning to associate democratic values with Romanticism as shown with phrases like "egotism of motive." Additionally, the abrupt association of the "incapacity for surrender or allegiance to something outside of oneself" seems quite close to the definition of asceticism as "a *formula* to be imposed upon him from above" in the aforementioned essay on More (*Prose* I.407). It seems evident that a dissatisfaction with democracy precedes an explicit adoption of monarchism, but this distaste is couched in terms associated with the Romantic impulse which is in opposition to both the ascetic ideal and Classicism.

While asceticism is an undercurrent to some of the major themes of Eliot's early prose, there is a lot of interdependence. Eliot's ideals of Impersonality seem based on the idea of a supra-personal community from his readings on primitive religion, and this slowly transforms into the literary Tradition. When

---

12    Cf. *Prose* I.674.

Eliot's Classicism develops, the exclusively literary Tradition is subsumed into a larger project of "allegiance to something outside the self" with both religious and political dimensions (*Prose* II.525).

Having examined how impersonality, Tradition, Classicism, and, religious and political concepts are tied to the ascetic ideal, I will show how these ideas begin also to blur with each other. First is the overlap between impersonality and religion. Eliot's early book reviews on primitive religion display an interest in community with an emphasis on impersonality. Summarizing Durkheim's argument, Eliot states that

> The instinct for association and community with other men is [...] a religious instinct. For the savage or the civilised man, a solely individual existence would be intolerable; he feels the need of recreating and sustaining his strength by periodic refuge in another consciousness which is supra-individual.
>
> *Prose* I.421.

While Eliot is summarizing, he is also highlighting and phrasing Durkheim's argument in terms of his own reading on mysticism. Underhill's chapter on psychology begins with discussing the soul's means of "escape from the prison of the sense-world, transcend its rhythm, and attain knowledge of—or conscious contact with—a supra-sensible Reality" (Underhill 52). This idea is repeated throughout the book review. Primitive man is described as "[living] in two worlds, the one commonplace, practical, a world of drudgery, the other sacred, intense, a world into which he escapes at regular intervals, a world in which he is released from the fetters of individuality" (*Prose* I.422). This foreshadows Eliot's aside in "Tradition and the Individual Talent" about escaping from personality (*Prose* II.111). This comment is not unique to his review of Durkheim. In his first review of *Religion & Science*, Eliot summarizes that the isolated individual "is the earlier and truer aspect of our *personality*, contact with other personalities leads us out of it. [...] The awareness of a group of personalities gives us law and morality. The awareness of a supreme spiritual pressure gives us religion" (*Prose* I.434). He explicitly insists personalities are experienced "as influences, as spiritual pressures" (*Prose* I.434). Although Eliot is discussing another's work, his conclusion is more than flattering: "[t]hose who feel that not only their own creed but religion itself stands in need of defence, should not neglect the aid which this book offers them" (*Prose* I.435). This, at least, suggests some sympathy with the work. Clearly, there is a colocation between these early reviews on religion and the idea of an escape from the personality.

INTEGRATING 51

Even before "Tradition and the Individual Talent," Eliot strikes on the integration of the asceticism-derived concept of impersonality with Tradition. In a 1917 review of the letters of J. B. Yeats, Eliot first quotes a passage containing the line "[a poet] does not seek the original, *but the truth*"; before editorializing that

> Mr. Yeats understands poetry better than anyone I have ever known who was not a poet[.] [...] Ordinary writers of verse either deal in imagination or in "ideas"; they escape from one to the other, but neither one nor the other nor both together is truth in the sense of poetic truth. Only old ideas "part and parcel of the personality"[24][13] are of use to the poet."
>
> *Prose* I.552.

This prefigures, in adumbrated form, "Tradition and the Individual Talent." But this passage also contains the beginning of the fusion of Tradition and impersonality. Note the term "escape" seen in previous discussions of impersonality combined with the need to integrate "old ideas" until they become "'part and parcel of the personality'" (*Prose* I.552). This latter idea, implicit in this particular essay, is made explicit in the editorial portion of a review published a few months later. In this essay, Eliot begins, "Each of us, even the most gifted, can find room in his brain for hardly more than two or three new ideas, or ideas so perfectly assimilated as to be original" (*Prose* I.608). Even at this early stage in his prose-career, Eliot is moving toward "Tradition and the Individual Talent." A few sentences later, Eliot gives an inchoate definition for Tradition: "All the ideas, beliefs, modes of feeling and behaviour which we have not time or inclination to investigate for ourselves we take second-hand and sometimes call Tradition" (*Prose* I.608). This is less than the full complexity of the historic sense from "Tradition and the Individual Talent," but it does contain the early element of impersonality; the Tradition is a repository of knowledge outside the self.

After "Tradition and the Individual Talent," the fusion of the idea of impersonality and Tradition becomes more emphatic and more ascetic in nature. The personality becomes increasingly negatively portrayed. For example, he comments that "[i]n the man of scientific or artistic temper the personality is distilled into the work, it loses its accidents, it becomes, as with Montaigne, a permanent point of view, a phase in the history of mind" (*Prose* II.135). Again, the scientific imagery is reflected in the term distillation, but there is also an

---

13    Eliot is here quoting and citing from Yeats' letters.

increase in the amount of references to mysticism. Eliot, in a review of Native American poetry, states that "the artist is, in an impersonal sense, the most conscious of men; he is therefore the most and the least civilized and civilizable; he is the most competent to understand both civilized and primitive." (*Prose* 11.138). The connection is, admittedly, not obvious. A few sentences earlier, Eliot had stated that the artist "should be aware of all the metamorphoses of poetry that illustrate the stratifications of history that cover savagery" (*Prose* 11.138). This seems a version of the comments in "Tradition and the Individual Talent" where Eliot refers to the "Magdalenian draughtsmen" in the same breath as Homer and Shakespeare (*Prose* 11.107). Thus, Eliot is consistent about integrating the prehistoric and the primitive into the idea of the Tradition. This is also where the connection to mysticism is. In his second review of C. J. Webb's group theories, Eliot, explaining the concept of totemism, notes that primitive man

> is capable of a state of mind into which we cannot put ourselves, in which he *is* a parrot, while being at the same time a man. In other words, the mystical mentality, though at a low level, plays a much greater part in the daily life of the savage than in that of the civilised man."
>
> *Prose* I.431.

The implication is that the artist, as the least civilized man, may have a greater part of the mystical mentality than the average man. This ties crisply to Underhill's conception of the artist having a mystical nature as well, which will be discussed at length in the next chapter. By the time, Eliot is writing "Tradition and the Individual Talent" the two are almost merged.[14]

The interweaving of Tradition and Classicism begins in Eliot's earliest book reviews, particularly in his review of *Group Theories of Religion and the Individual*, by Clement Webb, which Eliot characterizes as "an original polemic in an important struggle" (*Prose* I.417). Eliot insists that "Mr. Webb stands for the humane tradition; his opponents, for the novelties of science. This is a chapter in the history of classicism and romanticism" (*Prose* I.417). Thus, while it is not the fullness of the concept of Tradition, it does indicate that the two were

---

14  While this will be discussed at some length later, it is important to note that these ideas occur elsewhere than in "Tradition and the Individual Talent." In "The Preacher as Artist," Eliot comments that "a great deal in Donne's predicatory style is traditional, and that some of the most praised passages are produced by a method which is more than traditional, which is immemorial, almost imposed by the sermon form." (*Prose* 11.165). Here, Donne's personal role is deprecated, the work rendered impersonal by the form, the Tradition of the literary sermon.

INTEGRATING

53

associated at least even at the beginning of his criticism. As Eliot continues in
these early years to write about Tradition, he positions it, at first, as an opposite
to Romanticism rather than as a component of Classicism. For instance, Eliot,
in the review "Professional, or..."[15] comments that

> An attitude which might find voice in words like these is behind all of
> British slackness for a hundred years and more: the dislike of the special-
> ist. It is behind the British worship of inspiration, which in literature is
> merely an avoidance of comparison with foreign literatures, a dodging of
> standards.
>
> *Prose* I.698.

The two sub-elements of Tradition and Classicism are combined here. The
phrase "worship of inspiration" is suggestive of the Romantic view of literary
creation in opposition to Eliot's more scientific metaphors and focus on impersonal creation. The insistence on examining foreign literature as part of
Tradition is fairly consistent throughout his work. Yet, the comment on foreign
literatures is associated, via an appositive, with "dodging of standards." Classicism is associated with rational, objective standards, as previously seen. Eliot,
at nearly the same time, writes that "[a] poet, like a scientist, is contributing
toward the organic development of culture: it is just as absurd for him not to
know the work of his predecessors or of men writing in other languages as
it would be for a biologist to be ignorant of Mendel or de Vries" (*Prose* I.719).
Here, the scientific metaphor appears again, associated with the literature of
other languages. This metaphor will also be applied to the rational work of the
Classicist critic: "If the critic has performed his laboratory work well, his understanding will be evidence of appreciation; but his work is by the intelligence,
not the emotions" (*Prose* I.760). Thus, it appears that even before "Tradition
and the Individual Talent," Classicism and the literary Tradition are, at the very
least, united against Romanticism.

The religious and political dimensions of Classicism do not begin to receive
their full statement until "The Function of Criticism" and will only grow in
importance until they eclipse Classicism altogether. However, even in the early essays there are some suggestions that Eliot's conception of Classicism is
deeper than an aesthetic philosophy. In the previously quoted second review

---

15    This particular essay also foreshadows Eliot's comments about the "great labor" to acquire
      the historical sense in "Tradition and the Individual Talent"; Eliot notes that "[t]echnique
      is more volatile; it can only be learned, the more difficult part of it, by absorption" (*Prose*
      II.106, I.699).

of Webb's *Group Theories of Religion*, Eliot concludes that the reader "ought to realise that the struggle of "liberal" against "orthodox" faith is out of date. The present conflict is far more momentous than that" (*Prose* I.432). As mentioned previously, this book has been associated with the battled between Classicism and Romanticism; in other words, Classicism and Romanticism have subsumed a religious debate. Additionally, this comment associates, implicitly, Romanticism with the liberal Christianity of Eliot's upbringing which he had rejected roundly even in the mid 1910s. For another example, in his second review of *Religion and Science*, Eliot comments that "[a]s for romanticism in theology, we find one fundamental assumption: there is something called religion, independent of articulate creeds" (*Prose* I.706). This is connected to the aesthetic components of Classicism explicitly by the preceding comment that "[t]o be in love with emotion has been our affliction since Rousseau; to believe in belief is a form of the same malady" (*Prose* I.706). Thus, Romanticism and Classicism early on acquired religious dimensions, which only grew after "Tradition and the Individual Talent." These religious elements slowly color the aesthetic components. Even before "The Function of Criticism," Eliot would make comments such as

> All first-rate poetry is occupied with morality: this is the lesson of Baudelaire. More than any poet of his time, Baudelaire was aware of what most mattered: the problem of good and evil. What gives the French Seventeenth Century literature its solidity is the fact that it had its Morals, that it had a coherent point of view. Romanticism endeavoured to form another Morals"
>
> *Prose* II.306.

Here, the religious elements, with hints of the ascetic background, are rendered explicit. Seventeenth-century French literature is highlighted as being mature and Classical in "The Function of Criticism" (*Prose* II.462). Thus, Eliot is specifically connecting a cogent, moral point of view as a feature of Classicist aesthetics in contrast to Romanticism.

There are very few discussions of the political implications of Classicism early, but there is a very interesting quotation in his review of Georges Sorel's *Reflections on Violence*. Towards the end of the piece, Eliot states that Sorel

> is representative of the present generation, sick with its own knowledge of history, with the dissolving outlines of liberal thought, with humanitarianism. He longs for a narrow, intolerant, *creative* society with sharp divisions. He longs for the pessimistic, classical view. And this longing is

INTEGRATING                                                                                        55

healthy. But to realize his desire he must betake himself to very devious
ways. [...] It is not surprising that Sorel has become a Royalist."

> *Prose* I.559.

It is not clear to me whether Eliot would place himself in this category in 1917.
Additionally, "the pessimistic, classical view" does not seem to be quite the
same as Classicism. Nonetheless, the "dissolving outlines of liberal thought" is
suggestive of Romanticism, and the "knowledge of history" does seem a precursor of the historical sense of "Tradition and the Individual Talent." As it is,
Eliot seems to find this combination of desires the logical precursor to Royalism which would be the path that Eliot himself will follow years later.

Before a detailed analysis of the seminal essays "Tradition and the Individual Talent" and "The Function of Criticism," let me briefly recapitulate the position of these two within the evolution of Eliot's thought already charted. In
"Tradition and the Individual Talent," the fusion of impersonality and tradition
is largely completed and couched in ascetic, if largely non-religious, terminology. Eliot returns to "Tradition and the Individual Talent" as the starting point
to broaden his argument in "The Function of Criticism," where the concepts of
Classicism, religion, and royalism are further integrated. Throughout each of
these, the ascetic ideal is clearly evinced in Eliot's phrasing.

While most discussions of "Tradition and the Individual Talent" focus on
either the historical sense or the catalysis metaphor, the less-examined context
surrounding these ideas, though, shows the origin of impersonality and Tradition in the ascetic ideal.[16] In fact, his idea of a historical sense and its connection to asceticism may have been suggested by Underhill:

> [A]s in all the other and lesser arts which have been developed by the
> race, education consists largely in a humble willingness to submit to the
> discipline, and profit by the lessons, of the past. Tradition runs side by
> side with experience; the past collaborates with the present.
>
> UNDERHILL 359.

While I am not necessarily suggesting that Eliot is *consciously* imitating Underhill, the resemblance to "Tradition and the Individual Talent" is startling.
The idea of an artist's being willing "to submit to the discipline [...] of the past"
is not unlike the "great labour" necessary to acquire the historical sense, a resemblance that will deepen as Eliot develops this thought in "The Function of

---

16    Ellmann touches on similar ideas, although her intersection with the ascetic ideal is brief,
      given her interest in psychoanalytic criticism (Ellmann 38–9).

Criticism" (Underhill 359; *Prose* II.106). Underhill's statement that "the past collaborates with the present" reflects the idea of how "the timeless and the temporal together" are required for originality in art (Underhill 359; *Prose* II.106). Eliot, of course, extends this concept from Underhill to include the present's alteration of the past which is his innovation on Underhill, but clearly Underhill's mystical tradition, one that comprised authors and poets, seem to have influenced his thinking.

As he transitions out of his discussion of the historical sense, Eliot comments that "[w]hat happens is a continual surrender of himself as he is at the moment to something which is more valuable. The progress of an artist is a continual self-sacrifice, a continual extinction of personality" (*Prose* II.108). Here, the artistic act is defined in clearly ascetic terms which aligns with Underhill's discussion of the artist progressing in a manner similar to the mystic. As Underhill says, "[t]he death of selfhood in its narrow, individualistic sense is, then, the primary goal" of any ascetic practice, and Eliot seems to be casting the artistic progress in similar terms (Underhill 266). Later in the essay, Eliot reworks Wordsworth's definition of poetry according to this distinctly ascetic approach to artistic achievement.

> Poetry is not a turning loose of emotion, but an escape from emotion; it is not the expression of personality, but an escape from personality. But, of course, only those who have personality and emotions know what it means to want to escape from these things.
>
> *Prose* II.111.

Underhill explicitly casts ascetic ideal as an escape: "[t]o have arrived" at the goal of purgation "is to have escaped from the tyranny of selfhood" (Underhill 261). Eliot's aside at the end of the quotation mirrors not only his reading but earlier comments on the nature of ascetic practice. In the previously quoted letter to Brigit Patmore, Eliot commented in critique of her work that she "had got thoroughly *inside* the feelings, but hadn't quite got *out* again," but he later backpedals that "*stupid* detachment is so much the rule, that [his interest in cold detachment] may be only a particular taste" (*Letters* I.220). Again, Underhill illuminates this comment; she concludes that her catalogue of absurd acts of asceticism is merely evidence that "[t]o say that some have fallen short of this difficult ideal and taken refuge in mere abnegation is but to say that asceticism is a human, not a superhuman art, and is subject to 'the frailty of the creature'" but that "on the whole, these excesses are mainly found amongst saintly types who have not exhibited true mystic intuition" (Underhill 260). Eliot seems to have integrated a similar idea of an intrinsic quality of an artist—if perhaps not quite to the extent of Pound's idea of a poetic Apostolic Succession—that must be perfected through the ascetic ideal of self-surrender.

In the less-examined conclusion of "Tradition and the Individual Talent," Eliot self-consciously does not follow his logic through to its conclusion, which is a task that "The Function of Criticism" will, in a different stage of his thought, fulfill. In analyses of "Tradition and the Individual Talent," the quotation from Aristotle's *De Anima* is rarely examined As Eliot read Aristotle in Greek, the reader will forgive the analysis of the Greek. The germane adjective ἀπαθές has the word for suffering (πάθος) with a distinctive emphasis on passivity as its root. Liddell, Scott, and Jones quote this specific passage from *De Anima* as an example under a subdefinition which emphasizes freedom from emotion and disinterestedness. Additionally, the strong copulative καὶ links this aspect clearly to divinity. After this excursion, Eliot's cryptic comment that he "proposes to halt at the frontier of metaphysics or mysticism" is a cursory acknowledgment that his ideas of Tradition and impersonality have at least some underpinning in the ascetic ideal from his reading on mysticism (*Prose* II.112). The actual quotation is ambiguous, though. It is generally understood to mean that to pursue any farther would be to trespass upon metaphysics or mysticism, and that may have been what Eliot intended. However, the word "frontier" here could imply that to pursue it farther would be to leave the well-traveled areas of metaphysics or mysticism. The ambiguity suggests that Eliot may be aware that his essay has a deep mystical background. The essay's conclusion, though, emphasizes this basis in ascetic ideals by insisting that "the poet cannot reach this impersonality without surrendering himself wholly to the work to be done" (*Prose* II.112). Here, again, at the essay's conclusion is the focus on self-surrender to achieve impersonality, to escape from the self, which is the hallmark of the ascetic ideal. Yet, at this stage in the development, this is not the labor of love, the "dreadful joy" that Underhill describes[17] and religion, Classicism, and Royalism have yet to be fully integrated. "Tradition and the Individual Talent" is thus an important and cogent step, but its ideas are still inchoate; it is not Eliot's final statement on the matter.

In "The Function of Criticism," Eliot begins by quoting from "Tradition and the Individual Talent" and deliberately characterizing his topic then as "a problem of order; and the function of criticism seems to be essentially a problem of order too" (*Prose* II.458). Thus, he is encouraging his readers to see "The Function of Criticism" as an extension of "Tradition and the Individual Talent" and summarizes his previous article: "There is accordingly something outside

---

17    Cf. Underhill 243.

58 CHAPTER 3

of the artist to which he owes allegiance, a devotion to which he must surrender and sacrifice himself in order to earn and to obtain his unique position" (*Prose* 11.458). The wording emphasizes the ascetic aspects of Eliot's conception of the artistic experience and also the exteriority of the Tradition as a standard, which is a feature, perhaps the defining one, of Classicism. Eliot insists, then, that what must be true about art must be true of criticism as the latter is dependent on literature and not "an autotelic activity" (*Prose* 11.459). Thus, the ascetic ideal expressed in art is transferred to the critic. Eliot emphasizes the point that "[t]he critic, one would suppose, if he is to justify his existence, should endeavour to discipline his personal prejudices and cranks—tares to which we are all subject" (*Prose* 11.459). Again, the asceticism-associated word, "discipline," is used to emphasize the process of creating impersonality. Also, "tares" has strong biblical overtones. The second and third portions of the essay are devoted to the contrasting viewpoint: that of the Romantic critic exemplified in his friend John Middleton Murry. Eliot's own viewpoint, particularly regarding the religious and political dimensions is here largely defined by opposition.

Quoting as "an unimpeachable definition," Eliot states that "'Catholicism,' [Murry] says, 'stands for the principle of unquestioned spiritual authority outside the individual; that is also the principle of Classicism in literature'" (*Prose* 11.460). This is an idea that has been seen in both veiled and unveiled terms throughout Eliot's early prose, the existence of an external authority to which a person must submit. It is part of the definition of asceticism. Yet, what had previously been hinted at darkly, Eliot here makes clear:

> If, then, a man's interest is political, he must, I presume, profess an allegiance to principles, or to a form of government, or to a monarch; and if he is interested in religion, and has one, to a Church; and if he happens to be interested in literature, he must acknowledge, it seems to me, just that sort of allegiance which I endeavoured to put forth in the preceding section [*i.e.* Tradition].
> *Prose* 11.461.

In short, Eliot has here embraced, if perhaps not expressly for himself, what More stated nearly a decade earlier: Royalist politics, Anglo-catholic religion, Classicism, and the literary Tradition have one root and sap. Eliot, then, interrogates the opposite ideology, Romanticism with its focus on Murry's "inner voice." This will show that the ascetic ideal is key to this complex of intellectual conservatism.

Eliot tackles the moral and religious definition first, snidely commenting that "the inner voice, in fact, sounds remarkably like [...] 'doing as one likes'"

INTEGRATING 59

and that "[t]he possessors of the inner voice ride ten in a compartment to a football match at Swansea, listening to the inner voice, which breathes the eternal message of vanity, fear, and lust" (*Prose* II.461). Thus, it is clear that Eliot associates the inner voice with not merely a literary failing but with a distinctly moral and religious one; vanity, fear, and lust are not generally issues associated with literary criticism. Eliot admits that Murry would object to the football-hooligan characterization "with some show of justice" before proceeding (*Prose* II.461). "[Murry] says: 'If they (the English writer, divine, statesman) dig *deep enough* in their pursuit of self-knowledge [...] they will come upon a self that is universal'" (*Prose* II.461). In his response to this, Eliot shows how deeply he has integrated the ideas in his mystical readings, stating that such a practice of self-interrogation "was of enough interest to Catholicism for several handbooks to be written on its practice. But the Catholic practitioners were, I believe, with the possible exception of certain heretics, not palpitating Narcissi; the Catholic did not believe that God and himself were identical" (*Prose* II.461). The several handbooks to which Eliot refers is not clear; there is a list of descriptions of interior prayer by Catholic saints in Underhill, but it might also refer to books Eliot read himself like Poulan and Jeffries (Underhill 368–9). What is more of note is Eliot repeating Underhill's rather defensive insistence that "[t]he greatest mystics, however, have not been heretics but Catholic saints" (Underhill 126). The later-edited comment about "heretical experts who were often Teutonic" seems a comment on the excessive emphasis on immanence associated with German mysticism embodied by Meister Eckhart who "preached immanence in its most extreme and pantheistic form" mentioned on the page prior to the above-cited quotations (Underhill 126). Eliot's dislike of Eckhart will be discussed in later chapters, but his objection is that it leads the same place that Eliot accuses Murry's doctrine of the inner voice of leading: "a form of pantheism which I maintain is not European" (*Prose* II.461). While it is hard to extract precise details from a one-sided argument, Eliot's interest in religion at this phase has not only deep roots in his mystical readings but some moral urgency.

As Eliot proceeds through the essay, a political dimension is added to his characterization of Romanticism. In the third section of "The Function of Criticism," Eliot writes:

> the search for perfection is a sign of pettiness, for it shows that the writer has admitted the existence of an unquestioned spiritual authority outside himself, to which he has attempted to *conform*. [...] Thus speaks the Inner Voice. It is a voice to which, for convenience, we may give a name: and the name I suggest is Whiggery.
>
> *Prose* II.462–3.

Here, the political angle not only takes a distinctly Royalist tone but also begins the integration of the political and religious. Referring to the inner voice as Whiggery suggests not only the democratizing element in the English Civil War—as contrasted to the Metaphysical Poets and Dryden—but also to puritanism. A reference to *Hudibras* earlier in the essay confirms that Eliot intends the collocation.

In conclusion, Eliot, as he developed as a critic, seems to have embraced Paul Elmer More's definition of intellectual conservatism as requiring "an askesis, an external *formula*" (*Prose* I.407). Initially, this tendency is rather divorced from its origins in religious texts; however, by the time Eliot has assumed the editorship of *The Criterion*, More's integrated approach has been fully embraced. In his *apologia* for the magazine, Eliot asserts that "a literary review should maintain the application, in literature, of principles which have their consequences also in politics and in private conduct" (*Prose* II.446). By the time he writes his essay on Lancelot Andrewes, Eliot could easily write about how Andrewes' "passion for order in religion is reflected in his passion for order in prose" (*Prose* II.821). This ideal of order, rooted in asceticism, expressed themselves in Eliot's devotion to the literary Tradition, his war of words with his friend Middleton Murry over Classicism and Romanticism, his interest in Anglo-Catholicism, and his emergent Royalism.

CHAPTER 4

# Bridging

While Eliot is publicly engaging with asceticism through his prose, he is also privately exploring the more esoteric aspects of the ascetic ideal from his reading on mysticism. Eliot was fascinated by the mystical communion of souls and the ascetic preparation required to achieve it at this period of life. This is first evident in the 1919 review "Beyle and Balzac." This aspect of the ascetic ideal is also apparent in his 1926 Clark Lectures. Between these prose works, Eliot's poetry between 1919 and his conversion in 1926 also explores the ascetic ideal but through its failure: sin leading to social and spiritual isolation. The purpose of this chapter is to provide the background to prove this idea is at work in some of Eliot's greatest poetic works. The logic is that if Eliot learned of the ascetic ideal at Harvard, his responses and critiques of Bradley resonate with the same ideas, and they appear, endorsed, in his Clark Lectures in 1926, then they could not have been entirely absent while he was writing "Gerontion," *The Waste Land*, and "The Hollow Men." Thus, this chapter will track each major component from the mystical readings, through F. H. Bradley, and to the Clark Lectures. Let me be frank—this is a prolonged, technical exegesis of recondite aspects of Eliot's education and thought; the actual application to his poetry must wait until Chapter 5. The reader who is happy to take me at my word may proceed to the close-readings; however, I am obligated to "show my math," nonetheless. Since many of these sources are obscure, I have taken the liberty of quoting more heavily as to not leave the reader searching for rare volumes.

The influence of F. H. Bradley is why the ascetic ideal has less prominence in Eliot's poetry and prose at this time. After finishing "*La Figlia*" at the end of 1912, Eliot turned his attention from poetry and engaged for a time with philosophy and specifically, Bradley's *Appearance and Reality*. The poetry written when Eliot resumes writing in 1914–5 and the way that the ascetic ideal is presented in those poems are clearly influenced by Bradley's philosophy. His hegemony, though, seems to have waned by the time "Gerontion" is written in 1919. Two aspects of his philosophy are important for my purposes here: his skepticism and his denial of the ascetic ideal.[1] It should be noted that I have

---

1  Two other aspects of Bradley's philosophy, solipsism and the conflation of spiritual and mental health, will be discussed later. A deeper theological examination of Bradley's Absolute in comparison with other theisms that Eliot encountered would certainly be probative but lies beyond the scope of this study.

© KONINKLIJKE BRILL NV, LEIDEN, 2020 | DOI:10.1163/9789004375826_006

taken the liberty of glancing toward Eliot's post-conversion work in this section as much of what he writes on Bradley's influence is from that time. Rather than speculate, I have elected to step out of my temporal frame briefly; there is simply not enough solid, contemporaneous evidence for a full examination of Bradley's influence on Eliot's theological views in the 1910's and early 1920's.[2] This will explain why the ascetic ideal is diminished during this time.

Eliot's first encounter with Bradley's work was not as a doctoral student in philosophy during the summer of 1913. Rather, he likely first encountered Bradley as an undergraduate studying religious manifestations in 1909. In A. A. Caldecott's *The Philosophy of Religion*, which is one of the orthodox mystical readings, Bradley is uneasily classified as a theologian under the heading of "Quasi-Theisms" (Caldecott 392). Caldecott justifies this by substituting "the term 'Divine Being' for 'Reality'" in Bradley's arguments (Caldecott 392). Having made this assumption, Caldecott proceeds to prove that Bradley's conception of Reality is both Immanent and Transcendent, which are the two qualities which he deems necessary for a proper Theism (Caldecott 395). He concludes that "Bradley works as a philosopher and uses philosophical terminology for the most part. But as Aristotle called Theology what was afterwards known as Metaphysics, we are making no strain in calling this a Theological treatise; and in regarding it as a most important contribution to nineteenth century Theism" (Caldecott 396). Caldecott asserts that the admission of "the canon of 'application of terms of human thought to the Deity,' [...] might relieve the vacillation and inconsistency which is the great defect of Mr. Bradley's work as it stands" (Caldecott 396). Eliot seems to have absorbed this belief in the theological underpinnings of Bradley's work. For instance, Eliot, at one point, speaks of a "transition from one point of view to another which is known to Mr. Bradley's readers as transcendence" (*Prose* 1.468). The exact referent is exceedingly unclear but seems close to Caldecott's discussion. In "Leibniz' Monads and Bradley's Finite Centers," Eliot asserts that "just as Leibniz' pluralism is ultimately based upon faith, so Bradley's universe, actual only in finite centers, is only by an act of faith unified" (*Prose* 1.465). Eliot's statement reiterates Caldecott's previously-quoted criticism of Bradley, which is that a leap of faith is required for the world of Bradley's philosophy to be anything other than "the isolated finite experiences out of which it is put together" (*Prose* 1.465). The Absolute, Eliot contends, is "[p]retending to be something which makes finite centers cohere[;] it turns out to be merely the assertion that they do. And this

---

2   Child's discussion of "Appearances, Appearances," while relevant, relies on what is likely a student satirizing his course reading. Though probative, I am wary of applying the poem as a definitive, nuanced statement of Eliot on Bradley (Childs *Mystic, Son, and Lover* 86–7).

BRIDGING                                                                 63

assertion is only true so far as we here and now find it to be so" (*Prose* 1.465). In short, Eliot finds Bradley's Absolute to be not a philosophical necessity derived from reason, but, in accordance with his mystical readings, a by-word for the Divine. The Absolute, then, requires faith to be actual, a faith that Eliot did not, as yet, possess in the 1910's.

The most lasting feature of Bradley's philosophy upon Eliot is, of course, not the content of Bradley's work, but rather his own skeptical mindset. Eliot writing many years later of writers who influenced him mentions "F. H. Bradley, whose works—I might say whose personality as manifested in his works—affected me profoundly" ("To Criticize the Critic" 20). This is the core of his influence on Eliot's writing: an attitude rather than a list of beliefs. In 1927 and over ten years from his dissertation, Eliot writes that "Bradley is thoroughly empirical, much more empirical than the philosophies that he opposed. He wished only to determine how much of morality could be founded securely without entering into the religious questions at all" (*Prose* III.311). Dogmatism of any variety was especially antithetical to Bradley's thinking. At the start of *Appearance and Reality*, he states that metaphysics should be studied, "even if it end in total skepticism" as it

> is, so far as I can see, [the only] certain way of protecting ourselves against dogmatic superstition. Our orthodox theology on the one side, and our common-place materialism on the other side [...] vanish like ghosts before the daylight of free skeptical enquiry. I do not mean, of course, to condemn wholly either of these beliefs; but I am sure that either, when taken seriously, is the mutilation of our nature. Neither, as experience has amply shown, can now survive in the mind which has thought sincerely on first principles; and it seems desirable that there should be such a refuge for the man who burns to think consistently, and yet is too good to become a slave, either to stupid fanaticism or dishonest sophistry.
>
> BRADLEY 5

That Eliot in the 1910's would have considered himself one of those "who burn to think consistently" seems likely; however, Bradley's thinking was not mere iconoclasm. It is essential to his thought that "sentient experience [...] is reality, and what is not this is not real" (Bradley 144). This sort of skepticism is exemplified in Bradley's contempt for spiritualism, even in an era laden with it.[3]

---

3  Bradley is not the only place where Eliot also encountered condescension towards occultism. He also read it in Inge who was much less a skeptic than Bradley (Inge *Mysticism* ix). Cf. Bradley's additional note on spiritualism (Bradley 506–7).

64                                                                    CHAPTER 4

Unlike most of Bradley's influences, this disdain for the occult would be life-long.[4] This disdain extends into Eliot's turn to Christianity ("The Dry Salvages" v.1–16). On the other hand, Bradley considered religion and God to be appearance; he later concludes that an afterlife is also unlikely (Bradley 443–8, 506–10). What Eliot learned from Bradley, though, was not any particular doctrine, but a mindset of skepticism that, in the end, brought him to belief.[5] What Eliot, at the time, thought of the passage from Hume he read near the end of Caldecott's work is unknown. Yet, in the end, he came to agree that "[t]o be a philosophic skeptic is, in a man of letters, the first and most essential step to being a sound believing Christian" (Hume qtd. in Caldecott 405).[6]

Unlike in his earlier readings on mysticism, the ascetic ideal is disparaged by Bradley—something that must, at least partially, account for its temporary disappearance from Eliot's poetry. While Bradley never touches on asceticism in so few words, he posits many ideas which areantithetical to it.[7] In Bradley's philosophy, "[e]very flame of passion, chaste or carnal, would still burn in the Absolute unquenched and unabridged, a note absorbed in the harmony of higher bliss" (Bradley 172). Additionally, Bradley, while denying Hedonism, defines the good as "that which satisfies desire" (Bradley 402).[8] The ascetic ideal, of course, asserts the opposite: the good requires the extinguishing of selfish desire.[9] Similarly, Bradley's denial of free will, while a minor point in *Appearance and Reality*, is also deeply problematic to asceticism, which involves "a *deliberate* recourse to painful experiences" [emphasis added] (Bradley 435, Underhill 247). Finally, Bradley attempts to solve the problem of pain in the Absolute by denial; he simply does "not admit the possibility of an Absolute perfect in apprehension yet resting tranquilly in pain" (Bradley 158). This is, of course, directly counter the assertion of the mystical writers that Eliot read but also contrary to Eliot's own thinking, even at that time. In an oft-quoted 1914 letter to Conrad Aiken, Eliot states that "[s]ome people say that pain is necessary ('they learn in suffering' *etc*), perhaps others that happiness is. Both beside the point I think: what is necessary is a *certain kind* (could one but catch it!)

---

4   For an example from the period in question, cf. Eliot's letter to Eleanor Hinkley on March 23rd 1917 (*Letters* I.185–6).
5   Cf. *Prose* III.308.
6   In 1948, Eliot writes "[o]ne may become a Christian partly by pursuing skepticism to the utmost limit" (*Prose* VII.112).
7   Cf. Bradley 6.
8   Cf. Bradley 406–7 *et al.*
9   Cf. Underhill 264–7 *et al.* Bradley's conceptions are not always wholly clear on the matter. Cf. Bradley 441.

BRIDGING 65

of *tranquility,* and *sometimes* pain does ~~buy~~ bring it" (*Letters* 1.44–7). While not the universal statement that Bradley is making, this letter does suggest that Eliot *could* conceive of tranquility in pain. In his 1929 essay on Dante, Eliot states that "[i]n purgatory the torment of flame is deliberately and consciously accepted by the penitent. [...] The souls in purgatory suffer because they *wish to suffer,* for purgation. And observe that they suffer more actively and keenly, being souls preparing for blessedness, than Virgil suffers in eternal limbo. In their suffering is hope" (*Prose* III.716). Eliot follows this statement with the speech of Daniel Arnaut from the ending of Canto XXVI. These comments seems at least consonant with his explanation to Aiken. While his statements about suffering cannot be applied directly, Eliot titles the first edition of the 1920 poems with a quotation from that speech by Daniel Arnaut, which clearly indicates that he was thinking on such passages even at that time.[10] As seen in the last chapter, Eliot was clearly not wholly at ease with Bradley's antipathy to ascetic thought as the 1910's were coming to an end, and though he is under the influence of Bradley for a time, Eliot clearly returned to the ascetic ideal's potential to allow the communion of souls by 1919.

Eliot's education on this part of the ascetic ideal may be summarized as follows: The divine λόγος[11] allows, with sufficient personal, spiritual preparation, for connection between not only the individual and God but his fellow man; sin severs this link which results in isolation. Thus, ascetic purification, self-denial, is the remedy. This becomes one of the most enduring but also the most intricate aspects of the ascetic ideal. I will examine the essay "Beyle and Balzac" to show Eliot's interest in the mystical communion at the end of asceticism. Then, I will track each of the four main components through Eliot's readings and into his 1926 Clark Lectures. The four requirements are sin, personal isolation, spiritual monadism, and the λόγος. This will not only show the continued applicability of the mystical readings but also reveal the depth and intricacy of the ascetic ideal. As a caveat, I am not suggesting that Eliot necessarily *held* any of these beliefs before his conversion; rather, they offer a discourse from which he is drawing and an ideal with which he is interacting.

---

10    The original epigraph to "Prufrock" is also from this speech by Arnaut, so it had been on his mind since before "*La Figlia*" was written (*Poems* 1.376).

11    As nigh every conceivable permutation of transliteration and formatting of the term λόγος has been used by the authors quoted in this chapter, I have, for consistency, rendered all of them in this way to maintain both the polyvalence and synonymy that Eliot would have seen. In his Harvard notes, Eliot did not generally transliterate the Greek, although he was not consistent in its pointing Cf. "Notes on Aristotle (16)" 6.

66                                                                                    CHAPTER 4

The first thread to examine in this aspect of the ascetic ideal is found in the two curious and relatively unexamined final sentences of the oft-quoted review "Beyle and Balzac":

> Beyle and Flaubert do not point, but they suggest unmistakably the awful separation between potential passion and any actualization possible in life. They indicate also the indestructible barriers between one human being and another. This is a "mysticism" not to be extracted from Balzac, or even Miss Underhill. "Ainsi tout leur a craqué dans la main."
>
> *Prose* ii.50.

Eliot's discussion of the inexorable division of finite centers is unsurprising and frequently linked by critics, I believe correctly, to the citation of Bradley in *The Waste Land* notes. What *is* surprising is that he refers to this as a kind of mysticism and off-handedly mentions Underhill, and it is surprising in two ways: first, the inability of individuals to connect to each other is indeed a theme that Eliot encountered in his mystical reading, but it was far from a common one, mostly residing as an undercurrent. He is quite correct that it very rarely, if ever, appeared in Underhill. Second, it is striking that he would refer to Underhill at all. There is no evidence that he had read her work in over six years at the time of "Beyle and Balzac." This off-handed comment may indicate, in line with my previous discussion, that even abstract and theological aspects of the ascetic ideal were returning to Eliot's mind. It is, after all, one of the core arguments of this study that the ascetic ideal is an occasionally submerged but permanent substratum of Eliot's thought. I have no other explanation for this odd aside about Evelyn Underhill in a book review nearly a decade after his Harvard studies.

The equally probative final sentence of the paragraph is from Flaubert's plan for the ending of *Bouvard et Pécuchet*.[12] While most of this summary is simply bulleted plot points, this line begins the final summation of the work as a whole.[13]

> So everything has gone to pieces in their hands.
> They no longer had any reason to live.

---

12    Though not always included in early editions of *Bouvard et Pécuchet*, this "epilogue" of sorts was published in *La Nouvelle Revue* in 1881 where Eliot could have seen it.

13    To the best of my knowledge, the tantalizing parallel between this first line, which Eliot repeatedly quotes, and *The Waste Land* 30 has never been properly explored.

BRIDGING

A good idea cherished secretly by each of them. They conceal it from each other. From time to time, they smile when it comes into their heads; then at last communicate it to each other:
*To copy as in former times.*

*Bouvard and Pécuchet* 99–100.

Why exactly Eliot would choose this phrase to punctuate the reference to the mysticism of spiritual monadism is exceedingly unclear from the context of the article. An explanation could be extracted from another use of this line in his 1921 essay on Andrew Marvell:

> Gray and Collins were masters, but they had lost that hold on human values, that firm grasp of human experience, which is a formidable achievement of the Elizabethan and Jacobean poets. This wisdom, cynical perhaps but untired (in Shakespeare, a terrifying clairvoyance), leads toward, and is only completed by, the religious comprehension; it leads to the point of the *Ainsi tout leur a craqué dans la main* of Bouvard and Pécuchet.

*Prose* II.313.

This quotation from Flaubert seems to be the only part of those ending notes which sounds like an actual line from a novel as opposed to the author's notes. The denouement of the novel has Bouvard and Pécuchet commissioning a desk built for two so they could copy side-by-side. It is a renewal of intimacy and of connection.Eliot insists, oddly, this a religious turn which is absent from Flaubert utterly. Returning to the quotation as it appears in "Beyle and Balzac," the presence of the phrase at the end of the paragraph implies that the phrase represents the final result of this mystical understanding of isolation.

Moreover, Eliot was quite right in stating that spiritual monadism was not found in Underhill as she never discusses the concept directly; however, several other authors in Eliot's reading do so, notably Inge. This is possibly the source of the slightly critical tone in mentioning her. Eliot seems to have encountered this idea of spiritual monadism mostly in Bradley. In addition to the famed passage from *The Waste Land* notes, there are a number of other places where Bradley discusses it in greater detail.[14] For example, Bradley, in an exploration of the body-soul duality, states that:

---

14    Discussion of the passage in *The Waste Land* is delayed until Chapter 5.

> The way of communication between souls, and again their sameness and difference, are points on which we must be careful to guard against error. It is certain, in the first place, that experiences are separate from each other. However much their contents are identical, they are on the other hand made different by appearing as elements in distinct centers of feeling. The immediate experience of finite beings cannot, as such, come together; and to be possessed directly of what is personal to the mind of another, would in the end be unmeaning.
>
> BRADLEY 342–3.

Bradley concludes that "[s]ouls seem to influence one another only by means of their bodies" (Bradley 353). These two statements may underlie Eliot's comments in "Beyle and Balzac"; there are impermeable barriers between two individuals, which results in the inability "to actualize any real passion"[15] since "[s]ouls seem to influence one another only by means of their bodies" (Bradley 253).[16]

Although Eliot read and may have believed that individuals were spiritual monads, this does not mean that this idea was pleasing to him. His studies in mysticism and subsequent reading in Greek philosophy contradicted the idea, and in the 1926 Clark Lectures, he directly espouses these ideas rather than Bradley's. To this end, I will begin to trace the discourse from Eliot's readings and then locate these same themes present in his Clark Lectures.[17] If he first encountered this idea of mystical communion at the end of the ascetic ideal between 1909–15 and then comes to suggest it himself in 1926, then the ascetic ideal could not have been utterly forgotten when he was writing "Gerontion," *The Waste Land*, and "The Hollow Men." I will occasionally highlight general points of overlap to display the relevance of such abstract material more clearly to Eliot's poetry. By this act of triangulation, the ascetic ideal as an escape from solipsism will be evident as a substratum of Eliot's thought even through a very secular period of his life.

Now, the repeated invocation of Inge in the following discussion requires justification as many years separated Eliot's reading at Harvard from the writing of his greatest works; however, Eliot wrote two fairly laudatory letters to his mother concerning meeting Inge in December 1920 (*Letters* 1.522–3).

---

15  It is possible that this may have struck a chord in light of Eliot's marital difficulties, but such biographical inquiries are beyond the scope of this study.

16  Cp. Bradley 342–3.

17  I am assuming familiarity with the concepts and contents of Clark Lectures on the part of the reader and will only highlight unusually probative instances.

BRIDGING                                                                 69

Additionally, in 1924, Eliot devoted a section of his April commentary in *The Criterion* to criticizing one of Inge's recent newspaper columns (Harding *Criterion* 131–2). While, upon first inspection, this might seem to argue against Inge's continued influence, Eliot's phrasing shows the respect that he held for Inge; the commentary seems to express primarily disappointment in the lack of insight and sensitivity provided by Inge on Byron (*Prose* II.534).[18] For instance, Eliot notes that "Dean Inge attacks culture from within," a statement which presupposes him to be part of a cultural elite and implies a responsibility that Eliot feels Inge is misusing (*Prose* II.533). Eliot goes on to note that the Evening Standard's public "deserves a little better food from a writer whose scholarship and ecclesiastical preferment command respect" (*Prose* II.534). The praise for and familiarity with Inge's academic works is clear. Moreover, Jason Harding reminds that Eliot wrote to Bonamy Dobrée in 1926, the same year as the Clark lectures, calling Inge "a heretic & as a social philosopher [...] a humbug" (*Letters* III.286).[19] However, such views are not found in the works by Inge that Eliot read during his time at Harvard, and this is suggested by a later letter where in contrast to his social theories, which Eliot finds "wholly reprehensible[,] [Inge's] relation to neo-Platonism, and also his relation to Christianity, are yet to be considered" in the *Criterion*. Eliot, earlier in life, seems to approve for Inge's 1899 condemnation of St. Bernard's homily on the Song of Solomon as against the authority of the church in his notes on Inge's *Christian Mysticism*, calling it "Romantic mysticism," presumably opposed to Inge's own classical position ("Notecards" 1). Thus, it seems that Eliot is accusing Inge of heresy for altering his views from the ones Eliot first encountered, the heavily neo-Platonic ones quoted in this study. Additionally, to prepare Dobrée for a column on Inge, Eliot "instructed Irene Fassett to send copies of [Inge's] books," the precise identities of which have not survived (Harding *The Criterion* 131). Again, this suggests continued familiarity with Inge and his work, if less than approval of his current intellectual course. Fascinatingly, it appears that Eliot increasingly disapproves of who Inge had become as Eliot increasingly becomes who Inge had been when Eliot first read his books—the conservative, Greek-philosophy-focused Anglo-Catholic public intellectual.

Additionally, there is further influence of Inge on Eliot's thought. When Eliot asserts in his essay on Leibniz's Monads that "Leibniz does not succeed in establishing the reality of several substances. On the other hand, just as Leibniz'

---

18    This disappointment is also evident in the discussion of Bertrand Russell's thoughts on the same topic that forms the first part of the same commentary and which receives the same scathing treatment as Inge's (*The Criterion* II.233–4).

19    Cf. Harding *Criterion* 132.

pluralism is ultimately based upon faith, so Bradley's universe, actual only in finite centers, is only by an act of faith unified" (*Prose* 1.465). Compare this to Inge's comment that

> [s]uch a monadism as that of Leibnitz is no improvement on frank pluralism, though it professes to be a compromise between pluralism and monism. The spiritual atoms of which his world are composed are said to form a system "ideally," *i.e.* for the mind of an all-wise spectator. There is no reciprocal action between monads, but a pre-established harmony which is due to the will of God, who, as in most philosophical systems of this type, is not really God, but a finite spirit. Leibnitz seems to have *started* with the assumption that human souls are impenetrable, indiscerptible atoms, and then to have built up his theory to have built up his theory of monads to account for it.
>
> INGE *Personal Idealism* 115.

Eliot seems to echo Inge in this matter,[20] and my argument here is, of course, based on an intellectual history and an underlying discourse rather than wholly on direct citation. This will, as I have said before, require extended citation of a great deal of technical material, but it is necessary to chart the course of the ascetic ideal.

Let me also remind of the four interrelated concepts which underpin how the ascetic ideal relates to personal communion. The first concept is the possibility of mystical communion of souls in opposition to the spiritual monadism of Bradley; the second is that this idea of mystical communion is derived from Plato's doctrines of Love; the third is the λόγος as the means of relation between souls; the final is the destructive power of sin in severing this link.

First, Bradley's view of souls as impenetrable monads was staunchly rejected in some of Eliot's mystical readings. The idea that real communion with others is possible is one that Eliot seems to have desired and thought unattainable based on his comments in "Beyle and Balzac." It also forms the ground of the defective asceticism in "Gerontion," *The Waste Land,* and "The Hollow Men." Consider the following passage from Inge:

---

20    Cf. Eliot's comment in one of his graduate essays that "[i]t is true that the monads have no windows, that the finite centres, as long as they last, are impervious, but not that the finite centre is a soul, not that the whole of reality is simply the sum of these centres" (*Prose* 1.174).

BRIDGING

Let us just compare this doctrine of impervious selves, *solida pollentia simplicitate*, with the absolutely fluid conception of personality which we find in the New Testament. Jesus Christ was seriously suspected of being Elijah, or Jeremiah, or even John [the] Baptist, who had just been beheaded. And unless we are willing to sacrifice the whole of the deepest and most spiritual teaching of St Paul and St John, unless we are prepared to treat all the solemn language of the New Testament about the solidarity of the body and its members, the vine and its branches, as fantastic and mis-leading [sic] metaphor, we must assert roundly that this notion of "impervious" spiritual atoms is flatly contrary to Christianity.

INGE *Personal Idealism* 94–5.

Inge asserts that the Greek "ὑπόστᾶσις and [Latin] *persona* by no means corresponded in meaning" so that two beings could be the same in essence in the minds of the ancients (Inge *Personal Idealism* 93).[21] Thus, physical dimensions have no bearing on the actions of the soul and the nature of identity. I suspect that this influenced Eliot's discussion of the synonymy of persons in his notes to *The Waste Land*.[22] In his most extended discussion on the concept which will be helpful to quote in full, Inge states that

it is possible to save personality without regarding the human spirit as a monad, independent and sharply separated from other spirits. Distinction, not separation, is the mark of personality; but it is separation, not distinction, that forbids union. The error, according to the mystic's psychology, is in regarding consciousness of self as the measure of personality. The depths of personality are unfathomable, as Heraclitus already knew;[23] the light of consciousness only plays on the surface of the waters. [...][24] So far is it from being true that the self of our immediate consciousness is our true personality, that we can only attain personality,

---

21 For a brief discussion of the term ὑπόστᾶσις, cf. Spicq 421–3.

22 "Tiresias, although a mere spectator and not indeed a 'character,' is yet the most important personage in the poem, uniting all the rest. Just as the one-eyed merchant, seller of currants, melts into the Phoenician Sailor, and the latter is not wholly distinct from Ferdinand Prince of Naples, so all the women are one woman, and the two sexes meet in Tiresias. What Tiresias *sees*, in fact, is the substance of the poem" (*The Waste Land* Note to ln.218).

23 Heraclitus Fr. 71. [Inge's note].

24 The intervening portion in this already excessively long quotation contains a lengthy citation of Jean Paul Richter which is the source for Laforgue's phrase, "*L'Afrique intérieure.*" I am indebted to Ferguson for confirmation of the Richter quotation as the source for Laforgue (Ferguson 29).

as spiritual and rational beings, by passing beyond the limits which mark us off as separate individuals. Separate individuality, we may say, is the bar which prevents us from realizing our true privileges as persons. And so the mystic interprets very literally that maxim of our Lord, in which many have found the fundamental secret of Christianity: "He that will save his life—his soul, his personality—shall lose it; and he that will lose his life for My sake shall find it." The false self must die—nay, must "die daily," for the process is gradual, and there is no limit to it. It is a process of infinite *expansion*—of realizing new correspondences, new sympathies and affinities with the not-ourselves, which affinities condition, and in conditioning constitute, our true life as persons. The paradox is offensive only to formal logic. As a matter of experience, no one, I imagine, would maintain that the man who has practically realized, to the fullest possible extent, the common life which he draws from his Creator, and shares with all other created beings,—so realized it, I mean, as to draw from that consciousness all the influences which can play upon him from outside,—has thereby dissipated and lost his personality, and become less of a person than another who has built a wall round his individuality, and lived, as Plato says, the life of a shell-fish.

INGE *Christian Mysticism* 30–2.

One important facet is this: unlike Underhill, Inge does not limit this concept of union merely to the soul and God but includes the union of other souls as a significant possibility—even a necessity—by noting the separation from an indistinct "other spirits." Elsewhere, Inge states that this kind of union *is* something associated with personal intimacy, but one existing within a communal, religious context:

[T]he Christian life is to be considered as, above all things, a state of union with Christ, and of His members with one another, love of the brethren is inseparable from love of God. So intimate is this union, that hatred towards any human being cannot exist in the same heart as love to God. The mystical union is indeed rather a bond between Christ and the Church, and between man and man as members of Christ, than between Christ and individual souls. Our Lord's prayer is "that they all may be one, even as Thou, Father, art in Me, and I in Thee, that they also may be one in us."[25] The personal relation between the soul and Christ is not to be denied; but it can only be enjoyed when the person has "come to himself"

---

25    Cf. 1 John 4:19–21.

BRIDGING 73

as a member of a body. This involves an inward transit from the false isolated self to the larger life of sympathy and love which alone makes us
persons.

INGE *Christian Mysticism* 51.

Such a communion is the antithesis of the state found in "Gerontion," *The
Waste Land*, and "The Hollow Men" with "each in his prison" (*The Waste Land*
414). It is also in direct opposition to what Eliot wrote in his Harvard essay
"Finite Centres and Points of View" where a "finite centre is exclusive, in that
you cannot go in or out with impunity. You cannot, without completely abandoning your own point of view, completely understand that of another. I do
not say that a point of view may not be transcended, or that two points of view
may not melt into each other; but in this transformation the ingredients have
ceased to exist." (*Prose* I.175). Eliot's objections to such communion of souls are
interesting. For instance, he does not assert that they are impenetrable and in
fact makes many very strange allowances, but he disallows the possibility of,
as Inge says, distinction without separation. This latter option, which is modeled on the hypostatic union, is inherently mystical, and Eliot at the height
of his philosophical skepticism in all likelihood would not have considered it.
However, the solipsistic state without any ability to connect, with God or others, is consistently portrayed, no matter the author, as a deficient existence—a
horror rather than a sad reality. As Eliot read, this state of isolation is also one
of thwarted potential. Inge states that

> The fact that human love or sympathy is the guide who conducts us to the
> heart of life, revealing to us God and Nature and ourselves, is proof that
> part of our life is bound up with the life of the world, and that if we live in
> these our true relations we shall not entirely die so long as human beings
> remain alive upon this earth.
>
> INGE *Christian Mysticism* 327.

This image of expansion stands in stark contrast to the lifeless, unreal states
of the figures in Eliot's poems, who are cut off from both human and divine
love by their inability to surrender themselves. For a brief example, compare
the statement by Inge that "[w]ords were invented to communicate our ideas
to others; but where the barrier between persons is broken down by love and
devotion, words are as unnecessary as they are inadequate" to Sweeney's paradoxical cry to Doris "I gotta use words when I talk to you" (Inge *English Mystics*
120, *Sweeney Agonistes* "Agon" 132). Here, the very act of needing words represents the unbridgeable gaps between individuals. In his 1914–15 essay "Notes

74                                                                          CHAPTER 4

on Logic," Eliot writes that "[t]his world however is so far only a dream world. It need not be real. The cognitive powers, whatever they can do for us, cannot bring us into contact with anything real [...] We cannot intuit or observe anything successfully without the aid of words" ("Notes on Logic" (15) 25–6).[26] The self is imprisoned within its spiritual monad and is unable to directly contact other beings or God; this is the state to which the ascetic ideal is a remedy.

Spiritual monadism appears repeatedly in the Clark Lectures. Eliot emphasizes that "[o]ne of the capital ideas of Donne, the one which is perhaps his peculiar gift to humanity, is that of the union, the fusion, and identification of *souls* in sexual love. [...] how many centuries of intellectual labour were necessary, how much dogma, how much speculation, how many systems had to be elaborated, shattered and taken up into other systems, before such an idea was possible! The soul itself had to be constructed first: and since the soul has disappeared we have many other things, the analysis of Stendhal, the madness of Dostoevski" (*Prose* II.616) Of particular note is the reference to Stendhal in relation to "Beyle and Balzac." Eliot, then, ties this idea of Donne's to Bradley's immediate experience by stating that this poetic experience is "*one form* of an enlargement of immediate experience which, in one form or another, is a general function of poetry" (*Prose* II.616). Eliot gives the example from the *Iliad* "[w]hen Helen looks out from Troy and thinks she sees her brothers in the host, and Homer tells us that they were already dead, we partake at the same time of her feelings and of those of an omniscient witness, and the two form one" (*Prose* II.616–7). This immediate experience seems to be a single, intangible moment when subject and object are one, which is a kind of spiritual communion.

The origin of the concept of the imprisoned self across all these various authors appears to be, primarily, "the life of a shell-fish" from Plato's *Phaedrus*, among other writing. Now, Eliot's letters reveal he was writing weekly papers on Plato for Harold Joachim in 1915, and a piece of onionskin paper inserted into his "Notes on Philosophy (9)" contains a list of Plato's works with checkmarks by various dialogues and some of those are the ones which he discusses in his notes (*Letters* I.91, 92, 118; "Notes on Philosophy (9)" 37). This suggests the insert to be some of sort of reading list including *Phaedrus*, *Symposium*, and *Gorgias*. Unfortunately, none of Eliot's notes relating *specifically* to the *Phaedrus* and *Symposium* survive. However, as will be seen later in this chapter, a significant and probative summary of Eliot's philosophical conclusions on

---

26      In the absence of a scholarly edition of Eliot's notes (the ones quoted here are likely from Bertrand Russell's lecture series), I have endeavored to reproduce them as exactly as possible and will burden the reader with textual notes explaining when I have made editorial emendations. I have, though, not marked [sic] in most of these quotations.

BRIDGING 75

them is extant. Plato's influence on the mystical writers is almost impossible to understate. "Plato is the father of European mysticism," Inge plainly states, and none of the other authors Eliot read would conceivably have disagreed (Inge *Christian Mysticism* 78). Underhill, notably, unites the Platonic ideals of Love with the ascetic ideal, or as she calls it "The Purgative Way." Let me quote the single best example[27] fully:

> What must be the first step of the self upon this road to perfect union with the Absolute? Clearly, a getting rid of all those elements of normal experience which are not in harmony with reality: of illusion, evil, imperfection of every kind. By false desires and false thoughts man has built up for himself a false universe: as a mollusk by the deliberate and persistent absorption of lime and rejection of all else, can build up for itself a hard shell which shuts it from the external world, and only represents in a distorted and unrecognisable form the ocean from which it was obtained. This hard and wholly unnutritious shell, this one-sided secretion of the surface-consciousness, makes as it were a little cave of illusion for each separate soul. A literal and deliberate getting out of the cave must be for every mystic, as it was for Plato's prisoners, the first step in the individual hunt for reality.
>
> In the plain language of old-fashioned theology "man's sin is stamped upon man's universe." We see a sham world because we live a sham life. We do not know ourselves; hence do not know the true character of our senses and instincts; hence attribute wrong values to their suggestions and declarations concerning our relation to the external world. That world, which we have distorted by identifying it with our own self-regarding arrangements of its elements, has got to reassume for us the character of Reality, of God. In the purified sight of the great mystics it did reassume this character: their shells were opened wide, they knew the tides of the Eternal Sea. This lucid apprehension of the True is what we mean when we speak of the Illumination which results from a faithful acceptance of the trials of the Purgative Way.
>
> UNDERHILL 240.

While it does tie together the concepts of sin, isolation, and asceticism, this seems to be a more reductive use of Plato, as will be seen below, and I think

---

27    I will not further proliferate examples from the mystical readings of this sort of direct derivation of ideas from Plato as it was ubiquitous. Cf. Cutten 380, Inge *Christian Mysticism* 18–19, 22, 93, *Personal Idealism* 21–2, Jones 60, 74, 76, 211–2, Récéjac 86, Underhill 25, 55, 87, 287.

76                                                                      CHAPTER 4

further cause of Eliot's assertion that Underhill omitted this "type" of mysticism. Since Eliot not only read Underhill but also the Platonic original,[28] it is important to quote the original source as well. In Plato, the "madness" of the lover is akin to divine inspiration, and this revelation of earthly beauty leads to the contemplation of higher things provided there is detachment from the lower.

> Thus far I have been speaking of the fourth and last kind of madness, which is imputed to him who, when he sees the beauty of earth, is transported with the recollection of the true beauty; [...] For, as has been already said, every soul of man has in the way of nature beheld true being; this was the condition of her passing into the form of man. But all souls do not easily recall the things of the other world; they may have seen them for a short time only, or they may have been unfortunate in their earthly lot, and, having had their hearts turned to unrighteousness through some corrupting influence, they may have lost the memory of the holy things which once they saw. [...] For there is no light of justice or temperance or any of the higher ideas which are precious to souls in the earthly copies of them: they are seen through a glass dimly; and there are few who, going to the images, behold in them the realities, and these only with difficulty. But beauty could be seen, brightly shining, by all who were with that happy band,—we philosophers following in the train of Zeus, others in company with other gods; at which time we beheld the beatific vision and were initiated into a mystery which may be truly called most blessed, celebrated by us in our state of innocence, before we had any experience of evils to come, when we were admitted to the sight of apparitions innocent and simple and calm and happy, which we beheld shining in pure light, pure ourselves and not yet enshrined in that living tomb[29] which we carry about, now that we are imprisoned in the body, like an oyster in his shell."
>
> *Phaedrus* §249d–250c[30]

---

28    I have quoted the most prominent Late-Victorian translation, that of Benjamin Jowett, as I am unclear if Eliot read Plato in the original Greek.

29    The relation between body and tomb is more apparent in Greek due to the closeness between σῶμα and σῆμα. The former, though meaning corpse in the time of Homer, broadened to mean the body in general. Eliot would have known of this due to the distinct pun on this in *Gorgias* §492, one of the dialogues highlighted in his notes. The passage as a whole bears a powerful resemblance to portions of *Sweeney Agonistes*, a resemblance which has not been adequately explored, to my knowledge.

30    This is, of course, not the only place that this concept is developed in Plato. It is even more prominently displayed in *Symposium* where during Socrates hears from Diotima that the:

BRIDGING                                                                                    77

Here is clearly displayed the idea of the lower beauty leading to the higher—
something seen before to which the argument here will return again. The ascetic undertones to this are quite evident as Plato emphasized a selfless, not a
self-serving, form of love and goodness. Importantly, some generalizations on
Plato's conception of Love remain in Eliot's Harvard notes, which show that he
contemplated these ideas. Eliot's notes record:

> Plato [unclear word] question of origin ethics of love & turns to me to
> Physic. & constructs the object of love. He assumes that there is an object
> corresponding to the need. He wishes to put the good in the centre of
> his existential realities. Anything that we want points towards this good,
> but is not itself necessarily good or true. Any need promises[31] some kind
> of growth. The reproductive instinct is the tendency toward immortality.
> [unclear symbol]
>
> The object of love becomes less temporal; the mind becomes inter-
> ested in the immortal.
>
> Plato begins by asking for a system of values; but he turns the system
> values into ~~the~~ a cause of life.
>
> "Notes on Philosophy (9)" 55.

As is typical for his notes, Eliot is interested in the ethical implications of Greek
philosophy throughout his notes, but there is a clear absorption of this understanding of Platonic love, which is all the argument here requires.

The relation between Plato's philosophy of Love and more ordinary forms
of love is complicated in Eliot's case, but it does provide an important background for so much of the ascetic ideal. The admitted messiness derives from
the fact that Eliot was reading Plotinus at the same time as Plato, according
to his letters, but many of the orthodox mystical readings have a strong Neo-
Platonic bent, particularly Inge, so Eliot was reading the actual sources for

---

"life above all others which [a] man should live, [is] in the contemplation of beauty absolute; a beauty which if you once beheld, you would see not to be after the measure of gold,
and garments, and fair boys and youths, whose presence now entrances you; and you and
many a one would be content to live seeing them only and conversing with them without
meat or drink, if that were possible—you only want to look at them and to be with them.
But what if man had eyes to see the true beauty—the divine beauty, I mean, pure and
clear and unalloyed, not clogged with the pollutions of mortality and all the colors and
vanities of human life—thither looking, and holding converse with the true beauty simple and divine? Remember how in that communion only, beholding beauty with the eye
of the mind, he will be enabled to bring forth, not images of beauty, but realities (for he
has hold not of an image but of a reality), and bringing forth and nourishing true virtue to
become the friend of God and be immortal, if mortal man may. (*Symposium* §211b–212a)".

31    A doubtful reading.

78  CHAPTER 4

ideas he had already encountered[32] (*Letters* I.91–2). For instance, the previous idea of Beauty leading upwards is combined with a forerunner to Bradley's Absolute in the first *Ennead*:

> The born lover has a certain memory of Beauty but, severed from it now, he no longer comprehends it; spell-bound by visible loveliness, he clings amazed about that. His lesson must be to fall down no longer in bewildered delight before some one embodied form; he must be led to beauty everywhere and be made to discern the One Principle underlying all.
>
> *Enneads* I.iii.2[33]

This is, then, distinctly Christianized by many of the mystical authors. During a discussion of Robert Browning, Inge states that "[t]rue love may begin with a large element of bodily appetite; but it issues in a communion of souls in which each makes the other see 'new depths of the Divine'" (Inge *English Mystics* 220). Eliot's aforementioned notes on Plato essentially reiterate this statement of Inge's, albeit in a compressed form. This is further complicated by the fact that, in his reading, interrelation between divine and carnal love is not always the causal one espoused by Plato, Plotinus, and Inge; sometimes, it is merely one of emanations. For instance, Cutten states that "[t]his all-embracing [mystical] love has its prototype in the consuming passion of the lover for his mistress" (Cutten 33). When speaking of the "mingling of joy and sorrow" experienced in prayer, *Père* Poulan blandly notes that "[s]omething of the kind is felt in human love when it is violent" (Poulan 145, 144). Eliot explores this relation further elsewhere in his notes on Plato when he states that "Plato proceeds on two ∥ lines.[34] 1. Point of view of Knowledge 2. Point of view of

---

32  As for Inge, in his 1917 lectures, *The Philosophy of Plotinus*, Inge states "[n]o other guide even approaches Plotinus in power and insight and profound spiritual penetration. I have steeped myself in his writings ever since [writing *Christian Mysticism*], and I have tried not only to understand any other intellectual system, but to take them, as he assuredly wished his readers to take them, as a guide to right living and right thinking" (Inge *Plotinus I* 7).

33  This, unsurprisingly, is echoed by Inge when, as quoted in a previous chapter, he stated that it is a great mistake to shut our eyes to the world around us, "and all beautiful things." The love of beauty will lead us up a long way—up to the point when the love of the Good is ready to receive us. Only we must not let ourselves be entangled by sensuous beauty. Those who do not quickly rise beyond this first stage, to contemplate [the] "ideal form, the universal mold," share the fate of Hylas; they are engulfed in a swamp, from which they never emerge. (Inge *Christian Mysticism* 93).

34  These are Eliot's double-vertical lines. I believe they should be read as "parallel" with the mathematical usage.

BRIDGING                                                                                          79

Ethics.[35] The outcome of this is the mystical doctrine of divine love. Value as a standard of this divine love. Two lines fuse in this highest abstraction, wh. includes[36] a dozen or so different categories" ("Notes on Philosophy (9)" 62). He continues this, noting that

> The particulars are relevant to an extent that they can all point away from themselves to the divine love—they [can exalt][37] a love which is not of themselves. The notion of the idea[38] drawing all existence towards itself—this notion has prevailed. Present situation is, what substitutes for this can we discover which will give to life an equal coherence and importance. Or there is some transcendental organism of thinking. Or evolutional. —These are all attempted substitutes for the divine love— Aristotle substitutes by his discussion[39] of the nature of happiness. To which the introduction lies in the *Philebus*, a ‖ to the *Parmenides* in terms of ethics.
>
> "Notes on Philosophy (9)" 63.

In this passage, Eliot ties the strands of the argument I am presenting together here himself. The concept of the compelling higher love and that a particular person or love somehow points beyond itself to this higher ideal is mystical and is connected with the ascetic ideal. This shows Eliot's absorption of a relational connection between the higher and the lower forms of love. The important thing is that Eliot considered there to be a substantial connection between earthly and divine loves because the figures in Eliot's poems cannot pass beyond the prisons of their own bodies and desires due to their lack of purification and so cannot rise to the rarified zones of love discussed by the authors he read. Plato helps form the ideal that the figures in Eliot's poems fail to realize.

This discussion of love is mirrored in his Clark Lectures when Eliot states that "such poetry," which temporarily fuses subject and object, "though it may find a partial gospel in the *Banquet*[40] of Plato (a work which influenced Donne indirectly through neoplatonism), finds no place in the ancient world" (*Prose* II.617). In the passages here, Eliot is, of course, speaking of Donne; however,

---

35    Eliot has ditto marks here, obviously referring to the phrase "point of view of Knowledge" which lies directly above in the manuscript.

36    Reading doubtful.

37    This word is unclear. It could be read as communicate as well.

38    Probably a transliteration of ἰδέα.

39    A questionable reading.

40    Another name for the *Symposium*.

80 CHAPTER 4

the application of these as an ideal to be sought is easily seen elsewhere in his Clark Lectures and his other work on Dante. Eliot juxtaposes the concept of mysticism and Plato's *Symposium* with the poetry of immediate experience. This suggests that Eliot had absorbed the connection found in his mystical readings, and he expands on this concept in his commentary on the following lines in Donne's "Extasie":

> When love, with one another so
> Interinanimates two soules,
> That abler soul, which thence doth flow,
> Defects of lonelinesse controules.
> DONNE "Extasie" 41–4 qtd. in *Prose* II.657.

Eliot states of these lines that "[t]he idea of this quatrain is perhaps the cornerstone of the whole structure—an idea perhaps suggested to him by the *Banquet* of Plato—the isolation of soul from soul, its craving for the rare moments of semblance of fusion with another" (*Prose* II.658). It is interesting that Eliot qualifies the possibility as "semblance of fusion," even then doubting the possibility. He goes on to muse if "from a strictly orthodox Christian point of view" or even from "the point of view of a mystes[41] of Eleusis," "this union of human soul with human soul is intelligible" (*Prose* II.658). The wording here is important. Eliot does not question whether or not this is desirable—that seems to be taken for granted. Rather, he wonders if it is "intelligible"; in other words, if such a union of souls can be framed logically, dogmatically defined, or even merely apprehended with the mind. The attempted and failed apprehension of the communion of others is *precisely* the problem that faces "Gerontion" and many of the other figures in Eliot's poems from this period. Eliot goes on further to display the Platonic view explicitly. In discussing the dichotomy of body and soul, he states

> [t]he only difference there is between higher and lower, more and less worthy loves; in the distinguishing and experiencing of which differences it must be said that Dante and his friends were consummately expert. There is no imagined struggle of soul and body, only the one struggle toward perfection.

---

41 Cf. "A mystic (μύστης) is one who has been, or is being, initiated into some esoteric knowledge of Divine things, about which he must keep his mouth shut (μύειν); or, possibly, he is one whose *eyes* are still shut, one who is not yet an ἐπόπτης" (Inge *Christian Mysticism* 4).

BRIDGING

The separation of soul and body in this way is a modern conception; the only ancient parallel that occurs to me is the attitude of Plotinus toward the body as quoted by Porphyry; and in the form employed by Donne represents a far cruder state of philosophical speculation than that of Aquinas. [...] [T]he conception of the ecstasy of union between two souls is not only philosophically crude but emotionally limiting. The expression of love as contemplation of the beloved object is not only more Aristotelian, it is also more Platonic, for it is the contemplation of absolute beauty and goodness partially revealed through a limited though delightful human object.[42] What is there for Donne? This union of ecstasy is complete, is final; and two human beings, needing nothing beyond each other, rest on their emotion of enjoyment. But emotion cannot rest; desire must expand,[43] or it will shrink. Donne, the modern man, is imprisoned in the embrace of his own feelings. There is little suggestion of adoration, of worship.

*Prose* II.659–60[44]

This passage suggests that Eliot has, it seems, absorbed the Platonic concept of love to which the ascetic ideal strives.[45] Here, Eliot appears to be insisting that need for a spiritual union with another is important, but as in Plato, it is only the *beginning*. The desire must lead outside the self, through self-abnegation, or the result is the imprisonment within the self. Eliot continues on to note that this self-imprisonment of Donne's "leads in fact to most of modern literature; for whether you seek the Absolute in marriage, adultery, or debauchery, it is all one—you are seeking in the wrong place." (*Prose* II.660). This concept of failing to find the Absolute in merely earthly, sensual communion is something Eliot deals with obliquely in "Gerontion" and *The Waste Land*, but explicitly in

---

42  Eliot elsewhere notes that "Dante and his contemporaries were quite aware that human love and divine love were different, and that one could not be *substituted* for the other without distortion of the human nature. Their effort was to enlarge the boundary of human love so as to make it a stage in progress towards the divine" (*Prose* II.707).

43  Cf. "Dante had, in this respect, the art of a Platonic lover: he could enlarge the object of his passion, and keep the warmth and ardor of it" (Santayana 91).

44  Cf. Eliot in his notes "Evil flowering from spurious [questionable reading] love—"the[sic] higher kind of love between non-lovers. Degrees of _____ and the inferior drags down the other" ("Notes on Philosophy (9)" 47).

45  Furthermore, Eliot had previously quoted, with no disapproval, Remy de Gourmont's comments on the Provençal ideal of love: "*L'amour des poètes deivent pur, Presque impersonnel; son objet n'est plus une femme, mais la beauté, la fémininité personifée dans une creature idéale*" (Gourmont qtd. in *Prose* II.648). The Platonic implications in this are obvious.

82                                                                                            CHAPTER 4

"The Hollow Men." It is, as he says, the "vain effort to find the permanent by fixing the transient" (*Prose* II.660).

As mentioned above, the most prominent effect that Eliot read of such unions, whether corporal or spiritual, is the dissolution of the otherwise inexorable divisions between subject and object. In his mystical readings, the capacity for bridging subject and object is a property of the λόγος. While an implication in many of the above-quoted passage, it is discussed explicitly in a number of locations. In his explication Plotinus and his mystical visions, Jones comments that "the last mount [to climb in the journey to God] is the complete return to the Divine Center, to a *vision* in which the subject and object, knower and known, are one. But *that is a state beyond consciousness*; that is beyond the subject-object type of consciousness," and to this, Jones adds that "[w]e often have such experiences in some degree. All our high moments of beauty, of love, of worship are experiences beyond the subject-object type of consciousness" (Jones 76).[46] The ability to bridge the division in subject and object, however momentarily, is an attribute of the λόγος[47] according to Eliot's reading. As Inge explained, "[t]he Stoics also taught that we have communion with each other through our participation in the [λόγος], which remains *one* and the self-same spirit, though he divides to every man soverally as he wills.[48] (Inge *Personal Idealism* 44).[49] The [λόγος] is, as Eliot also read, the bridge between mankind and God *i.e.* between immanence and transcendence (Underhill 124–6).

> [I]n the Person of Christ, St. Teresa isolated and distinguished the [λόγος] or Creative Word;[50] the expression, or outbirth, of the Father's thought. Here is the point at which the Divine Substance first becomes

---

46   There are suggestions here of Dante's *Epistle to Can Grande, q.v.* Ch. VII.

47   This concept may be implied by the more pedestrian use which Aristotle employs to the word. In his notes, Eliot states that "[t]his passage introduces us to word [λόγος]. Primary meaning = a verbal expression of a thought, & acc. to J. A. Smith it have [questionable reading] loses sight of this sense" ("Notes on Aristotle (16)" 6).

48   Eliot's Harvard notes record sketches of questions on the Stoics and their ideas of good and evil as well as the division of body and soul, noting only "inconsistencies" (Pencil loose-leafs pg. 2 in "Notes on Philosophy 12").

49   Inge does not elaborate further on the matter, though his Hellenistic derivation of the λόγος concept is typical of the time, as seen by Underhill's works. This view finds its apotheosis in the *Das Evangelium des Johannes* of Rudolf Bultmann, Cf. Bultmann 13–83. Much contemporary scholarship derives the Johannine λόγος from Jewish Wisdom Literature *i.e.* Proverbs 8:1–31, Baruch 3:36–4:1, 1st Enoch 42:1–2, Sirach 24:7–12 *et al.* Cf. Richards 162–9.

50   Like Inge, Underhill has no difficulty associating this with Heraclitus. In her discussion on Vitalism *i.e.* Bergson, she states "this 'new' way of seeing the Real goes back to [Heraclitus], whose [λόγος] or Energizing Fire is but another symbol for that free and living Spirit

apprehensible by the spirit of man; that mediating principle "raised up between heaven and earth" which is at once the Mirror of Pure Being and the Light of a finite world. The Second Person of the Christian Trinity is for the believer not only the brightness or express image of Deity, but also the personal, inexhaustible, and responsive Fount of all life and Object of all love: Who, because of His taking up (in the Incarnation) of humanity into the Godhead, has become the Bridge between finite and infinite, between the individual and the Absolute Life, and hence in mystic language the "true Bridegroom" of every human soul.

UNDERHILL 131.

This bridging capacity forms the paradigm seen in "Gerontion," *The Waste Land*, and "The Hollow Men," and Eliot repeats it in a truly striking metaphor in his Clark Lectures. He refers to the type of thought, "which occurs when an idea, or what is only ordinarily apprehensible as an intellectual statement, is translated in sensible form; so that the world of sense is actually enlarged" (*Prose* II.616). As an example, Eliot cites the passage on the union of souls previously discussed (*Prose* II.616). "[T]his type of thought, the *Word made Flesh*,[51] so to speak, is more restricted in the times and places of its avatar than is immediately evident. [...] The characteristic of the type of poetry I am trying to define is that it elevates sense for a moment to regions ordinarily abstract, or on the other hand clothes the abstract, for a moment, with all the painful delight of flesh.[52] To call it mystical would be facile, and I hasten to discountenance the use of this word" (*Prose* II.616–7). This is a clear indication of Eliot's assumption of the incarnational conception of the λόγος and its connective power.

The final aspect and the one most closely connected to the ascetic ideal is the ability of sin to destroy the communion with man and God established by the λόγος; again, this is developed by some of Eliot's readings on mysticism. Inge writes that "[t]he world as it is, is the world as God sees it, not as we see it. Our vision is distorted, not so much by the limitations of finitude, as by sin and

---

of Becoming, that indwelling creative power, which Vitalism acknowledges as the very soul or immanent reality of things" (Underhill 33).

51   This was not a singular comment as Eliot says elsewhere of Cowley that "[h]e fails to make the Word flesh, though he often makes it bones" (*Prose* II.620).

52   Cf. the comment in his notes that "[νοός] is like sense in being a kind of immediate apprehension," and "[f]lesh has a λόγος [...] it feels heat, & may be destroyed by excessive heat. But mind is pure δύναμις [this final word is difficult to read and lacks pointing] ("Notes on Aristotle (16)" 24–5). The synonymy of νοός and λόγος in Eliot's reading will be discussed later in this chapter.

84 CHAPTER 4

ignorance" (Inge *Christian Mysticism* 24). This idea is drawn out in more detail in another work where Inge states that

> Redemption must be vicarious; it must be wrought by the suffering of the just for the unjust. And the redemption wrought by One is efficacious for many, because we are united to Him by closer bonds than those of ethical harmony. Sin is that which cuts us off from all this. It erects an image of the false self, the isolated, empirical self, which has no existence, and makes this idol its god. [...] Does this view demand an impossible detachment from personal, living interests? It seems to me that it does just the opposite. We *are* what we are most deeply interested in. We are what we love. And what we love, because we love it, is not external or alien to ourselves. "*Amate quod eritis*," says St Augustine. Outside interests are only outside because we make them so. In the spiritual world there is no outside or inside, no mine and not mine; all is ours that we can make our own. All is ours if we are Christ's. For Christ, as the [λόγος], the Power of God, and the Wisdom of God, is the life of all that lives, and the light of all that shines. Is it not always just that fatal reference to our own interests that cramps our sympathies, warps our activities, and blinds our perceptions?
>
> INGE *Personal Idealism* 178–80.

Here we find a convergence of the strands of this theme. Of particular interest here is the concept of sensual failure that occurs several times within Eliot's poems of this time. This is also seen in the aforementioned passage in the *Symposium* when Diotima says "[b]ut what if a man had eyes to see the true beauty—the divine beauty, I mean, pure and clear and unalloyed, not infected with the pollutions of the flesh and all the colors and vanities of mortal life" (*Symposium* §211d-e).[53]

---

53  This is the same assertion in the *Phaedrus* where he states that "we were admitted to the sight of apparitions innocent and simple and calm and happy, which we beheld shining in pure light, pure ourselves and not yet enshrined in that living tomb which we carry about, now that we are imprisoned in the body, like an oyster in his shell" (*Phaedrus* §250c). Cf. the equally ascetic statement that "he who is not newly initiated [νεοτελὴς rather than μύστης] or who has become corrupted, does not easily rise out of this world to the sight of true beauty in the other, when he contemplates her earthy namesake, and instead of being awed at the sight of her, he is given over to pleasure, and like a brutish beast he rushes on to enjoy and beget; he consorts with wantonness, and is not afraid or ashamed of pursuing pleasure in violation of nature" (*Phaedrus* §250e–251a).

This is the bridge between the basic understanding of the ascetic ideal in Eliot's earliest poetry and the more complicated, intricate usage in his later works. Because these ideas are present in his education and are evident in his Clark Lectures, they could not have been wholly forgotten when he was writing the greatest of his early poetry.

CHAPTER 5

# Pining

As late as his writing of "The Hollow Men," Eliot was fascinated by the most abstruse aspect of his ascetic ideal. He had read that the λόγος allowed for the mystical communion of souls if they properly purified. Like in the "Saint" poems, Eliot explores this through failure Thus, he explores the ascetic ideal in three overlapping areas: a failure of ascetic purification, an explicit omission of the λόγος, and isolation from both a lover and the Divine, often in terms of a failure of vision. This should not be read reductively. I am not suggesting this is, necessarily, a conscious creation of Eliot's; however, all three of these elements, sin, isolation, and the absent λόγος, are present in "Gerontion," *The Waste Land*, "The Hollow Men." These components of ascetic failure occur separately in "Gerontion" while they are largely fused in "The Hollow Men." Eliot presents these ideas in his synthesized state in his Clark Lectures. This slow fusion occurs in parallel with the combination of the strands of his intellectual conservatism discussed in Chapter 3. Thus, ascetic failures occur roughly near failures of vision and the absence of the λόγος in "Gerontion," but they are synonymous by the time Eliot writes "The Hollow Men." As this is still a skeptical period of Eliot's life, the ascetic ideal is not overtly endorsed, but, unlike in the "Saint" poems, the failure of asceticism is portrayed in a negative light.

In all three of the major poems considered in this chapter, the first aspect of the ascetic ideal discussed is the absent λόγος followed by sin then isolation. In "Gerontion," unlike in the later poems, this chain of ascetic failure occurs in disparate sections, and in "Gerontion," the absent λόγος is located in lines 17–33. In this passage, Eliot begins with an altered quotation from Lancelot Andrewes' Sermon XII and traces a path of religious decay from a failed Incarnation to occultism to Gerontion himself who is sunk in skepticism.[1]

Before I examine this in detail, there is constructive contrast to a poem written just a few years before. Eliot portrays a similar pattern of decay from λόγος to a figure of impotence in "Mr. Eliot's Sunday Morning Service," and the comparison is instructive. There are very distinct differences in Eliot's treatment of the ascetic ideal between this earlier, more skeptical period and the one that

---

1  The reason for Eliot's familiarity with Andrewes at such a secular period in his life is unexplained to the best of my knowledge. It may, at the very least, be reasonably inferred that this is further evidence for a return to his thinking on spiritual matters.

# PINING                                                                87

"Gerontion" inaugurates. The passage in question in "Mr. Eliot's Sunday Morning Service" reads:

> Polyphiloprogenitive
> The sapient sutlers of the Lord
> Drift across the window-panes.
> In the beginning was the Word.
>
> In the beginning was the Word.
> Superfetation of τὸ ἕν
> And at the mensual turn of time
> Produced enervate Origen.
>> "Mr. Eliot's Sunday Morning Service" 1–8.

Let me trace the poem's line of erudite logic. Eliot begins with the "sapient sutlers" but quickly notes that they are the result, not the beginning, stating that "[i]n the beginning was the Word." This quotation of John 1:1 is from the most important source of λόγος-Christology (John 1:1–18). Here, it also serves as a rather nuanced critique of the "sapient sutlers." With his extensive knowledge of Greek, Eliot knew, in Inge's words, that "the same word [λόγος] in [the Greek] language should mean [both] *speech* and *reason*" (Inge *Personal Idealism* 38).[2] However, the English translation "Word" has lost this second connotation, a fact which Eliot knew.[3] This may be an arcane joke on those "masters of the subtle schools" who have made speech without reason ("Sunday Morning Service" 31). Nonetheless, the second stanza is what encapsulates the ideas of religious decay. The quotation from John 1:1 is repeated but defined as the "[s]uperfetation of τὸ ἕν" ("Sunday Morning Service" 6). This loaded phrase encapsulates a vast array of Eliot's more recondite reading. First, the Greek τὸ ἕν[4] while best translated as "The One" has several different meanings in ancient philosophy. It can be a reference to material monism or to the transcendant deity of Plotinus, both of which Eliot encountered during his Harvard years.[5]

---

2   Cf. "Notes on Aristotle (16)" 6, 18, 69.

3   Eliot read of the debate on the appropriate translation of λόγος among the church fathers which resulted in the choice of the Latin *Verbum*, from where the traditional English is derived, in Inge *Personal Idealism* 37–9. His notes contain a vague suggestion of it as well. Cf. "Notes on Aristotle (16)" 6.

4   As with λόγος, to avoid the idiosyncrasies of translation and transliteration across the various sources, I have returned the multiplicity of terms to the original Greek to highlight the unity of thought Eliot would have seen.

5   Mostly in Burnet. Eliot's notes on the topic are found in "Notes on Philosophy 14a."

In Plato's *Parmenides*, the words τὸ ἕν specifically are used to describe what Jowett translates as "The One" (*Parmenides* §137c). In his notes on this section of that dialogue, Eliot writes "[p]aradoxically, in the *Parmenides*, the absolute is attacked at the same time that it is set up" (*Notes on Philosophy* (9) 62). Thus, the phrase τὸ ἕν may also be associated with Bradley's Absolute within Eliot's personal philosophical views. In the context of the poem, this implies that the λόγος is an emanation from the Absolute. This is an idea which Eliot likely encountered in Plotinus. In 1914, Eliot attended J. A. Stewart's seminar on Plotinus (*Letters* I.73, 91, 92, 118). Yet, the explicit identification of Plotinus's One with the Absolute is made in Inge (Inge *Personal Idealism* 71). The explanation of the λόγος could be the superfetation of τὸ ἕν is rather complicated: in Plotinus, the "[νοός] stands as the image of [τὸ ἕν], firstly because there is a certain necessity that the first should have its off-spring, carrying onward much of its quality" (*Enneads* v.i.7).[6] The use of the word "superfetation" enforces this generative metaphor in Plotinus by implying a multiple pregnancy, particularly the impregnation of a womb already pregnant.[7] This, I believe, is a reference to the fact that in Plotinus, τὸ ἕν "is a unity, but [a] Unity which is the potentiality of all existence," and so already contains all things in potential including the νοός. Meanwhile, the νοός is itself a plurality as "it is the sum of an Intellectual-Being with the object of its Intellection, so that it is a duality" (*Enneads* v.i.7, III.viii.9). Thus, to generate a plurality from within something that contains the potentiality of all things including the generated plurality would be a superfetation. In "Mr. Eliot's Sunday Morning Service," the λόγος (or νοός) then decays or emanates "at the mensual turn of time" to "enervate Origen" ("Sunday Morning" 7–8).[8] This is analogous to the emanation of the νοός to individual souls (*Enneads* IV.i.1–ii.2). Moreover, the choice of Origen is a pointed one. The self-castrating church father was known for his unique and neo-Platonic interpretations of John 1 as well as having studied under Ammonius

---

6  The term νοός was, as early as Anaxagoras, associated with the λόγος of Heraclitus (Burnet 310). Plotinus freely associates them in *Enneads* v.i.9. Associating the λόγος with the νοός is mentioned by Inge as common in Christian Neoplatonism Cf. "Christian Neoplatonism tended to identify the [λόγος], with the [νοός], 'Mind' or 'Intelligence,' of Plotinus, and rightly; but in Plotinus the word [λόγος] has a less exalted position, being practically what we call 'law,' regarded as a vital force" (Inge *Christian Mysticism* 94). There are diverse ways of spelling the word νοός in Greek; I have employed the headword in LSJ as opposed to the Attic contraction. I have, as with λόγος, altered the source texts for synonymy.

7  As opposed to an emanation in the style of Jewish Wisdom literature or Arian Christology, which Eliot learned of in Inge *Personal Idealism* 39–40.

8  The manuscript read "menstrual"; however, this was deleted by Pound (*Poems* I.537). Given the general translation of νοός (Divine-Mind) and the general focus on idle cerebration, I believe mensual to be a polyglot pun based on the word for mind in Latin, *mens*.

PINING                                                                              89

with Plotinus.[9] Thus, the Absolute and λόγος has become reduced to a figure of stagnation and impotence and doctrinal casuistry.

A similar pattern functions in "Gerontion"; however, there are a number of important differences. The most important is that while "Mr. Eliot's Sunday Morning Service" recapitulates the emanations of Plotinus' theosophy as parody, "Gerontion" traces the decay of an abortive revelation, to ritual, and finally to impotent unbelief. The ascetic aspect of this disintegration may be found in differences between the quotation in "Gerontion" and the original sermon by Lancelot Andrewes.' The figures in the poem show an unwillingness to undergo hardships for spiritual gain *i.e.* ascetic preparation. The poem reads:

> Signs are taken for wonders. "We would see a sign!"
> The word within a word, unable to speak a word,
> Swaddled with darkness.
> GERONTION 17–9.

Whereas the passage in Andrewes' sermon reads:

> Signs are taken for wonders. "Master, we would fain see a sign," that is a miracle. And in this sense it is a sign to wonder at. Indeed, every word here is a wonder. *Tò βρέφος*, an infant; *Verbum infans,* the Word without a word; the eternal Word not able to speak a word; 1. A wonder sure. 2. And the *σπαργανισμὸς,* swaddled; and that a wonder too. "He," that (as in the thirty-eighth of Job he saith) "taketh the vast body of the main sea, turns it to and fro, as a little child, and rolls it about with the swaddling bands of darkness";—He to come thus into clouts, Himself!
> ANDREWES 204.

One of the first probative pieces of information comes from the abbreviation of the quotation from the Pharisees.[10] In Andrewes, the title "Master" is used, but this honorific is removed when Gerontion speaks. As Andrewes notes, the Pharisees are asking for a miracle, confuting the concept of signs and miracles, which is more clear from the Matthew 16 iteration of the pericope. Andrewes discusses this confusion earlier in the sermon where he says, "[f]ind Him we cannot, if first we find not a sign to find him by. *Erit vobis signum,* and *hoc erit,*

---

9    Eliot's notes record that he knew Plotinus and Origen studied under Ammonius together ("Notes on Philosophy (9)" 103).

10   Andrewes cites Matthew 12:38. This, or at least a very similar, pericope also occurs in Matthew 16:1–4, Luke 11:29–32.

90                                                                                    CHAPTER 5

saith the Angel, 'a sign ye shall have;' and 'This shall be it;' 'ye shall find Him swaddled and laid in manger'" (Andrewes 199). The meaning behind the sign[11] is one of humility—

> For *loquitur signis*, "signs have their speech," and this is no dumb sign. What saith it then to us? Christ, though as yet He cannot speak as a new-born babe, yet by it He speaks, and out of His crib, as a pulpit, this day preaches to us; and His theme is *Discite a Me*, "Learn of Me for I am humble"—humble in My birth ye all see [...] But then, as St. Augustine saith well, *Signum vobis, si signum in vobis,* "A sign for you, if a sign in you."
>
> ANDREWES 205

In short, the ability of the sign to speak which would enable the hearers to find the λόγος lying in the manger depends upon humility—self-abnegation. Andrewes makes this explicit when he states: "If it be *signum vobis* to some, it is for some others *signum contra vos;* and that is the proud" (Andrewes 206). That Gerontion in Eliot's poem misses the sign is certain based on the phrasing of his own version. There is not the capital to denote the word as the λόγος. Instead of Andrewes' "the Word without a word; the eternal Word not able to speak a word," Gerontion speaks of "[t]he word within a word, unable to speak a word" (Andrewes 204, "Gerontion" 18). Since the sign is unable to speak to Gerontion, the λόγος is functionally absent. The lines thereafter explore the consequences of this aborted revelation.

The phrase "swaddled with darkness" in line 19 is again a notable departure from Andrewes; the simile from the book of Job becomes concrete reality. Additionally, it represents the first step of decay. Eliot seems to be drawing on imagery of the *Deus Absconditus*, the darkness hiding knowledge of God, seen in his early readings. It was sometimes connected with Bradley's Absolute. To reiterate, it had been nearly ten years since Eliot had read most of this material. So, the quotations here are not direct citations of particular passages but rather references to concepts that formed the basis of his knowledge on the subject. A more detailed understanding of these concepts from Eliot's own reading provide a nourishing context for interpretation of the poem. As Eliot read of Pseudo-Dionysius the Areopagite, "[t]he mystic [...] must leave behind

---

11    Cf. one of Eliot's Harvard papers where he states "When Mr. Bradley asserts that a sign differs from another existence in having besides existence and content, *meaning*, I agree; but I should not admit that these three characters are found in the same way in the idea. For in the idea, existence and meaning fall together—that is, the existence *is* nothing over and above meaning. It is just the separate existence, the fact that a sign might be interpreted as other, or simply not recognized as a sign, that makes it a sign." (*Prose* I.184).

PINING                                                                                      91

all things both in the sensible and in the intelligible worlds, till he enters into the darkness of nescience that is truly mystical" (Pseudo-Dionysius qtd. in Inge *Christian Mysticism* 109). Poulan states, along a similar line, "the *fourth character* of the mystic union consists in the fact that the knowledge of God, of which it is partly composed, is *obscure* and *confused*. Hence these expressions: to enter into the *divine obscurity* (*oratio in Caligine*), or into the *divine darkness*" [bold and italics his] (Poulan 118).[12] This nescience is connected explicitly to the unapproachability of the Divine by St John of the Cross who characterizes God as having "made darkness His secret place, His pavilion round about Him with dark water, and thick clouds to cover Him" (St John of the Cross qtd. in Inge *Christian Mysticism* 227). This darkness of God is analogous to the unapproachable Absolute of Bradley by Jones in his discussion of Meister Eckhart: "'In the Naked Godhead there is never form nor idea,' *i.e.* there is nothing thought can seize. 'He is an absolute, pure, clear *One*'—'the impenetrable Darkness of the eternal Godhead.'"[13] (Eckhart qtd. in Jones 226). Thus, the concept of the λόγος has decayed to the concept of the Absolute through its unfathomability and the emphasis on mere knowledge.[14] Eliot thought enough of Eckhart to mention him twice in the Clark Lectures, and referring to him casually as "a heretic" in the latter occurrence (*Prose* II.637, 651). Given that Eliot is discussing an idiosyncratic division between Romantic and Classical mysticism in this part of the Clark Lectures, I doubt he is referring to the 1329 papal bull condemning 17 of Eckhart's teachings and is expressing a more private displeasure with his conceptions of the Deity.[15] In Eliot's phrase, "Meister Eckhart and his followers—appropriately, in Germany—reasserted the God of the Abyss; the God, in short, of Mr. D. H. Lawrence" (*Prose* II.651). Eliot is, in 1926, objecting to the inscrutable Divine Darkness of the Absolute with the full weight of the integration of Classicism with religion and the ascetic ideal. In 1919, I doubt if his objection would be as vehement or cogent, but, as was shown in Chapter 3, these ideas were present, if inchoate. In "Mr. Eliot's Sunday Morning Service," Eliot merely apes the theosophy of Plotinus. Eliot, in

---

12   Eliot read something equivalent in Inge *Studies in English Mystics* 105–6.

13   The relation between the Absolute and God is one that troubled Eliot and the authors he read. Eckhart's solution is discussed in Jones 225–9; Bradley's critiques the disparity between the two in *Appearance and Reality* 444–7. Both of these bear strong similarities to *Parmenides* §132e–135b which Eliot in his notes on Philosophy comments "Does God know only the essence & not the individual? Paradoxically, in the *Parmenides*, the absolute is attacked at the same time that it is set up" ("Notes on Philosophy (9)" 62).

14   Inferior to love as a power of perception in most of the mystical thought Eliot read. Cf. Underhill 54–7.

15   Although, Eliot did read of this ignominious end to Eckhart's career in Jones 239–41.

92                                                                                CHAPTER 5

"Gerontion," is clearly making an explicit point, though, by having the λόγος decay into the Absolute.

The following lines in "Gerontion," "[i]n the juvescence of the year / [c]ame Christ the tiger," show a further decay away from the Incarnate λόγος. The line seems a compound of a phrase from Andrewes and the Blakean Tiger (*Poems* I.475–6). The context of the Andrewes is once again germane:

> If rugged or uneven the way, if the weather ill-disposed, if any never so little danger, it is enough to stay us. To Christ we cannot travel, but weather and way and all must be fair. If not, no journey, but sit still and see farther. As indeed, all our religion is rather *vidimus,* a contemplation, than *venimus,* a motion, or stirring to do ought
>
> But when we do it, we must be allowed leisure. Ever *veniemus,* never *venimus;* ever coming, never come. We love to make no very great haste. To other things perhaps; not to *adorare,* the place of the worship of God. Why should we? Christ is no wild-cat. What talk ye of twelve days? And if it be forty days hence, ye shall be sure to find His Mother and Him; she cannot be churched till then. What needs such haste? The truth is, we conceit Him and His birth but slenderly, and our haste is even thereafter.
>
> ANDREWES 258.

The application of spiritual sloth, *acedia,* an important concept in Dante and a term Eliot himself employed, to these lines in the person of Gerontion is worth exploration. The double-inversion of the quotation with the unspiritual speaking in Andrewes and then Gerontion distorting the Christ-as-wildcat/tiger image does create a hermeneutical tangle. Frankly, Eliot's tendency to misquote these particular lines[16] makes me leery of drawing detailed conclusions. Regardless, this seems another step further away from full knowledge of divinity that the ascetic ideal promises. The next section of lines (21–3) begins the next stage of decay as the figure of the Deity fades to mere ritual.

> In depraved May, dogwood and chestnut, flowering judas,
> To be eaten, to be divided, to be drunk
> Among whispers.
>
> "Gerontion" 21–3.

The first line indicates the passage of time. If Christ came at Christmas, then slid to the Tiger in the juvescence of the year, which would surely be in February and March, then "depraved May" would be the next step chronologically. The

---

16    Cf. *Poems* I.475.

# PINING

adjective "depraved" signals that this is a decay. Line 22 refers to the Eucharist. Now, Eliot's reading included a discussion of the history of the Lord's Supper as a spiral from a communal meal to a magic ritual by a prominent Quaker author (Jones 28–36). Jones summarizes this transformation:

> As soon as the sense of the Divine presence vanished from men's hearts, the religion which Christ had initiated underwent a complete transformation. Magic and mystery took the place of the free personal communication. The real presence of Christ was sought in the bread and wine and in the bath of regeneration, rather than within the soul itself. With this change of faith the administration of these rites became supremely important. Once the "Lord's Supper" had been a common joyous meal, now it became a mysterious rite by which immortality was imparted.
>
> JONES 36.

This line of thought seems to be echoed in "Gerontion." Even the partial and inadequate revelations of the Absolute and Christ the Tiger fade to rite and ceremony. Importantly, Jones places the emphasis on personal communion being lost, which ties thematically to the ascetic ideal. From here, the passage in "Gerontion" begins to list the participants of this ceremony in an equivalent spiral of decay. Like many of the figures—to call them characters might be overreaching—in Eliot's earlier works, there is little that can be attached to them. Still, it seems possible to trace this as a descent through them.[17] The Eucharist is consumed

> by Mr. Silvero
> With caressing hands, at Limoges
> Who walked all night in the next room;
>
> By Hakagawa, bowing among the Titians;
> By Madame de Tornquist, in the dark room
> Shifting the candles; Fräulein von Kulp
> Who turned in the hall, one hand on the door. Vacant shuttles
> Weave the wind. I have no ghosts,
> An old man in a draughty house
> Under a windy knob.
>
> GERONTION 23–33.

---

17    Mayer reads these figures similarly but instead as discrete occurrences of failure rather than a downward trend (Mayer 230). Bush's reading is less convincing (Bush 40).

The figure of Mr. Silvero seems to me concerned with sensuality as shown by his "caressing hands" and his "walk[ing] all night in the next room" (Gerontion 24–5). John Mayer's suggestion of this latter comment indicating a kind of existential angst in the face of an unsatisfying ritual seems germane (Mayer 230). Line 24, "Hakagawa, bowing among the Titians" inspires more diverse readings from critics ("Gerontion" 24).[18] Within the context, it is best, I think, to read this as someone giving obeisance best suited to religion to cultural artifacts, which might be read as a decay from devotional object to iconography to "mere" art. Madame de Tornquist, whose name is perhaps a play on tourniquet, is the figure of the occultist. Eliot, whose dislike of such was consistent, would likely think this a perversion of mysticism and religious thought in general. Finally, Fräulein von Kulp, whose name is likely a pun on the Latin for sin, lingers at the door, not opening it. The use of opening a door for the acceptance of belief is Biblical, so the symbolic implication is one of sin preventing the door from opening.[19] The phrase "vacant shuttles weave the wind" seems to squint. It simultaneously provides a summation of the previous figures *i.e.* Hakagawa, Tornquist, Kulp, but also looks forward to Gerontion himself who reenters the poem.[20] Finally, Gerontion speaks of himself in line 33–4, saying "I have no ghosts, / [a]n old man in a draughty house" ("Gerontion" 33–4). Located at this point in the list, he is even farther from the λόγος than those partaking in a ritual. The phrase "I have no ghosts" also squints. It suggests that he is not haunted, but also that he is lacking in the Holy Spirit. His house has no spirits, merely draughts, showing his condition of doubt. This unbelief tempered with *acedia* is the ultimate result of the failed revelation exemplified by the absent λόγος, which is crucial to the mystical communion part of the ascetic ideal.

It is unsurprising, given Eliot's skepticism while he was writing "Gerontion," that the concept of sin is vague. These components of the failure of the ascetic ideal: isolation, the sense of sin and the absent λόγος, while present in "Gerontion," will expand into major components of *The Waste Land* and "The Hollow Men." Nonetheless, the speaker in the poem can be easily seen, as previously mentioned, as embodying *acedia*, an insufficient attempt at goodness which results in a failure of vision due to lack of ascetic preparation. *Acedia*

---

18    I am unconvinced by Mayer's assertion of this as representing the divorce of religion from nation (Mayer 230). Ricks' interpretation overturns many older readings but provides little positive direction (Ricks *Prejudice* 123–5).

19    Rev. 3:20 is particularly relevant; however, Cf. Matthew 7:7–8, Luke 11:9, Luke 13:24–5, Acts 12:12–7, 14:27, 2nd Corinthians 2:12, Colossians 4:3. The attachment of this to a female figure is interesting; however, it is beyond the scope of this study.

20    Whether this phrase is derived from the Book of Job or Joyce's *Ulysses* is irrelevant to the current argument.

PINING 95

is a concept derived from Dante, which Santayana in his *Three Philosophical Poets*, defined as

> A possibility of general moral sluggishness and indifference. This Dante, with his fervid nature, particularly hates. He puts the Laodiceans in the fringe of his hell; within the gate, that they may be without hope, but outside of limbo, that they may have torments to endure, and be stung by wasps and hornets into a belated activity.
>
> SANTAYANA 111–2[21]

Such a description may help clarify the situation of Gerontion. He confesses himself to have been "neither at the hot gates / [n]or fought in the warm rain / [n]or knee deep in the salt marsh, heaving a cutlass, / [b]itten by flies, fought" ("Gerontion" 3–6). The biting flies suggests the passage in Canto III of the *Inferno*. Gerontion has not fought at all but rather sits in a state of decay like the self-apotheosized god of love in "Exequy," "[a] bloodless shade among the shades / [d]oing no good, but not much harm" ("Exequy" 13–4). At the risk of anachronism, Gerontion embodies what Eliot accuses Baudelaire of: "a true form of *acedia*, arising from the unsuccessful struggle towards the spiritual life" (*Prose* IV.158). Gerontion receives a revelation but does not grasp it. He does not struggle towards spiritual truth, through ascetic purification; in Andrewes' words, his "religion is rather *vidimus*, a contemplation, than *venimus*, a motion, or stirring to do ought" (Andrewes 258). Gerontion thinks but does not act. This dichotomy is one that Eliot encountered in Underhill to whose work his thoughts had returned during the period he was writing "Gerontion." She reiterates that love, desire, conation is required of the mystics that "there is no sense in which it can be said that the desire of love is merely a department of perfect knowledge: for that strictly intellectual ambition includes no adoration, no self-spending, no reciprocity of feeling between Knower and Known. Mere knowledge, taken alone, is a matter of receiving, not of acting: of eyes, not wings: a dead alive business at best" (Underhill 55).[22] This properly describes Gerontion who has knowledge without desire and as such misses the revelation. Importantly, there is in this mere cognition, no ability to interact between Knower and Known. It ends in the imprisonment of the self.

The isolation in "Gerontion," while similarly obvious, is also more nuanced than the conception of sin. This is best seen in the poem's penultimate strophe:

---

21  This passage in Dante eventually becomes the *locus* of "The Hollow Men."

22  It is possible that this may have influenced *The Waste Land* 40.

96 CHAPTER 5

> I that was near your heart was removed therefrom
> To lose beauty in terror, terror in inquisition.
> I have lost my passion: why should I need to keep it
> Since what is kept must be adulterated?
> I have lost my sight, smell, hearing, taste and touch:
> How should I use them for your closer contact?
>> "Gerontion" 55–60.

The passage is often read as addressing the Divine; however, the previous line "The tiger springs in the new year. Us he devours" contradicts this reading as Christ the Tiger is distinct from the "us" ("Gerontion" 48). This other person is likely to be the referent in the following discussion as it is still "we have not reached conclusion" ("Gerontion" 49). The phrase "new year" in context of the previous stanza may indicate a new line of disintegration away from a physical beloved parallel to the fall away from the Divine previously occurred. The "we" of the precious stanza is quickly sundered into a you and I, so that the one that was "near your heart" has become separated. Intimacy becomes isolation. This loss has not only personal but spiritual implications as the last chapter's discussion of Plato has shown. The association of this with sensual failure is intriguing, but again, one that occurs in Eliot's mystical readings. For example, in his section refuting the idea that mystic contemplation could be produced by sensible images, Poulan quotes St. John of the Cross as saying:[23]

> If [the soul] attempt to seek them [sweetness and fervor], not only will it not find them, but it will meet with aridity, because it turns away from the *peaceful and tranquil good* secretly bestowed upon it when it attempts to fall back on the operations of sense. In this way it loses the latter without gaining the former, because the senses have *ceased to be the channel of spiritual good* … for the gift being so grand, and an *infused gift*, cannot be received in this scanty and imperfect way.
>> ST. JOHN of the Cross qtd. in Poulan 135.

The loss of terror is a bit more troublesome, but I believe it is found in Proverbs 2:5, where if wisdom is found "then you will understand the fear of the Lord and find the knowledge of God" (Proverbs 2:5).[24] Thus, losing the terror is the

---

23    Eliot also encountered St John of the Cross in Inge *Christian Mysticism* 222–30.

24    The personification of Wisdom as a source for the λόγος in Jewish Wisdom literature is discussed briefly by Inge but largely discounted; however, the connection is rather tenuous, I think. Cf. Inge *Personal Idealism* 38–40.

PINING 97

loss of even the knowledge of God where the Beauty is the loss of Love. Love and Knowledge are vehicles of experience in Eliot's reading (Underhill 54–5). By inquisition, I think this is continual philosophical questioning. Thus, the creeping doubt is at the root of the divorce between the self and other *and* the self and the Divine. This is one of the distinct differences in "Gerontion." The isolation from another person only *mirrors* that of the separation from the Divine. In *The Waste Land*, as will be seen, the two occur simultaneously while in "The Hollow Men" the two are rendered as one. Yet, going farther than the "Narcissus" and "Sebastian" poems, Eliot presents an example of asceticism gone wrong. Pain in Underhill's phrasing "plunges like a sword through creation leaving on the one side cringing and degraded animals and on the other side heroes and saints" (Underhill 23). Eliot is here presenting the former, the failure of asceticism, suffering which results not in the divine union but in aridity and ultimately solipsism. Such themes in "Gerontion" will be associated explicitly with a failure of the ascetic ideal in *The Waste Land* and "The Hollow Men." Thus, this is the first, inchoate evidence of this personal application of the ascetic ideal in Eliot's work. The sin is more limited,—Gerontion makes none of the superhuman efforts to attain the Good that the saints in the mystical readings performed, and the result is isolation.

Let me reiterate the overarching argument of this chapter. The poems of this period interrogate the most complex aspect of the ascetic ideal, the mystical communion of souls that follows purification, by exploring failure to attain it through three recurring images: isolation, sin, and the absent λόγος. In *The Waste Land*, these themes are more interconnected than in "Gerontion." As in the earlier poems, the absent λόγος presents the most exegetical difficulty and will be dealt with first. The absence of the λόγος in *The Waste Land* is presented in diverse instances, scattered throughout the poem. This is unsurprising as there is nothing programmatic about Eliot's preoccupation with the ascetic ideal.[25] Let me enumerate the instances of absent λόγος, which I will discuss: the first is the scene in The Hyacinth Garden; the second the absence of the Hanged Man; the third and fourth are two other instances of spiritual failure though without a specific tie to the λόγος; the fifth the mysterious voice of the Thunder. This is completely separate from the pedestrian observation that

---

25    As a procedural matter, however, it is worth mentioning that I am omitting "The Resurrection and the Life" fragment from the manuscript from my discussion. Rainey dates it from October 1913 which has approached critical consensus (Rainey 200–1). Additionally, that poem itself seems to be merely a liberal rendition of an unattributed Baudelaire poem found in a footnote on page 447 of Bradley's *Appearance and Reality*. The reason for its inclusion among *The Waste Land* manuscripts being unknown, I am hesitant to draw upon it for my argumentation.

98                                                                      CHAPTER 5

"What the Thunder Said" is partly a crucifixion scene where the crucifixion occurs completely off-stage, so the Word never appears. The sixth and final is the
OM missing from the benediction in the poem's final line. The sense of all of
these is one of abortive revelation. To be poetic, though words are spoken, the
Word is unheard. Let me first examine the fullest instance of failed revelation
in the Hyacinth Garden:[26]

> 'You gave me hyacinths first a year ago';
> 'They called me the hyacinth girl.'
> —Yet when we came back, late, from the Hyacinth garden,
> Your arms full, and your hair wet, I could not
> Speak, and my eyes failed, I was neither
> Living nor dead, and I knew nothing,
> Looking into the heart of light, the silence.
> *Oed' und leer das Meer.*
> > *The Waste Land* 35–40.

The imagery of sensual failure as a part of the mystical experience is not an
uncommon one. Underhill states that "'the bodily sight stinted,' says Julian [of
Norwich], 'but the spiritual sight dwelled in mine understanding, and I abode
with reverent dread joying in that I saw.' The heart outstrips the clumsy senses,
and sees—perhaps for an instant, perhaps for long periods of bliss—an undis-
torted and more veritable world" (Underhill 310).[27] The phrase "neither living
nor dead" is, among other things, a reference to *Inferno* XXXIV:25 at the fear
of Dante gazing upon the face of Satan at the very bottom of Hell. Despite the
quotation from Julian above, I believe, in line with "Gerontion," this failure of
the senses should be interpreted negatively.[28] The next phrase "heart of light,
the silence" is usually referred to as a mystical vision; however, it does not seem
to refer to any specific incident in any of Eliot's mystical readings. Curiously,
the vision of the transcendent is more commonly referred to as one of darkness

---

26    Just before the Wagner quotation, there is a curious tie between the dry scholasticism of
      Gerontion and the powerfully multivalent phrasing of *The Waste Land* 30. In one of his
      graduate essays "The Relativity of Moral Judgment," Eliot writes "[t]o reduce the world to
      set of formulae is to let it slip through our fingers in a fine dust; but to fly into an emo-
      tional orgy or retire into a sunlit stupor is to let the world slip through our fingers in a thin
      smoke" (*Prose* I.198). The connection is tantalizing and, to my knowledge, has never been
      properly explored.
27    Cf. Poulan 167–8, 176, St Bernard qtd. in Underhill 293.
28    Cf. St Augustine qtd. in Récéjac's 128, Underhill 161.

PINING 99

than light.[29] Occasionally, the element of silence is added as well. Eliot certainly read of mystic vision as "the luminous darkness of a silence which is full of profound teaching: a marvelous darkness which shines with rays of splendor" (Underhill 301).[30] It is also possible that Eliot is synthesizing one of the visions of Suso which features a heart of glass with the river of light in Dante as these two are discussed on the same page in Underhill (Underhill 342).[31] This seem no less unlikely as a source than those listed by Ricks and McCue (*Poems* 1.609). On the whole, though, I believe that the phrase "the heart of light, the silence" refers to a mystical experience broadly without any particular referent.

What is important about the phrase is the abortive nature of this vision. The speaker knows *nothing*. He is not initiated by this experience and is compared to how the shepherd watching over the dying Tristan sees nothing on the vast sea (*Poems* 1.609.).[32] This is, of course, not surprising, given Eliot's reading. As Inge notes in a poetic flourish, "[i]t is always 'in his light' that 'we see light'" (Inge *Christian Mysticism* 7). He continues by stating that "[t]he vision is inseparable from *likeness* to Him, which is a hope, not a possession, and is only to be won by 'purifying ourselves, even as He is pure'" (Inge *Christian Mysticism* 8). The vision fails due to a lack of purification from sin *i.e.* a failure of ascetic preparation. The exact nature of this sin will be discussed shortly.

The second instance of the absent λόγος is shortly thereafter in the Tarot card scene.

> Here is the man with three staves, and here the Wheel,
> And here is the one-eyed merchant, and this card,
> Which is blank, is something he carries on his back,
> Which I am forbidden to see. I do not find
> The Hanged Man. Fear death by water.
> I see crowds of people, walking round in a ring
>> *The Waste Land* 51–6.

---

29　Cf. Underhill 263, Pratt 161.

30　Cf. "'In the midst of silence, a hidden word was spoken to me.' Where is this Silence, and where is the place in which this word is spoken? It is in the purest that the soul can produce in her noblest part, in the Ground, even the Being of the Soul" (Eckhart qtd. in Underhill 45). Cf. Underhill 253, 530, Inge summarizing Philo in *Christian Mysticism* 83.

31　Cp. A similar convergence of imagery with reference to two disparate passages in St Augustine in Inge *Christian Mysticism* 131.

32　"A mystic (μύστης) is one who has been, or is being, initiated into some esoteric knowledge of Divine things, about which he must keep his mouth shut (μύειν); or, possibly, he is one whose *eyes* are still shut, one who is not yet an ἐπόπτης" (Inge *Christian Mysticism* 4).

The absence of the Hanged Man is specifically mentioned. Eliot, in one of his more dubious notes, associates him with the Hanged God of Frazer, which in itself unsurprising as the card of The Hanged Man is traditionally associated with the concept of sacrifice. More importantly, in his chapter on The Hanged God, Frazer draws comparisons between the Adonis and Attis legends of The Hanged God with the death of Christ, the incarnate λόγος (Frazer 362–4).[33] Thus, we have a deliberate omission of the λόγος and one with evidently dire consequence as the next line in *The Waste Land* mentions the inevitable death by water and the awaiting inferno. Now, as always, I am not asserting that any of this is programmatic on Eliot's part; *The Waste Land,* as his letters and the manuscript attest, had a more organic generation.[34] Rather, the continual pattern of such incidents shows that the ascetic ideal was on Eliot's mind through this phase of his career.

Although they are not *truly* instances of an absent λόγος, it may be instructive to consider two further possible sources for failed revelation. Since I am not arguing that Eliot necessarily intended this, such partial appearances are not surprising. The first is a curious source for the phrase "a heap of broken images" in l. 22. The second is the city dissolving in the sky in ll.371–2. The former seems to originate from a phrase in Inge's *Personal Idealism and Mysticism* where Eliot read that

> severe moral and mental discipline brings its own reward in its own partial supersession. Dualism is, after all, appearance and not reality. Apparent contradictions in the nature of things, when faced perfectly fairly, can be lived down. And so the inner discord of flesh and spirit is attuned, and even sin itself, whether in ourselves or in the world, is partly seen to be "behovable" as Julian of Norwich says. The will, no longer divided against itself, passes into intelligence; we become fellow-workers with God, rather than day-laborers in His service. The broken images of order and beauty, which we have trained ourselves to observe and reverence in the world, begin to form themselves into a glorious universe of gracious design, though which the Divine Wisdom [*i.e.* the λόγος] passes and penetrates, mightily and sweetly ordering all things.
>
> INGE *Personal Idealism* 15–6.

---

33  This material was removed from the early abridgements but would likely have existed in the editions in which Eliot seems to have read Frazer. Cf. Frazer 675–6.

34  E.g. *Letters* 1.625–30.

PINING                                                                            101

Compare this to *The Waste Land* where Eliot wrote:

What are the roots that clutch, what branches grow
Out of this stony rubbish? Son of man,
You cannot say, or guess, for you know only
A heap of broken images, where the sun beats,
And the dead tree gives no shelter, the cricket no relief,
And the dry stone no sound of water.
> *The Waste Land* 19–24.

The echo seems compelling enough that I think this is at least an unconscious allusion, and the context is suitably germane. In the state of aridity and spiritual desolation from the failure of "severe moral and mental discipline," the isolated fragments do not coalesce into a single cogent, beautiful world.[35]

As to the second instance, Eliot read in Jones of "the visible coming of the heavenly Jerusalem" expected by the Montanists which "appears with unabated vividness in the writings of Tertullian" (Jones 54). The passage is, in full:

The word of the new prophecy, which is a part of our belief, attests how it foretold that there would be, for a sign, a picture of this very city exhibited to view previous to its manifestation. This prophecy, indeed, has been very lately fulfilled in an expedition to the East. For it is evident from the testimony even of heathen witnesses in Judea there was suspended in the sky a city, early every morning for forty days. As the day advanced the entire figure of the walls would wane, and sometimes it would vanish instantly.
> TERTULLIAN qtd. in JONES 54.

This is quite similar to lines 371–6 of *The Waste Land*:

What is the city over the mountains
Cracks and reforms and bursts in the violet air
Falling towers

---

35   Sristava asserts that the "collocation of images of the valley of bones, the red rock, and the shadow is vitally charged with the tone of prophecy which promises a visualized understanding or the universal truths of death and rebirth" (Sristava 113). I do not see how the vatic tone might promise any of that; Tiresias provides no answers, certainly. While the expectation of resurrection is implied, there seems to be no evidence of it in this or, indeed, any section of the poem. Contra Sristava 112–3.

# CHAPTER 5

> Jerusalem Athens Alexandria
> Vienna London
> Unreal.
>
> *The Waste Land* 371–6.

A subconscious allusion to a very striking image he had read many years earlier is not beyond belief, and this certainly seems a better explanation than many others.[36] What I think is mopre interesting is the inability of the speaker to identify it as a heavenly Jerusalem, which is only one of the possibilities listed. While not a conclusive statement of divine absence, these two allusions indicate that the ascetic ideal and the places he encountered it were on Eliot's mind.

At the poem's end, the Divine voice speaks from the Thunder in one of most poem's most difficult pericopes. While remarkably polyvalent, this passage also contains an abortive revelation. Interestingly, the poem itself is vaguer than the cited Upanishad where it is specifically Prajapati who speaks *through* the Thunder. Eliot first read of Prajapati in J. B. Pratt's *The Psychology of Religious Belief*, one of the skeptical mystical readings. Pratt describes Prajapati as one step on the road between the polytheism of the Rig Veda and the Brahman, whom Pratt identifies with the Absolute (Pratt 86). The idea of the divine speaking from the Thunder is not exclusively Eastern, though, as Yahweh is depicted as speaking from or as the thunder in several places in the Old Testament: Jeremiah 10:13, Psalms 18:13, 77:17, and Job 37:4, most notably. Additionally, a relation between the thunder and Yahweh is drawn by Santayana who speaks, poetically, of "the thunders and the law of Sinai," and Pratt, as well, who quotes the song of Deborah in Judges 5:4–5 where Yahweh's victory is described in a water-giving fashion, which is not dissimilar from that of Indra in the Rig-Veda (Santayana 81, Pratt 117).[37] Additionally, Inge quotes a passage from an obscure poem "Bibliolatres" by Eliot's ancestor James Russell Lowell as an epigraph to his chapter on Nature-Mysticism and Symbolism in *Christian Mysticism*. Whether or not Eliot paid any attention to the poem or would have even recalled its existence when he was writing *The Waste Land* is unknown; however, it does encapsulate many of the ideas and images seen in "What the Thunder Said":

> "God is not dumb, that He should speak no more.
> If thou has wanderings in the wilderness,

---

36  Cf. *Poems* 1.694–5.
37  Cf. Rig-Veda qtd. in Weston 24–5, Marett 163.

PINING                                                                                        103

> And Find'st not Sinai, 'tis thy soul is poor;
> There towers the mountain of the voice no less,
> Which whoso seeks shall find; but he who bends,
> Intent on manna still and mortal ends,
> Sees it not, nor hears its thundered lore."
>
> LOWELL qtd. in INGE *Christian Mysticism* 248.

This poem does touch on the ascetic issues inherent in the poem that the materialism of focusing on the world's "manna still and mortal ends" will result in a failure to hear the "thundered lore." This passage may be one of the largest hermeneutical difficulties of *The Waste Land*. If the voice of God speaks, why does no one listen? Why is the speaker left "upon the shore / [f]ishing, with the arid plains behind him" like the scattered disciples after the crucifixion? (*The Waste Land* 424–5, John 21:1–14). The answer is that the λόγος is absent; the revelation of the Thunder is purely external. As Inge states,

> Revelation is the unveiling of some Divine truth which we could not have discovered for ourselves, but which, when it is shown to us by others to whom God has spoken, we can recognize as Divine. There can be no revelation which is purely external; such a communication would be partly unnoticed, and partly misunderstood. There must be the answering witness of the Spirit within us that this is the voice of God.
>
> INGE *English Mystics* 2–3.[38]

Or in Andrewes' words, "as St. Augustine saith well, *Signum vobis, si signum in vobis,* 'A sign for you, if a sign in you'" (Andrewes 205). In short, the poem is still faithless, the λόγος is absent, and the sign pointing to renewing revelation is completely ignored. This is also shown by the fact that in the Upanishad, Prajapati after giving each command responds with the word "*Om,*" which is some equivalent to the λόγος, to indicate that the group to whom it was directed understood, and in *The Waste Land,* no such response is heard (Kearns 222). To what degree, of course, Eliot was intending such a scheme is unclear and, somewhat, irrelevant. What is more compelling is the preponderance of small recurrences of the theme of the absent λόγος, and the persistent ties to ascetic failures occurring at the same time.

The final incident of the absent λόγος is shown by the poem's final ending. According to Kearns, "we must note that in the formal ending of an Upanishad proper, *shantih* is usually associated with the syllable *Om,* the [λόγος], or word

---

38    Cf. Acts 9:3–8, Acts 22:6–11.

of revealed truth, so that the full expression reads *Om shantih shantih shantih*" (Kearns 228).[39] The large indentation of the line in not only the first edition but even in both the manuscript and typescript suggests that Eliot intended this omission, by leaving space for the Word, but not including it (*Waste Land Manuscript* 80–1, 88–9, 146). Thus, the λόγος is absent from the poem's end. The revelation is abortive; the Divine voice spoke but went unheard or misunderstood. This is a firm example that an omission of the λόγος was deliberate by Eliot, although to what end is unclear.

In *The Waste Land*, the idea of sin is more explicit than in "Gerontion." The sin in the poem is best shown in the correspondence between the first three sections of *The Waste Land* and the commands of the Thunder in Part v.[40] In other words, I believe there to be a deliberate parallelism between the command *Datta* and "The Burial of the Dead," between *Dayadhvam* and "A Game of Chess," and between *Damyata* and "The Fire Sermon." This forms a pattern where ascetic failures occur simultaneously as themes of personal isolation. Unlike in "Gerontion" where isolation and sin are separate, in *The Waste Land* they occur in unison, distinct but not separate.

There is, of course, no definitive way of proving that Eliot intended such a structure; however, upon consideration of the evidence, I think it more likely than not that there was some intentionality. The most obvious element is that Eliot "has altered the order of the original text [*i.e.* The Brihadaranyaka Upanishad] from the sequence *damyata, datta, dayadhvam*" to the one currently in *The Waste Land* (Kearns 220).[41] Eliot did not seem to be in the habit of purposelessly altering the quotations he employed in the poem, so I find it difficult

---

39    Sristava asserts that the omission must be deliberate; however, he asserts that the lack of the λόγος should be taken positively, based on musical patterns, that it "closes the door of reversion to the arid plain [...] and marks a new beginning which has no end as is suggested by the total lack of any punctuation mark in the last line" (Sristava 57). Without musical patterning, it would be bad poetry, so I am not certain that proves anything, and it seems less than judicious to conclude such a dramatic positive turn for the poem on the basis of a missing period alone.

40    This has been noticed by others before, most completely by Childs; however, I arrived at this relation independently, and there has been little, if any, application of this correspondence. Cf. Childs *Mystic, Son, and Lover* 121–2, Sristava 49.

41    While I am indebted to Kearns for confirming this fact, she insists this is to emphasize *damyata, control* though better translated "practice self-control." This I do not dispute, but she marshals this in support of a Roycean reading where the Thunder's voice "renews [...] the community of the spirit of those who interpret" (Kearns 221). Given the result is the speaker sitting fishing alone on the shore of an arid plain with little, if any, evidence of understanding the Thunder, I do not see how the poem supports any part of the renewal of interpretive community. Contra Kearns 220–1.

PINING                                                                    105

to believe that he would have changed the order in this instance without reason.[42] Additionally, he often accepted changes in quotations from Pound when
there was an error and even made emendations after the *The Waste Land* was
published. For instance, consider the change to the Wagner lyric from the manuscript from *"Frisch schwebt"* to *"Frisch weht"* and the alteration of the original
*"Od' und leer"* to *"Oed' und leer"* in later printings as is done with the error in
the Latin *"Quando fiam ceu chelidon"* to *"Quando fiam uti chelidon"* (*The Waste
Land Manuscript* 7, 136, 146). Thus, I doubt that Eliot would have let a simple
error stand. On the whole, it is easier to believe that Eliot altered the order of
the commands deliberately.

The correspondence between the commands and the previous parts of the
poem are relatively simple, but they, nonetheless, provide the locus of sin in
the poem. In "The Burial of the Dead," the most probative location is the Hyacinth Girl's tacit request within the statement "You gave me hyacinths first a
year ago" (*The Waste Land* 35). It is to the speaker in this scene that the command *Datta*, be generous, seems to be directed. Interestingly, this seemingly
spurious connection is heightened by the strange extrapolation which follows
the command itself.

> What have we given?
> My friend, blood shaking my heart[43]
> The awful daring of a moment's surrender
> Which an age of prudence can never retract
> By this, and this only, we have existed
> Which is not to be found in our obituaries
> Or in memories draped by the beneficent spider
> Or under seals broken by the lean solicitor
> In our empty rooms.
> *The Waste Land* 401–9.

Here the idea of generosity is connected with the idea of "a moment's surrender," which initially seems to suggest a kind of sexual sin. Rather, I think that
the context for "*Datta*," the command for generosity, in view of the Hyacinth

---

42    I will not belabor with examples. Cf. *The Waste Land* 48, 63, 76, 199, *et al.* For examples of
lines with significant deviations, *vid. The Waste Land* 185, 197 *et al.*

43    This may be an unconscious allusion to Fr. 1 of Parmenides qtd. in Burnet 196–7: "Meet it
is that thou shouldst learn of all things, as well the unshaken heart of well-rounded truth,
as the opinions of mortals in which is no true belief at all."

Garden scene, places the emphasis is on a kind of self-surrender—at risk of anachronism, let me quote "East Coker":

> Do not let me hear
> Of the wisdom of old men, but rather of their folly,
> Their fear of fear and frenzy, their fear of possession,
> Of belonging to another, or to others, or to God.
> "East Coker" 94–7.

It is an unwillingness to give of the *self*, the inclusion of another person in love, "which an age of prudence can never retract" (*The Waste Land* 404). As Eliot read in G. B. Cutten, one of the more skeptical mystical readings, "the result of self-surrender, or a part of the process, is unification of the mind in contrast to the former divided self"; then, quoting William James, Cutten states that the process of unification "may come gradually, or it may occur abruptly; it may come through altered feelings or through altered powers of action; or it may come through new intellectual insights, or though experiences which we shall later have to designate as 'mystical'" (Cutten 246). The relation of this process of self-surrender to a mystical experience is interesting. What is more so is that the sensation of newness this conversion experience creates is likened to "the youth who has sung for the first time his love-tale to his lady and receives the assurance of requited life" (Leuba qtd. in Cutten 248). Thus, Eliot's readings have the same overlapping ideas: romantic connection, mystical communion, and self-surrender; however, what is portrayed in *The Waste Land* is, of course, a failure to attain this. In the poem, the generosity, the self-giving, has not occurred, the mystical vision has failed, and isolation is the result. Eliot portrays in this scene a failure of the senses and an inability to connect to someone else like he did in "Gerontion"; however, unlike the earlier poem where the two events are separate, in *The Waste Land*, they occur simultaneously, a progression which culminates in "The Hollow Men."

The second command "Dayadhvam," "be sympathetic," corresponds to "A Game of Chess." The applicability of this to the husband of the neurotic woman or to Lil's "friend" who preys upon her faltering marriage is obvious. The connection between a failure of sympathy, sin, and isolation was made explicit in a lengthy passage by Inge previously quoted in Chapter 4:

> love of the brethren is inseparable from love of God. So intimate is this union, that hatred towards any human being cannot exist in the same heart as love to God. The mystical union is indeed rather a bond between Christ and the Church, and between man and man as members

of Christ, than between Christ and individual souls. Our Lord's prayer is 'that they all may be one, even as Thou, Father, art in Me, and I in Thee, that they also may be one in us.'[44] The personal relation between the soul and Christ is not to be denied; but it can only be enjoyed when the person has 'come to himself' as a member of a body. This involves an inward transit from the false isolated self to the larger life of sympathy and love which alone makes us persons.

> INGE *Christian Mysticism* 51.

This passage connects all the strands of this argument. The concept of the λόγος is here merged with the possible consubstantial bond between others and there is an emphasis on purity *i.e.* on some form of ascetic preparation. The result of this failure of sympathy is isolation.

Finally, the phrase "Damyata" corresponds to "The Fire Sermon," and I will not weary the reader with a full demonstration of its applicability. The injunction to practice self-control to brothel-frequenting Sweeney, the sexual encounter of the typist and the clerk, and the shameless flirtation of Elizabeth and Leicester, implicitly before a bishop—so egregious that Leicester asks if they could be married on the spot[45]—seems obvious and equally so the resultant solitude. However, there is an instance worthy of extended discussion here. Excluding the "*ascétique*" in "*Lune de Miel*," this passage contains the only mention of the actual *word* asceticism in Eliot's published poetry ("*Lune de Miel*" 16). In his note to line 309, Eliot states "[t]he collocation of these two representatives of eastern and western asceticism, as the culmination of this part of the poem, is not an accident" (note to *The Waste Land* 309). Unfortunately, the note has that tone of mock pedantry which haunts many of the more dubious notes to *The Waste Land*, so I am loath to draw any direct conclusions based on the content. However, there are still some interpretive opportunities. The first is confirming that Eliot indeed thought about asceticism at all during this period. The second is that he clearly does not operate with a narrow view of the term as there is not a single instance of a self-mortifying medieval monk in "The Fire Sermon." Rather, it supports the mystical readings' assessment of ascetic ideal as the drive towards personal purity and selflessness. Notably, St Augustine in these works was primarily treated as a mystic, so it connects asceticism to the mystical process. The third is that curious comment about the meeting of the Eastern and Western asceticism is consonant with an aside by Underhill in her discussion of detachment.

---

44   John 17:21.

45   Cf. Eliot's note to *The Waste Land* 279.

108                                                                                                    CHAPTER 5

> Here East and West are in agreement: "Their science," says Al Ghazzali of
> the Sūfis, who practiced, like the early Franciscans, a complete renuncia-
> tion of worldly goods, "has for its object the uprooting of the soul of all
> violent passions, the extirpation from it of vicious desires and evil quali-
> ties; so that the heart may become attached from all that is not God, and
> give itself for its only occupation meditation upon the Divine Being."
>
> UNDERHILL 254.

What is portrayed in both the poem and this passage from Underhill is an appeal to the spirit for escape from the allures of the flesh (*The Waste Land* 309).
It is, of course, an abortive one as the last word of "The Fire Sermon" is "burning" (*The Waste Land* 311). The implication is that no relief from the fires of sin
has been found by the figures in the poem.

In *The Waste Land,* more so than in "Gerontion," there is an obvious link
through the concepts of the sin, isolation, and the absent λόγος. These elements all occur together, if not with the simultaneity which will be seen in
"The Hollow Men." This is still a scenario of failure as the sin of the characters
leaves no hope for communion at the end of purgation.

By way of conclusion, "The Hollow Men," like "The Function of Criticism" in
Chapter 3, displays how the disparate themes of the absent λόγος, sin, and isolation have become intricately, almost inextricably, interwoven. That the hollow men are figures of sin is obvious as they are self-confessed "lost / [v]iolent
souls" ("The Hollow Men" 1.15–6).[46] The uncertainty in the phrase "remember
us, if at all," seems to refer to the fact that, in Dante's *Inferno*, the world permits
no memory of the souls on the vestibule of Hell (*Inferno* III:49). Thus, within
the poem, the nature of the hollow men's sin is left indistinct, but it seems
more serious than the *acedia* seen in "Gerontion" and the lack of humanity and
self-control in *The Waste Land*.[47] Their isolation is equivalently self-evident—
they avoid meeting and speech—isolated but without solitude in the same
way that in *The Waste Land* "there is not even solitude in the mountains" (*The
Waste Land* 343). The final piece is the absent λόγος, and as with the other poems, it is the portion which requires the most exposition.

---

46   Dominic Manganiello has, for the most part, adequately treated the poem's Dantean ele-
     ments, and I will not recapitulate his argumentation. Cf. Manganiello 59–65.
47   Eliot's exchange with John Middleton Murry in his letters supports this increase in the
     feeling of sin in Eliot's own life; they would provide an excellent source to those more
     inclined to read Eliot's biography into this argument than I am.

PINING                                                                                          109

In "The Hollow Men," the Divine Revelation, the symbol and ability to communicate, is reduced to mere eyes, in line with the poem's minimalism. The image is a compression of the ideas of connection and sensual failure seen previously with the image of Beatrice from Dante. Eliot justifies this strange inclusion in his Clark Lectures where he comparies the *Vita Nuova* with Donne's "The Extasie." Most of the quotations in Chapter 4 were from this passage, in fact. Eliot asserts that the *Vita Nuova* is "a record of actual experiences reshaped into a particular form[,] [...] a kind of experience possible to a particular mental type, which persons of this type will always recognize" (*Prose* II.650). Eliot's comments are a recasting of Santayana's interpretation of the origin of the *Vita Nuova* in *Three Philosophical Poets* (Santayana 94–5). For all of Eliot's professed differences of opinion,[48] his Clark Lectures have strong resemblances with the "Dante" section of *Three Philosophical Poets*. Santayana's interpretation of Beatrice seems to inform Eliot's own:

> [i]f the *donna gentile* is philosophy, the *donna gentilissima*, Beatrice, must be something of the same sort, only nobler. She must be theology, and theology Beatrice undoubtedly is. Her very name is played upon, if not selected, to mean that she is what renders blessed, what shows the path of salvation. [...] It is certain, then, that Beatrice, besides being a woman, was also a symbol. But this is not the end. If Beatrice is a symbol for theology, theology itself is not final. It, too, is an avenue, an interpretation.[49] The eyes of Beatrice reflect a supernal light. It is the ineffable vision of God, the beatific vision, that alone can make us happy and be the reason and the end of our loves and our pilgrimages."
>
> SANTAYANA 96–8.

For merely the single most probative instance to "The Hollow Man," among a multitude: though Dante stares into the sun, it is only when he sees it reflected in Beatrice's eyes that he ascends to the Heavens (*Paradiso* I:64–72).[50] Beatrice as found in the image of eyes in "The Hollow Men" is not merely an example of the λόγος as a figure of speech but herself a kind of compression of the λόγος concept.

---

48    Cf. *Prose* II.613–4, 652ff.

49    This rather dubiously worded statement disguises an unmentioned accuracy. Beatrice, though Dante's guide all through the *Paradiso*, leaves him to the mystic St Bernard for the final guidance to the vision of God in *Paradiso* XXXI.

50    Eliot thought much of this passage, quoting it in both the 1919 and 1929 essays on Dante. Cf. *Prose* II.232, III.723–4.

110 CHAPTER 5

Now, it is important to note that the use of eyes as a stand-in for God himself in some way is not unique to Dante. St John of the Cross, as quoted in one of the mystical readings, says "of the 'Beloved:'[51] [...]

> The soul, because of its intense longing after the Divine eyes, that is the Godhead, receives interiorly from the Beloved such communications and knowledge of God as compel it to cry out, "Turn away, O my Beloved." Such is the wretchedness of our mortal nature that we cannot endure— even when it is offered to us—but at the cost of our life, that which is the very life of the soul and the object of its earnest desires, namely the knowledge of the Beloved. Thus the soul is compelled to say, with regard to the eyes so earnestly, so anxiously sought for, and in so many ways— when they become visible—"Turn them away[.]"
>
> ST JOHN of the Cross qtd. in POULAN 173.

This is tied intimately with the definition of Love defined in Plato but summarized in Underhill. The connection with Eliot's ideas in *Varieties of Metaphysical Poetry* will be apparent.

> Love's characteristic activity—for Love, all wings,[52] is inherently active, and 'cannot be lazy,' as the mystics say—is a quest, an outgoing towards an object desired, which only when possessed will be fully known, and only when fully known can be perfectly adored. Intimate communion, no less than worship, is of its essence. Joyous fruition is its proper end. This is true of all Love's quests, whether the Beloved be human or divine—the bride, the Grail, the Mystic Rose, the plenitude of God.
>
> UNDERHILL 55.

Here is Eliot's critique of the passion of "The Extasie," which is that Donne's poem has "little suggestion of adoration, of worship" (*Prose* II.660). The mystical communion of souls should include a closer connection to God, not just

---

51  Cf. "But where the metaphysician obtains at best a sidelong glance at that Being, 'unchanging yet elusive,' whom he has so often defined but never discovered, the artist a brief and dazzling vision of the Beauty which is truth, [the mystics] gaze with confidence into the very eyes of the Beloved" (Underhill 42).

52  Cf. "The wing is the corporeal element which is most akin to the divine, and which by nature tends to soar aloft and carry that which gravitates downwards into the upper region, which is the habitation of the gods. The divine is beauty, wisdom, goodness, and the like; and by these the wing of the soul is nourished, and grows apace; but when fed upon evil and foulness and the opposite of good, wastes and falls away" (*Phaedrus* §246d-e).

PINING                                                                                    111

the beloved. Additionally, this passage includes the image of the rose that is
the fullness of the divinity found in "The Hollow Men" IV.13, though obviously
it derives primarily from *Paradiso* XXX and XXXI.,

> Sightless, unless
> The eyes reappear
> As the perpetual star
> Multifoliate rose
> Of death's twilight kingdom.
> "The Hollow Men" IV.10–4.

Notably, the eyes are identified with and carry the power of the Divine Rose,
although they are not, strictly speaking, the rose itself. This is, in-and-of-itself,
a way of thinking of the λόγος. Of course, in "The Hollow Men" as in the earlier
poems, the λόγος is absent, the revelation does not occur as "there are no eyes"
("The Hollow Men" IV.2).

   The primary objection to this reading is likely to be that it places the sentiment of the poem much closer to the religious poetry. I am not arguing for
"The Hollow Men" as a conversion poem. In my opinion, the poem is ultimately faithless, an opinion that Eliot himself affirmed later in life as Eliot tells his
brother that it is his "one blasphemous poem" in a 1936 letter (*Poems* I.714).
Thus, the failure of the ascetic ideal is clearly a negative thing, but the ascetic ideal is not positively endorsed. After all, the poetic voice never manages
to pronounce "[f]or Thine is the Kingdom." The hollow men remain trapped
within their prisons of themselves by their sin because the λόγος is absent. As
such, I think the poem is more religious than is generally thought, again, a fact
on which Eliot himself would later insist.[53] The primary passage upholding the
more secular readings of the poem is III.12–3, "lips that would kiss / [f]orm
prayers to broken stone" ("The Hollow Men" III.12–3). This is read in a variety of
ways; however, all of these neglect the allusion to Dante within the phrase "to
broken stone." In *Paradiso* XVI, Caccaguida states that "[*m*]*a conveniesi, a quel-
la pietra scema / che guarda 'l ponte, che Fiorenza fesse / vittima ne la sua pace
postrema*"[54] (*Paradiso* XVI:145–7). Thus, the emphasis is not placed on the act
of the dichotomy between religion and personal intimacy but on the sudden

---

53    Eliot says in another 1936 letter that it would be more fitting under the label of "spiritual"
      rather than "social disease" in a contemporaneous anthology (*Poems* I.714).

54    Ciardi translates the passage: "it was fitting that to the broken stone / that guards the
      bridge, Florence should offer a victim / to mark the last day's peace she has ever known"
      (Ciardi 186).

reversion to human sacrifice *i.e.* the murder of Buondelmonti at the foot of the worn statue of Mars that guarded the bridge (Ciardi 192). Eliot thought enough on the Caccaguida episode to single it out, if not wholly laudably, from the rest of the *Paradiso* in his second Dante essay (*Prose* III.723). There is no substantial grounding for reading the poem as the last skeptical bastion of Eliot's secular period as opposed to part of a more gradual conversion.

In the last analysis, "The Hollow Men" exemplifies in almost inextricable ways, Eliot's involvement with the ascetic ideal in this period. The figure of eyes is the ideal to which the hollow men aspire—communion and adoration with and of an external and a Divine love. However, as in Chapter 2, the figures in the poem subsist in an unpurified state; this shatters the possibility of communion and leaves them imprisoned like oysters in the shell of themselves, to use Plato's metaphor from the *Phaedrus*. From the enervate solipsism of "Gerontion," *The Waste Land*, and "The Hollow Men," Eliot will after a number of years move to a serious consideration of this same aspect of the ascetic ideal, in works like *Four Quartets* particularly.

CHAPTER 6

# Dramatizing

As Eliot began his first forays into the theater, the ascetic ideal underlies the action in both the incomplete *Sweeney Agonistes* and his first success *Murder in the Cathedral*. Yet, the ascetic ideal is found more in the structure than in the plot.[1] In his earliest plays, Eliot derives the formal structure from the plays of Aristophanes. One of the distinct features of Attic Old Comedy of which Aristophanes is the exemplar is that an ideological struggle forms the core of the play. In Eliot's first two plays the ascetic ideal is the driving, victorious ideology.[2] As a note, the later plays written at the same time as the latter three *Quartets* use the ascetic ideal more like the works discussed in the next chapter than these early plays. While the incomplete nature of *Sweeney Agonistes* complicates the analysis, a lack of purification may be part of the play's thematic struggle. *Murder in the Cathedral* has no apparent relation to a comedy at first glance, but the two plays did have some connection in Eliot's mind. He is recalled as answering a question on the production of *Sweeney Agonistes* with a line that he used later in *Murder in the Cathedral* (Flanagan qtd. in *Letters* VI.569). Additionally, Cornford, Eliot's source for Aristophanic structures, notes that "a curious feature which distinguishes Aristophanes' plays from all other forms of Comedy," is "that they present a whole series of old men" who "undergo, in some sense, a similar rejuvenation" (Cornford 92–3). The modern popularity of *Lysistrata* obscures the fact that most plays by Aristophanes present an older man[3] who is disenfranchised from the prevailing political and social order, and his rejuvenation is effected by his reformation or defiance of this order. *Murder in the Cathedral* appears to follow this Aristophanic pattern.[4] Thomas, in his self-surrender, defies the prevailing political authority and conquers it to show the transcendence of the divine over human machinations.

---

1 This chapter extends research and argumentation from my article, "Aristophanic Structures in *Sweeney Agonistes*, *Hollow Men*, and *Murder in the Cathedral*." *T. S. Eliot Annual*, Clemson UP. 2017.

2 The later plays written at the same time as the latter three *Quartets* use the ascetic ideal more like the poems than these early plays.

3 Cornford highlights Trygaeus in *Peace*, Dikaiopolis in *Acharnians*, Demos in *Knights*, Strepsiades in *Clouds*, Philocleon in *Wasps*, Pisthetairus in *Birds*, Blepyrus in *Ecclesiazusae*, and Plutus in *Wealth* (Cornford 93).

4 *Contra* Spurr 41.

© KONINKLIJKE BRILL NV, LEIDEN, 2020 | DOI:10.1163/9789004375826_008

114                                                                CHAPTER 6

Eliot's engagement with Attic Old Comedy provides the background for these earlier plays, so a brief rehearsal of his understanding is necessary. A relatively sophisticated Aristophanic structure is displayed in the outline of "The Superior Landlord"; however, the dating of this manuscript is uncertain (*Poems* I.790–1). This fragment could easily be from a later attempt to finish the play and will not generally be considered before the discussion of *Murder in the Cathedral* (*Poems* I.790–1).[5] Eliot recounts in a 1932 letter that *Sweeney Agonistes* "was based upon the account of Aristophanic drama by F. M. Cornford in his *Origins of Attic Comedy*" (*Letters* VI.498). While it is obviously written years later, there is clear evidence that this is not revisionist history. Additionally, Eliot's engagement with Cornford's schema was not facile. One of the first apparent references to *Sweeney Agonistes* is in a 1923 letter to Ezra Pound wherein Eliot comments cryptically, "Have mapt out Aristophanic comedy, but must devote study to phallic songs, also agons" (*Letters* II.209). There are two matters of note here: the first is that Eliot conceived the play initially as a "comedy," which lessens the expectation of structural deviations from the play being labeled as a melodrama. The second is that Eliot devoted study and attention to the Aristophanic form; the attribution is not flippant. An offhand comment in the essay on "Ben Jonson" in 1919 reinforces this understanding of the importance of form to a work being Aristophanic in Eliot's mind:

> [T]he classification of tragedy and comedy, while it may be sufficient to mark the distinction in a dramatic literature of more rigid form and treatment—it may distinguish Aristophanes from Euripides—is not adequate to a drama of such variations as the Elizabethans.
>
> *Prose* II. 151.

This implies that, even before writing *Sweeney Agonistes*, Eliot considered the form a crucial component of Aristophanes' work.[6]

References to Aristophanes proliferate around the writing of *Sweeney Agonistes*; none seem to exist in the letters or *Collected Prose* before 1919, and there are very few in the published letters after 1925 and, generally, in response to a question about *Sweeney Agonistes*. Evidence of Eliot's interest in Aristophanes appears first in offhanded references in both the aforementioned essay on Ben

---

5   Scholarly opinion is divided. Buttram, Crawford, and Schuchard believe it is a draft of *Sweeney Agonistes*; Chinitz a later attempt to revise the play.

6   Buttram argues that Eliot was suspicious of the binary between comedy and tragedy (Buttram 181). The comment in "Ben Jonson" supports this with the caveat of Aristophanes, which complicates the application of this to *Sweeney Agonistes*.

DRAMATIZING 115

Jonson and in the influential "Philip Massinger" essay.[7] Additionally, a 1920 letter from his mother lists Aristophanes' *Birds* among his books, and in 1924 Eliot attempted to attend a performance of the play in the original Greek (*Letters* I.487, II.307, 23). However, the majority of mentions of Aristophanic topics in Eliot's writings are not to the plays alone but are combined with F. M. Cornford's *The Origin of Attic Comedy*.

That Eliot was, in the early 1920's, enamored of *The Origin of Attic Comedy* seems obvious.[8] One of the very first contributors he sought for the Criterion was Cornford of whom he asked "a contribution [...] on some subject which would be of interest to readers of your *Origin of Attic Comedy*" (*Letters* II.162). Eliot had glowingly praised the book in his essay "Euripides and Professor Murray," noting that "[f]ew books are more fascinating than those of Miss Harrison, Mr. Cornford, or Mr. Cooke, when they burrow in the origins of Greek myths and rites" (*Prose* II.197). Later in 1924, Eliot aligns Cornford as writing in the same vein as Jessie Weston (*Prose* II.514).[9] Current scholarly consensus is, understandably, skeptical about Weston's *actual* role in the structure of *The Waste Land*; however, this at least hints that Eliot considered using Cornford as an organizational frame at the time of *Sweeney Agonistes*. This is confirmed, though, by Eliot's own comments about Cornford's role in *Sweeney Agonistes* in which he explicitly references the book to someone performing the play and states that it "is important to read before you do the play" (Eliot qtd. in *Letters* II.162). This aligns with critical opinion on the structure of *Sweeney Agonistes* is based on Cornford's book.[10] I have yet to find any mention of other theorists or the like in conjunction with Aristophanes in either the published letters or the collected prose. While an excursion into Cornford's *The Origin of Attic Comedy* is not lightly undertaken, I feel justified in doing so, as Eliot uses the structure in *both* of these plays to dramatize his ascetic ideal.

---

7    Cf. *Collected Prose* II.151 ff., 254 ff.

8    It is equally obvious that Eliot thought very little of Cornford's 1912 monograph. Disparaging remarks, seemingly centered on the perceived Bergsonian elements in Cornford and the early work of the other Cambridge Ritualists, dot the earliest essays. Cf. *Collected Prose* I.114, 417, 420, 430. This is an unexamined problem with David Ward's application of Gilbert Murray to *Murder in the Cathedral.* Cf. Ward 71 ff.

9    Cf. Chinitz 72–5, whose argumentation is only supported by the discussion here. *Contra* Smidt 191, who dismisses primitive religious influences outside of *The Waste Land.*

10    Carol Smith in *T. S. Eliot's Dramatic Theory and Practice* emphasizes the importance of Cornford and the other Cambridge Ritualists; however, her interpretation is focused on an extension of the mythical method delineated in "Ulysses, Myth, and Order" using all of the Cambridge Ritualists and diverges from the structural argument presented here (Smith 40–7). Cf. Buttram 180.

To briefly summarize Cornford's theory,[11] all plays by Aristophanes, and presumptively all of Attic Old Comedy, follow a "canonical plot-formula" which "preserves the stereotyped action of a ritual or folk drama" (Cornford 3). The first half of the play contains three parts: a *Prologue*,[12] which consists of "exposition scenes," the *Parodos* (πάροδος) which is the entrance of the chorus and their initial song, and then the *Agon* (ἀγών), "a fierce 'contest' between the representatives of two parties or principles, which are in effect the hero and villain of the whole piece" (Cornford 2). After the *Agon* is the *Parabasis* (παράβασις), an idiosyncratic feature of Old Comedy, wherein the Chorus bids "farewell to the actors, who leave the stage clear till it is over, and then return to carry on the business of the piece to the end" (Cornford 3). During the *Parabasis*, the Chorus comes forward "to address the audience directly" (Cornford 3). After the return of the actors, there are scenes of "Sacrifice and a Feast" interrupted "by a series of unwelcome intruders," generally stock characters labeled by Cornford collectively as Impostors, "who are successively put to derision by the protagonist and driven away with blows" (Cornford 3). A second *Parabasis* may then be included which occurs primarily in Aristophanes' earliest plays. The play concludes with "a festal procession" called a *Kômos* (κῶμος) wherein the victorious party is celebrated in a scene which is often either directly or indirectly marital in nature; the chorus exits in a procession called an *Exodos* (ἔξοδος) (Cornford 3).

Only two of the listed scenes, the *Prologue* and *Agon*, are extant even in part in *Sweeney Agonistes*, and the structure is not so rigid as to allow extrapolation from what remains. Yet, analysis of Cornford suggests that Doris is the protagonist of the play, which will elucidate the presence of the ascetic ideal. The often tacit assumption that Sweeney is the protagonist seems based on his recurrence in Eliot's other poetry and being the titular character.[13] However, in Aristophanes, the only extant play clearly named for the protagonist is *Lysistrata*, whose redolent name, "dissolver of armies," is more likely the cause. Additionally, Sweeney is not included in the *Prologue*, and the extant plays of

---

11  For the purposes of my argument, what is important is that Eliot believed Cornford correct; whether his theories are considered accurate by contemporary Aristophanes scholarship is immaterial.

12  Cornford's transliteration of Greek terminology and names is rather idiosyncratic and occasionally inconsistent (including the capitalization and italicization), but it is followed here for internal consistency. The original Greek is supplied on the first instance.

13  Scofield, for instance, suggests that "it is the man's state of mind after the murder which is the moral centre of the piece" (Scofield 192). Again, "The Superior Landlord" is not being considered.

DRAMATIZING                                                                          117

Aristophanes usually open with the protagonist.[14] It is not clear that the passages preserved are the opening of the play, but I doubt we possess only the part of the prologue without Sweeney on stage.

Considering Doris the protagonist is corroborated by the extant "Fragment of an Agon" section of *Sweeney Agonistes*, where the ascetic ideal will be most largely figured. The *Agon* is to be understood as "a dramatized debate [...] in which the persons represent opposing principles" (Butcher qtd. in Cornford 73). Yet, it is also a tightly structured one; Cornford asserts, regarding the *Agon*'s form:

> The structure of the regular *Agon* is antiphonal, in two balanced halves. First comes the *Ode*, in which half the Chorus, according as their sympathies incline, encourage one or both the adversaries to do their utmost. Then the Leader, in the *Katakeleusmos*, calls on the Antagonist to speak first. The party who will ultimately be defeated always begins. He opens his case in the *Epirrheme*, usually interrupted by objections and questions from the [protagonist]. The passage ends in a *Pnigos*. The second part is parallel in form and contents. [...] Finally, in the *Sphragis*, the leader of the Chorus pronounces a verdict in favor of the [protagonist]."
>
> CORNFORD 72.

Let me briefly summarize. After an initial choral ode, the chorus leader invites the Antagonist to speak, although the protagonist interjects. This builds to a wild, shouting climax in the *Pnigos* (πνῖγος). There is another ode, and then the protagonist gives their own speech also ending in a *Pnigos*. Finally, the chorusleader declares victory for the protagonist. While the structure is rarely followed perfectly, it is consistent enough to determine, largely, what is missing from "Fragment of an Agon." As is obvious, we clearly have neither the initial *Ode*, the *Katakeleusmos* (κατακελευσμός),[15] nor the *Sphragis* (σφραγίς) of the *Agon* in *Sweeney Agonistes*. The definition of a *Pnigos* is sufficiently vague to allow the possibility of Sweeney's final long speech in lines 131–53 being one, though this is far from certain as Doris receives an interjection and Sweeney speaks again. The only evidence that the speech should be given in a single

---

14    In *Knights, Wasps,* and *Peace,* the main character is slightly delayed in appearance with the initial exposition carried by secondary characters, but this is quickly remedied on every occasion, certainly more quickly than would have to occur in *Sweeney Agonistes*; an argument could be made about Blepyrus in *Ecclesiazusae* given the *Kômos*, but Cornford clearly classifies Praxagora as the protagonist (Cornford 33–4).

15    The repeated invocation to "let Mr. Sweeney continue his story" may serve as a sort of *Katakeleusmos* or at least the ghost of one (*Sweeney Agonistes* "Agon" 101–2, 116).

breath, which is a requirement of the genre,[16] is the lack of punctuation after the third line of the speech—hardly definitive. Thus, the only portion which we possess appears to be all or most of Sweeney's *Epirrheme* interrupted by vaguely choral odes/songs,[17] which Cornford would mark as allowed under the genre by an example from the *Thesmophoriazusae*(Cornford 73). Returning to the issue at hand, Cornford is unequivocal that "[t]he party who will ultimately be defeated always begins" (Cornford 72). Thus, unless what remains is only the second half of the *Agon*, then, Doris is the protagonist and her speech would espouse an idea opposite to Sweeney. I theorize that this would favor, somehow, the ascetic ideal. I believe Sweeney's speech is not the rebuttal because of the length of the speeches. In Cornford's footnotes, *Epirrhemes* are between seventy and eighty lines (Cornford 72–3). The rebuttals are invariably and significantly shorter—usually only forty lines—which increases the likelihood that Sweeney's speech is the Antagonist's *Epirrheme*. Given the above circumstantial evidence and the established tradition of female protagonists in Aristophanes, the possibility that Doris is the protagonist should be entertained.

This identification is supported by one of the more puzzling passages in the "Fragment of an *Agon*," Sweeney's extended threat to cook Doris "[i]nto a stew" (*Sweeney Agonistes* "Agon" 10).[18] This is not merely the normal assortment of threats and invective that accompany an *Agon*,[19] nor is it a bizarre non-sequitur to the discussion of the murder in the second portion of the *Agon*. One of the core aspects of Cornford's thesis is the connection of the *Agon* to "ritual contests between the representatives of Summer and Winter, Life and Death" (Cornford 74). Cornford also connects this to the Mummer's Plays and

---

16    This is based on the cryptic line about the *Pnigos* in the *Scholia in Acharnenses* 659a: "ὥσπερ ἡ κατακλείς ἐκ διμέτρου μὲν ἑνὸς καταληκτικοῦ" (Dübner 19).

17    Buttram questions whether or not the last of these is the *Sphragis*, the pronouncement of the victor, and whether the last chorus "expresses [Sweeney's] perspective" (Buttram 189). I would suggest this may be the ode that transitions to the protagonist's *Antepirrheme*, if Sweeney's final speech be the *Pnigos*.

18    In addition to those listed in *Poems* 1.810–1, this passage may be a reference to Henry James's *The Ambassadors*, where Miss Barrace and Mr Bilham, gossiping in Madame de Vionnet's parlor, say:
       'Oh you, Mr Bilham,' she replied as with an impatient rap on the glass, "you're not worth sixpence! You come over to convert the savages—for I know you verily did, I remember you—and the savages simply convert *you*.'
       'Not even!' the young man woefully confessed: 'they haven't gone through that form. They've simply—the cannibals!—eaten me; converted me if you like, but converted me into food. I'm but the bleached bones of a Christian.' (James *The Ambassadors* 144).

19    Cornford in his chapter on the *Agon* reminds the reader of "Bdelycleon's passionate denunciations and his father's successive threats of suicide and murder" before noting that "[t]he *Agon* in the *Wasps* is one of the mildest" (Cornford 74).

DRAMATIZING

the myth of St. George with a distinct emphasis on the resurrection of the protagonist (Cornford 61–2). Cornford's folkloric focus is not irrelevant to Eliot's structural interests. In the 1923 review "The Beating of a Drum"—written during the coeval geneses of *Sweeney Agonistes* and "The Hollow Men," Eliot digresses, saying:

> The prototype of the true Fool, according to my conjecture, is a character in that English version of the Perseus legend, the Mummers' Play of St. George and the Dragon. The Doctor who restores St. George to life is, I understand, usually presented as a comic character. As Mr. Cornford suggests, in *The Origin of Attic Comedy*, this Doctor may be identical with the Doctor who is called in to assist Punch after he has been thrown from his horse.
>
> *Prose* II.472–3.

Eliot appears to concur with Cornford when the latter connects Punch to the core action of the folk-dramas that underlie the Aristophanic play: "the hero's simulated death and revival by the Doctor, and a fierce *Agon* with an adversary" (Cornford 147). This theme was even more pronounced in "The Superior Landlord" where Sweeney actually shoots Mrs. Porter who is eventually revived (*Poems* I.793–4).[20] It is not necessary to assume that such an event would have actually occurred in *Sweeney Agonistes*, though. Cornford states, in his discussion of the *Agon*, that "a dramatic death and resurrection of either adversary would be either too serious or too silly" (Cornford 75). Thus, the threat by Sweeney would be all that is required to retain this important thematic element. Additionally, the reference to the cooking of Doris carries an implication of resurrection. In his chapter on the *Agon*, Cornford explicitly connects the figure of the Cook in the *Knights* who boils and restores the aged Demos to youth with the resurrecting Doctor:

> a Cook who can perform such miraculous operations is manifestly a magician, and his profession coalesces with that of the Doctor in the primitive functions of the medicine-man—a figure who [...] stands out in the dim past behind the Doctor who revives the slain in the folk-plays.
>
> CORNFORD 90.

Thus, Sweeney's threats to cook Doris fulfill the death and resurrection theme of the protagonist to the *Agon* in Cornford's scheme; however, it is notably the

---

20    Cf. Kirk 112–3, Schuchard 87–100.

120                                                                                    CHAPTER 6

*protagonist* who is revived. Thus, this theme directed to Doris again implies
that she is the protagonist. As noted by Crawford, Sweeney's assertion that
"Life is death" seems to be, at least partially, a citation, centered on the death
and resurrection theme, from Aristophanes highlighted by Cornford (Crawford 151). Yet, this is an even deeper allusion than Crawford suggests. At the end
of the *Agon* in *Frogs* as Cornford summarizes,

> Euripides complains that he is 'left for dead' in the underworld [...].
> Dionysus replies to this appeal with a quotation from a play of Eurip-
> ides' own, the *Polyidos*,[21] which itself turned on a death and resurrection
> motive:
>    'Who knows if to be living be not death?'.
>    CORNFORD 82.

Even a cursory examination of the Greek text reveals that the applicable portion of the original line—"τὸ ζῆν μέν ἐστι κατθανεῖν"—is far closer to the simplicity of Eliot's own version than Cornford's flowery rendering (*Frogs* 1478).
Thus, viewing Doris as the protagonist who is threatened with death, with a
hinted possibility of resurrection, brings this passage in line with the Aristophanic structure found in Cornford's theory of the *Agon*. Eliot appears to
interweave not only the structure, but the relevant thematic elements from
Cornford into the "Fragment of an Agon."

The identification of Doris as the protagonist may also answer one of the
most perplexing aspects of the plays: the epigraph from St. John of the Cross,
whom Eliot read of extensively in his mystical readings. This is where the ascetic ideal is most obvious in *Sweeney Agonistes*. Buttram asserts that "Sweeney
is the only one to whom the epigraphs might even begin to apply unironically"
(Buttram 181). I find this unconvincing; Sweeney's speech seems only to support a brute, materialist existence driven by impulses to violence. The structure of the *Agon* is as an argument between principles rather than people, so
Sweeney as the antagonist is the representative of what the play is arguing
*against*. Since the fragment does not have the *Antepirrheme*, we do not appear
to have the statement of what principle will oppose and conquer Sweeney's
nihilism. I speculate that this is found in the epigraph from St. John of the
Cross. In the absence of other obvious referents, I think this the best option. It
is difficult to imagine where else that world-denying theme could be present
in the play. Thus, the core principle, the concept behind the *Agon* of the play,

---

21    As this is not one of Euripides' extant plays, I have no idea how else Eliot could have found
      this line except via Cornford and Aristophanes.

DRAMATIZING

121

appear to be ascetic: an ideal of self-denial against the skeptical materialism embodied by Sweeney. While Buttram's arguments about Doris's base nature are compelling, the Aristophanic structure is centered on the rejuvenation of the protagonist's malaise, often in a very literal sense as in the aforementioned restoration of Demos by cooking (Buttram 185). However, we do not know how Eliot may have intended Doris to divest herself of the love of created things or how this rejuvenation would have played out.[22] At least upon reflection, Eliot considered the play to have a moral focus; in a 1932 letter, Eliot states that *Sweeney Agonistes* "was to have been an Aristophanic ~~Morality~~ Miracle Play" (*Letters* VI.469). Obviously, had it been accomplished, this design would have rendered the play more religious than previously understood but probably not out of line with my previous reading of "The Hollow Men." This divergence is something that Eliot himself, in a 1935 letter, suggested: "[t]he present fragments would have looked very different in a complete text" (*Letters* VII.574). It would be speculation to insist that this religious tension is why the play remained unfinished, but it nonetheless foreshadows the direction that Eliot will take after his conversion when he returns to drama.

Eliot returns not only to the Aristophanic structure[23] in his first complete play, *Murder in the Cathedral* but also to the ascetic ideal as a driving force. Eliot dramatizes not only the initial phase of purgation, the detachment from worldly things, as in *Sweeney Agonistes*, but in *Murder in the Cathedral* the ascetic ideal includes the purification of the will *i.e.* the dark night of the soul. That the play follows the outline of an Aristophanic Comedy is not as absurd as might initially seem; Cornford's *The Origin of Attic Comedy* was rereleased in a second edition in the early 1930s, and Eliot also dismissed the idea of a Church pageant based on one of Aristophanes' plays, *Peace*, to the Dean of Chichester, largely on the grounds that it "would probably be too libelous to be produced at all" (*Letters* VII.465). Thus, Eliot still considered Aristophanes a viable form when he was writing *Murder in the Cathedral*. There is, additionally, a cryptic comment from Geoffrey Faber's journal suggesting that the masks, as in Greek plays, were considered for the production (Faber qtd. in *Letters* VII.670). In one of Eliot's later reflections on his own dramatic practice, he states: "[T]he vocabulary and style could not be exactly those of modern conversation—as in some modern French plays using the plot and personages of Greek drama" (Eliot

---

22  If the title "The Superior Landlord" does refer to this iteration of the play, it could be understood to refer to the turn to a landlord better than the exploitive Pereira.

23  In the rather idiosyncratic dialogue section of his work, Kenner touches, almost intuitively, on *Murder in the Cathedral*'s connection to Greek drama (Kenner 210). However, the matter is quickly dropped.

"Poetry and Drama 84–5). Eliot could be implying that not just the personages *i.e.* the chorus but the plot of *Murder in the Cathedral* stemmed from Greek drama, but none of these are definitive. E. Martin Browne, in his retrospect as the producer for Eliot's plays, discusses the genesis of *Murder in the Cathedral*. Unlike in the later plays, Browne was not privy to the earliest conceptions but concludes of the first draft because of the requirement of a chorus, that "the play is to be cast in a formal mould like that of Greek tragedy" (Browne 40). I suggest that Browne, who was not a scholar of Greek theater, is only half-right,[24] and that Eliot, a tentative dramatist by his own admission, returned to the same structure which he attempted earlier in *Sweeney Agonistes*.[25] In the extant letters, Eliot never comments to Browne about the Greek aspects of *Murder in the Cathedral*. I would speculate that Eliot may not have wanted to go over an intricate Aristophanic structure with a layman. He similarly rebuffs, with no explanation, Browne's attempts to restructure the play, which suggests that Eliot felt the order key (*Letters* VII.543). An examination of *Murder in the Cathedral* shows a large alignment with the Aristophanic structure established by Cornford and used by Eliot himself in the outline of "The Superior Landlord." This structure may also explain some of the more curious aspects of the play. As a reminder, the expected order of the Aristophanic play is *Prologue*, *Parodos*, *Agon*, *Parabasis*, Sacrifice/Feast, occasionally a second *Parabasis*, and then the *Kômos* followed by the *Exodos*. Following Cornford's definitions, each of these is not only present in *Murder in the Cathedral* but keyed to present an ascetic ideal of submission against worldliness and self-serving political interests. To help the reader grasp the large picture, a summarizing chart, like in Cornford's own appendices, is provided below before a detailed discussion of each element and its implication on the play's theme follows:

| Aristophanic Element | Summary of Element | Presence in *Murder in the Cathedral* |
| --- | --- | --- |
| *Prologue* and *Parodos* | Opening scenes and choral odes | Opening scenes and Thomas's entrance |
| *Agon* | Dramatized Debate | The Tempters |

---

24  I, for one, previously wondered why the play that we know to be based on Greek tragedy, *The Family Reunion*, has so little resemblance in structure and pacing with *Murder in the Cathedral*.

25  *Contra* Buttram who argues that "Eliot tiptoed diagonally away from his Cornfordian-Aristophanic approach" after *Sweeney Agonistes* (Buttram 181).

DRAMATIZING                                                                     123

| Aristophanic Element | Summary of Element | Presence in *Murder in the Cathedral* |
| --- | --- | --- |
| *Parabasis* | Direct address to audience at the play's halfway point | The Sermon |
| Sacrifice/Feast | Interrupted attempts to sacrifice to the gods | Death of Thomas |
| *Parabasis* II | A second direct address to the audience dividing the second act | The Knights' Defense |
| *Kômos* and *Exodos* | Departing chorus hailing victorious protagonist as the new divine ruler | Final odes celebrating Thomas as the new martyr and saint |

The play opens with an atypical element,[26] a choral ode, but otherwise follows the general pattern of the Aristophanic *Prologue* which is a brief series of dialogues designed to set the scene and introduce the primary actors. Cornford is not much concerned with the *Prologue*, and it is the only section to which he devotes no chapter which may explain Eliot feeling free to deviate. Yet, Cornford does contrast the Aristophanic and the tragic prologue traditions: "Whereas the Euripidean prologue will foretell the whole general course of the action to the end, the prologue in Aristophanes only states the main idea" (Cornford 199). Here, the Comic structure is present in *Murder in the Cathedral*. As Cornford notes, "[t]he proper term for the comic plot is not *mythos*, but *logos*" in other words, thematic conflict over narrative structure (Cornford 199). Thus, the prologue, instead of foreshadowing the web of events that will lead to Beckett's death as a tragic one would, focuses on the play's themes with the cryptic suggestion: "We wait / [a]nd the saints and martyrs wait, for those who shall be martyrs and saints," which hints of ascetic submissiveness to the divine will[27]

---

26   This is atypical for not only Aristophanes but all Greek tragedy; in the several dozen plays by Sophocles, Aeschylus, and Euripides I consulted, only Aeschylus's *Suppliant Women* and *Persians* open with a chorus. My own suspicion is that this is more of an Elizabethan feature than a Greek one. *Contra* Peter 158.

27   The Chorus's emphasis upon witnessing is closely allied with this same theme—even a basic knowledge of Greek provides that the word for witness is μαρτύριον. The chiasm in the lines hints at the theme of crucifixion, self-sacrifice.

(*Murder in the Cathedral* 13).[28] In fact, the events leading up to Beckett's death are downplayed by the Chorus's insistence that "Destiny waits in the hands of God, not in the hands of statesmen" (*Murder in the Cathedral* 13). This particular theme will return in the discussion of the play's ending as an *Exodos*.

The next portion of the play in the Aristophanic structure is the *Parodos*, the formal entry of the Chorus. This is, strictly, impossible in *Murder in the Cathedral* as the Chorus is already on the stage at the play's opening. Exigencies in the theatrical space may be the cause as "[t]he only door to the building was at the back of the auditorium, ninety feet from the stage. This meant that all entrances and exits must be made through the narrow central aisle between the seats" (Browne 56–7). The Chorus making such a long march would have been ridiculous in actual theatrical practice. One important part of the Chorus *does* enter here, and that is Thomas, who, as will be seen in the discussion of the *Agon* and the *Parabasis*, doubles as the Chorus-Leader. Such doubling is not unheard of in Aristophanes. Cornford asserts "[s]ince [Dikaiopolis] is both priest and congregation, he has not only to perform the part of 'Leader' of this Phallic Song, but also to act as his own Chorus"; the Chorus Leader also serves as the antagonist in the *Agon* of the *Birds*, the play by Aristophanes which Eliot seems to have known best (Cornford 38, 232). Thomas's narrative role as a spiritual leader of the women of Canterbury supports his structural identity within the play. Thus, the delayed entrance of Thomas serves as something of a *Parodos*.

As in the Aristophanic play, only a brief interlude separates the *Parodos* from the *Agon*, which in the case of *Murder in the Cathedral* is the long sequence with the Tempters.[29] This largely internalized action enforces the ascetic ideal as a core theme of the play: the resistance of temptation is the play's most memorable sequence. Cornford asserts that "[t]he *Agon* [...] occupies the first half of the play between *Parodos* and *Parabasis*" and that "[i]t is more like a sort of trial, with a strict rule of procedure" (Cornford 70, 71).[30] The most curious feature of the Aristophanic *Agon* is that its place in the play rather undermines the drama of the piece; "the *Agon* is often over and the victory proclaimed before the play is halfway through" (Cornford 71). This seems to

---

28    In the absence of the critical edition of Eliot's drama, the Harcourt Brace reprint is cited; mercifully for the reader, the pagination among these editions seems to be very consistent.

29    Grove touches on this, referring to the play as "Becket's *agon*," but this general usage glosses over the technical structure in Eliot's work (Grove 170).

30    Cf. Sultan who, arguing for *dedoublement* with the tempters, interprets this passage as largely an internal debate (Sultan 244).

DRAMATIZING 125

be what occurs in *Murder in the Cathedral*.[31] The audience might expect this "battle" with the Tempters and Thomas's resolution to be at a more climactic moment instead of so early in the play, and yet, this pacing offers compelling support for my hypothesis that Eliot is employing an Aristophanic structure over a more ordinary outline.

Let me proceed to the specifics of the form. The scene with the tempters shows the general outline of the Aristophanic *Agon*, which, as previously mentioned, is the *Katakeleusmos*, the antagonist's speech, the protagonist's rebuttal, and the verdict. If, as I have suggested, Thomas operates as both protagonist and chorus leader, this sequence follows the Aristophanic pattern, although it is repeated across the multiple tempters. The sequence does not begin with an ode by the full chorus, who has just recently spoken, but there is a short poetic passage by Thomas, which begins "For a little time the hungry hawk," and this introduces the antagonists and serves as the *Katakeleusmos*, the chorus leader's invitation to the adversary (*Murder in the Cathedral* 23). In Aristophanes, the *Katakeleusmos* is often similarly brief; When Cornford does a line-by-line exposition of an *Agon*, the *Katakeleusmos* is given only two lines (Cornford 73).

Because of the multiple antagonists, the *epirrheme* and *antepirrheme* are repeated four times. However, Eliot maintains the basic structure and proportions. Each time, the tempter speaks first and gives the longest speech and, as would be expected, is "interrupted by objections and questions from" the protagonist Thomas (Cornford 72). As previously mentioned, this is in line with the Aristophanic practice where the antagonist always speaks first. Finally, Thomas gives a short rebuttal, the *antepirrheme*. If the length for the protagonist's *antepirrheme* quoted in Cornford is taken and divided by four, it leaves an average length of thirteen lines, and Thomas's rebuttals, excluding the tempter's objections, fall reasonably within this span (Cornford 73). No odes interject between the *epirrhemes* and *antepirrhemes*, as might be expected in the longer structure, but, after the fourth tempter, when the pattern shifts to the next element, the chorus does deliver its two required odes. Additionally, the stichomythic interchange between the chorus, the priests, and the Tempters is what Cornford would call an "epirrhematic 'syzygy,' a closed system of balanced antiphonal parts" (Cornford 125).[32] Such an interchange with its rising energy, I believe, functions as a kind of *Pnigos*, which would be delivered with similar

---

31  Peter states as much, admitting that after this point "the play is (at least in one, not unimportant respect) virtually over" (Peter 165).

32  While Cornford only defines this term in his discussion of the *Parabasis*, the appendix indicates that it frequently occurs elsewhere in Aristophanes' extant plays. Thus, I do not believe the term's use here to be a misappropriation.

126 CHAPTER 6

rapidity (Cornford 121). Thomas's final speech would seem to be anomalous; the protagonist does not receive a concluding speech in the *Agon*. However, if Thomas is also the Chorus Leader, then this fits the pattern; his final speech functions as a *Sphragis* wherein "the leader of the Chorus pronounces the verdict in favor of the [Protagonist]" (Cornford 72).

As it follows the structure of the *Agon*, the sequence between Thomas and the tempters should possess some of the other features of the *Agon* in Aristophanes. The *Agon* is really a conflict between "two parties or principles" according to Cornford (Cornford 3). Thus, it should be possible to read Thomas's encounter with the Tempters in terms of a spiritual/philosophical conflict instead of as a dramatized personal reflection. The ascetic ideal, as will be seen, is the principle that Thomas argues for, although, in the case, of the fourth tempter, it is Underhill's fourth step of purgation, the dark night of the soul. The first tempter offers a distinctly epicurean temptation:

> Fluting in the meadows, viols in the hall
> Laughter and apple-blossom floating on the water
> Singing at nightfall, whispering in chambers
> Fires devouring the winter season,
> Eating up the darkness, with wit and wine and wisdom.
>> *Murder in the Cathedral* 24.

The substance of the argument seems, on the whole, suggested by Horace's Ode I:ix. Although the tempter suggests, unlike Horace, that the spring of life might come again (*Murder in the Cathedral* 24). Yet, Thomas rejects this out of hand, and the first tempter is advised to "[t]hink of penitence" (*Murder in the Cathedral* 25). Asceticism is his suggestion. Both the second and third tempters promise power, either as chancellor or allying with the barons against the king, and these are also rejected. All three are dismissed as "temporal tempters, / [w]ith pleasure and power at palpable price" (*Murder in the Cathedral* 39). To this point, Thomas represents an ascetic ideal of spirituality against the worldliness espoused by the tempters, but this is complicated by the fourth tempter.

The different character of the fourth tempter may seem to disrupt the pattern, but, as mentioned before, there is another aspect of the ascetic ideal discussed in Eliot's readings on mysticism. According to Underhill, purgation comes in two phases: a purification of the senses, but, later, for those of saintly aspiration, also, a purification of the will, a process which she refers to as the dark night of the soul[33] (Underhill 456–7). Eliot had become personally

---

33    At the risk of biographical speculation, this concept may have had some appeal to Eliot, personally. Underhill notes that "[m]any seers and artists pay in this way, by agonizing

DRAMATIZING                                                                127

acquainted with Underhill personally a few years before,[34] so it would not be
surprising that her ideas may recur. Within the Aristophanic framework, the
first three tempters dramatize the first phase of purgation, while the fourth
tempter dramatizes this second phase of purification. The Fourth Tempter
advises Thomas to "[s]eek the way of martyrdom, make yourself the lowest /
[o]n earth, to be high in heaven" (*Murder in the Cathedral* 39). The appeal
"[t]o do the right deed for the wrong reason" is a temptation not of the body
but of the heart (*Murder in the Cathedral* 44). Underhill states that "[f]or [such
temptations], a new and more drastic purgation is needed—not of the organs
of perception, but of the very shrine of self: that 'heart' which is the seat of
personality, the source of its love and will" (Underhill 464). Thomas is forced to
admit that he has thought of

> enemies dismayed
> Creeping in penance, frightened of a shade;
> [...] of pilgrims, standing in line
> Before the glittering jeweled shrine,
> From generation to generation
> Bending the knee in supplication.
> > *Murder in the Cathedral* 38.

Yet, he also recognizes the impermanence of these things in the face of the
glories of sainthood and admits his own desire for the glories that virtue and
martyrdom can win him in the hereafter. In her chapter on the dark night of
the soul, Underhill quotes from St Catherine of Genoa who states

> in all this show and glitter of virtue, there is an unpurified bottom on
> which they stand, there is a selfishness which can no more enter into the
> Kingdom of Heaven than the grossness of flesh and blood can enter into
> it. What we are to feel and undergo in these last purifications, when the
> deepest root of all selfishness, as well spiritual as natural, is to be plucked
> up and torn from us"
> > ST CATHERINE of Genoa qtd. in UNDERHILL 475.

The result of this knowledge is a "bitter self-contempt and sense of helpless-
ness which overwhelms the soul" (Underhill 476). This dramatization of the
dark night of the soul as part of the overall ascetic ideal also supports the

---

periods of impotence and depression, for each violent outburst of creative energy" (Underhill 457).

34    Cf. *Letters* V.511.

128                                                                                          CHAPTER 6

Aristophanic pattern. Drawing on the fertility rituals, Cornford additionally insists that there should be "some reminiscences of the death and resurrection motive clinging to the *Agônes*" (Cornford 75). The dark night of the soul is described, frequently, as a form of death in Underhill:

> Here, as in purgation, the condition of access to higher levels of vitality is a death: a deprivation, a detachment, a clearing of the ground. [...] The satisfactions of the spirit must now go the same way as the satisfactions of the senses. Even the power of voluntary sacrifice and self-discipline is taken away.
>
> UNDERHILL 478.

Eliot dramatizes both of these feelings in Thomas shortly before the transition to the concluding interchange of choral odes wherein he questions, "Can sinful pride be driven out / [o]nly by more sinful? Can I neither act nor suffer without perdition?" (*Murder in the Cathedral* 40). Eliot, in a letter to Browne, suggests that isolation and loneliness, which are features of the dark night, were intended emphasis of the play (*Letters* VII.544). Thus, Eliot, in accordance with his reading on mysticism and in Cornford, employs the Fourth Tempter to dramatize the dark night of the soul, the cleansing of the will, just as how the earlier tempters portray the purification from more worldly desires.

The *Sphragis*, the verdict by the chorus leader in the trial that is the *Agon*, also bears out the ascetic ideal being the dramatized concept in the play. While Thomas is speaking in his own voice at times, he also veers into more general, comprehensive statements in his role as the chorus leader such as his comment that "[t]he natural vigour in the venial sin / [i]s the way in which our lives begin" (*Murder in the Cathedral* 44). The pronoun use is pointed. In the plays of Aristophanes, there is an overriding social or moral concern intended to speak directly to the situation of the audience, and Eliot preserves this feature. At the conclusion of the *Sphragis*, Thomas, seemingly in his role as chorus leader, states:

> [F]or every evil, every sacrilege,
> Crime, wrong, oppression, and the axe's edge,
> Indifference, exploitation, you, and you,
> And you, must all be punished. So must you.
>
> *Murder in the Cathedral* 45–6.

The final "you" from Thomas may be directed out toward the audience. This is consonant with his role as chorus leader; Aristophanic drama, of course, was

DRAMATIZING 129

intended to speak directly to the audience's situation. The ascetic ideal, as portrayed in the *Agon*, is carried through the remainder of the play with an emphasis on not only the protagonist but this broader social applicability.

After the *Agon* is the *Parabasis*, a feature of Old Comedy that was already dying out in the days of Aristophanes, which Cornford describes as "a long passage which cuts the play in two about half way through its course and completely suspends the action. This passage is almost wholly undramatic" (Cornford 2). Cornford spends a good bit of time moderating contemporaneous scholarly dialogue on the *Parabasis* but concludes that its "essential character [...] should, perhaps, be found, not in the nature of [its] contents, but rather in the practice of directly addressing the audience" (Cornford 123).[35] The applicability of this to Thomas's sermon between Parts I and II seems obvious.[36] Cornford is unusually scathing about the formal place of the *Parabasis*, noting that "it has all the air of a piece of ritual procedure awkwardly interrupting the course of the play" and is "injurious to the conduct of a drama" (Cornford 122). This may explain why Eliot retains only the barest form of the *Parabasis* where the Chorus Leader, in this case Thomas, addresses the audience.[37] Since the ascetic ideal is one of the core themes of the play according to the structure, it should be present in this direct monologue with the audience. Eliot, toward the sermon's end, does have Thomas speak on the ascetic ideal:

> [Martyrdom] is never the design of man; for the true martyr is he who has become the instrument of God, who has lost his will in the will of God, and who no longer desires anything for himself, not even the glory of being a martyr. [...] so in Heaven the Saints are most high, having made themselves most low, and are seen, not as we see them, but in the light of the Godhead from which they draw their being.
>
> *Murder in the Cathedral* 49–50.

Eliot, via Thomas, is reflecting the radical concepts of asceticism found in the mystical readings. Consider how similar the above passage is to the following quotation by William Law:

---

35   I am, here, glossing over some *particularly* arcane technicalities of Attic Old Comedy irrelevant to the purposes of this study.

36   Browne has little to add on this front only noting that "[t]he sermon was an integral part of the original plan of the play" (Browne 46).

37   Peter's assertion that Becket is addressing "a hypothetical congregation (The Chorus)" is possible, but the emphasis should be placed more on the audience interaction (Peter 165).

This alone is the true Kingdom of God opened in the soul when, stripped of all selfishness, it has only one love and one will in it; when it has no motion or desire but what branches from the Love of God, and resigns itself wholly to the Will of God.

WILLIAM LAW qtd. in UNDERHILL 474.

As will be seen in the next chapter, Eliot is increasingly mirroring the opinions of the mystical readings, and here, he places a passage espousing a radical idea of self-denial, a denial of the will, in the mouth of Thomas. As Underhill says of the dark night of the soul, "this [is the] last and drastic purgation of the spirit; the doing away of separateness, the annihilation of selfhood, even though all that self now claims for its own be the Love of God" (Underhill 474).

According to Cornford, the scenes between the first *Parabasis* and the second are devoted to "a scene of Sacrifice and prayer, and the cooking and eating of a Feast," although many of the examples he quotes from Aristophanes require a good deal of casuistry to see (Cornford 94). Obviously, the presence of sacrifice in the scene of the martyrdom requires no justification. The presence of a feast may seem more far-fetched; however, the connection between the two in a Eucharistic, Anglo-Catholic context is more plausible, although a full exploration of such is beyond the pale of this argument. Additionally, the text itself motions towards the concept of the Aristophanic Feast when the knights are first invited to dinner upon their arrival. Feasting is also included in the refrain the knights sing when they enter drunk: "Come down Daniel and join in the feast" (*Murder in the Cathedral* 58, 745). These examples are far closer than some of the connections that Cornford draws. Yet, there is a further aspect to these scenes which fulfill the Aristophanic model, which is the presence of the Impostors, as Cornford calls them. "The scene of sacrifice, cooking, or feasting has no sooner begun than" these Impostors "interrupt the proceedings" (Cornford 132). In a 1932 letter on *Sweeney Agonistes,* Eliot refers to the "three *Intruders*" from an unwritten portion of the play, so he obviously considered this to be important to Aristophanic drama in general (*Letters* VI.498). Fascinatingly, he appears to retain even the number of intruders, which is not specified in Cornford, from his previous attempt. In *Murder in the Cathedral*, this part is played by the priests who repeatedly intercede to keep the knights from Thomas and then abscond with him to the cathedral. While this is more serious than in the Aristophanic comedy, "[t]heir common fate is a well-deserved rebuff" as Cornford suggests (Cornford 132). Like with the Impostors in the Aristophanic comedy, the priests' attempt to interrupt or halt the sacrifice of Thomas is ultimately futile.

DRAMATIZING

131

A second *Parabasis* occurs between the sacrifice and the *Exodos* in the "seven earliest plays" by Aristophanes (Cornford 130). Importantly, one of these is *Birds*, which is the play in which Eliot was most interested. A second *Parabasis* is also included in "The Superior Landlord" outline, which suggests that Eliot deemed it necessary (Eliot *Collected Poems* 792). Eliot signals that he intended the knights's defense as a *Parabasis* with the stage directions: "The Knights, having completed the murder, advance to the front of the stage and address the audience" (*Murder in the Cathedral* 78, italics omitted). Cornford insists in the *Parabasis* that the speakers "turn their backs on the scene of action and advance across the orchestra to address the audience directly—the movement from which the *Parabasis* takes its name" (Cornford 2). Reduced to summarizing the results of the seven plays featuring a second *Parabasis*, Cornford is vague on the content, alternately asserting that the second *Parabasis* often is an appeal to the judges or the audience in the form of an epirrhematic syzygy and also "practically a *débat*" between the opposing principles in the play (Cornford 130). Cornford also insists that reconciliation between divided halves of the chorus is another main purpose (Cornford 131). Eliot seems to have merged these disparate elements in Cornford in his own scene. The knights speaking in rounds, often building off each other, certainly would meet the qualification[38] of an epirrhematic syzygy. While there is an appeal to the audience, the Antagonist's representatives should attempt to reconcile its principle with the audience. This is seen, when one of the knights states,

> [Beckett] became more priestly than the priests, he ostentatiously and offensively adopted an ascetic manner of life, he affirmed immediately there was a higher order than that which our King, and he as the King's servant, had for so many years striven to establish; and that—God knows why—the two orders were incompatible.
> *Murder in the Cathedral* 81.

Here, Eliot is making clear that we are to understand Beckett's actions as ascetic in nature, although the word is included with Eliot's usual condescension to how the term ascetic was commonly understood. The comment about two orders, while appearing to reference the division of church and state, may also refer to the division between the worldly and the holy. Thus, the preference for one over the other is not a political preference, as the knights interpret, but

---

38    This does provide an interesting modulation to Badenhausen's understanding of the two *Parabasis* segments as collaborative (Badenhausen 163).

132                                                                      CHAPTER 6

would be an aspect of the ascetic ideal: the denial of the lower to attain the higher.

The final movement of the Aristophanic play is the *Exodos* wherein "the protagonist [...] is fêted in the torchlit *Kômos*" which is the chorus's song of praise of the victor (Cornford 24). At the most literal level, this is accomplished by the staging. As Malamud notes, "after the murder, Becket's body was carried out in a procession through the audience" (Malamud 244). Cornford states that Aristophanic "plays regularly end with a procession in which the Chorus marches out of the orchestra, conducting the chief character in triumph" (Cornford 8). Given that there was only one exit to the chapterhouse where the play was first staged, Eliot's procession seems to match identically. Yet, it is not merely the staging that matches the Aristophanic structure. To accomplish his fertility-ritual scheme, Cornford is eager to connect to a sort of Sacred Marriage. Obviously, nothing of the sort happens in *Murder in the Cathedral*; however, there is an important variation to this occurrence in Aristophanes and is what happens in the ending of *Birds*. In this variation, what occurs is not primarily a marriage but the inauguration of a new king and new Zeus,[39] in which the established temporal and religious authority is overturned and transferred to the protagonist. In this light, the ending of *Murder in the Cathedral* would seem to fit the pattern of the Aristophanic *Exodos*. Although obviously more subdued in tone than the jubilant endings—*Clouds* and *Frogs* excepted—in Aristophanes' comedies, *Murder in the Cathedral* still follows this pattern of indicating the reversal of the established order and the glorification of the victorious protagonist. The first priest's note of despair after the departure of the Knights is quickly rebuffed with the third priest insisting that the Church is "[t]riumphant in adversity" (*Murder in the Cathedral* 84). The second priest speaks of the unseen "glory of [Thomas's] new state," and the conclusion is that God "has given us another Saint in Canterbury" (*Murder in the Cathedral* 85–6). As in the Aristophanic play, the Chorus has the final passage of the play and ends with a request for prayer from Thomas as a saint—a sacred, Christian rendition of the proclamation of the new king and Zeus's authority in the Aristophanic model, particularly the last lines of *Birds*. Thus, the religious and temporal order at the play's beginning where a king may threaten the Church has been overturned. Thomas the exile has become the Saint displaying God's authority over all creation.

The triumph of the protagonist is only one portion of the Aristophanic comedy, though; the protagonist's ideology must also be victorious in its application to society. In the play's final sequence, the chorus declares itself to be

---

39    Cf. *Birds* 1706ff.

DRAMATIZING 133

speaking universally, "as type of the common man" and one of the components of this universality is that they "fear the blessing of God, the loneliness of the night of God, the surrender required, the deprivation inflicted" (Eliot *Murder in the Cathedral* 87–8). Here, Eliot is direct about the ascetic ideal present in the play, particularly the dark night of the soul, since what else could be meant by the phrase "the night of God"? The characterization of it as "loneliness" is typical in the mystical readings: "The greatest affliction of the sorrowful soul in this state [...] is the thought that God has abandoned it" (St John of the Cross qtd. in Underhill 465). The definition of the "dark night of the soul" is after all, a withdrawal of the feeling of divine presence from mystic (Underhill 464–5). The characterization of the dark night as a deprivation is also something Eliot encountered; Underhill describes the experience using some form of the word no less than sixteen times in her chapter on the dark night. The "surrender required" is not only the standard description of ascetic experience but also a comment on the "act of utter surrender" that is the end of the dark night (Underhill 481). By having the chorus highlight this, Eliot is emphasizing the universal applicability of Thomas's act to the common man. Not all are saints in the sense that Thomas is, but in speaking for the common man, the chorus is emphasizing the purification of the will necessary for holiness.

Eliot's interest in Cornford's *The Origin of Attic Comedy* and its influence on his understanding of Aristophanes obviously has farther reaching consequences than *Sweeney Agonistes*. Eliot seems to have found the Aristophanic structure a vitalizing one, which he employed in deep, technical detail. The depth of Eliot's interest in the Aristophanic structure in his earliest two plays has a distinct side-effect beyond the ordering of events. According to Cornford, Attic Old Comedy focuses not on conflict between characters but ideas, and the ideal that Eliot chose to dramatize was ascetic. In *Sweeney Agonistes*, the brute materialism—birth, copulation, death—of Sweeney is the principle which Eliot's play argues against. In *Murder in the Cathedral*, the play dramatizes not only the emptiness of sensuality and temporal power but also the abandonment of the individual will in the dark night of the soul. As is clear particularly from *Murder in the Cathedral*, Eliot's dramatization of the ascetic ideal reflects, in broad strokes, the ideas he first encountered in his mystical readings, but he is not speaking wholly in his own voice. Yet, when the detritus from the play was repurposed into poetry again in "Burnt Norton," the ascetic ideal that he had dramatized would be fully embraced.

CHAPTER 7

# Embracing

At the final stage of his poetic career, Eliot returns to many of the readings which influenced him at the beginning. In the latter three of the *Four Quartets* particularly,[1] the ascetic ideal presented reflects what Eliot had read in what I have termed orthodox mystical readings, particularly Inge, Jones, and Underhill, if only rarely in their own words.[2] Let me reiterate that I am using the term "orthodox" here to refer to the positions on mysticism and asceticism that Inge, Underhill, and Jones have in common. Nonetheless, the evidence from the letters and *Collected Prose* indicates that Eliot still valued these authors greatly. He was, by the time he was writing *Four Quartets* already a friend and correspondent of Evelyn Underhill, and her opinions on spiritual matters were prized. For instance, he had Underhill review a spiritual handbook on asceticism for *The Criterion* in 1932 that Eliot intended to purchase for himself (*Letters* VI.365–6). In 1934, he rushes to acquire a new translation of St John of the Cross because Underhill said "that it is much better" (*Letters* VII.233). Eliot's brother Henry in a lengthy letter on religious belief cites Dean Inge, in a paraphrase of an idea from *Christian Mysticism* 77–8 on the importance of Greek philosophy to Catholic doctrine. Henry then quotes Eliot's own words on that matter back to him (*Letters* VII.761). It would be speculation to say that Henry, who is not known to be particularly religious, had read Inge on Eliot's suggestion, but Henry *had* read Inge's work for whatever reason along with

---

1  Extending this argument to the late plays, particularly *The Cocktail Party*, would not be difficult, but it would be too lengthy an excursus. Additionally, the critical edition of the plays as well as the letters for those years are not yet available.

2  There is a very notable exception. In "Burnt Norton" III.23–4, Eliot states, "I can only say, *there* we have been: but I cannot say where. / And I cannot say, how long, for that is to place it in time." This appears to be a direct citation of a passage in Underhill's *Mysticism*: "A good map then, a good mystical philosophy, will leave room for both [Immanence and Transcendence]. It will mark the routes by which many different temperaments claim to have found their way to the same end. [...] The true mystic—the person with a genius for God—hardly needs a map himself. He steers a compass course across the 'vast and stormy sea of the divine.' It is characteristic of his intellectual humility, however, that he is commonly willing to use the map of the community in which he finds himself, when it comes to showing other people the route which he has pursued. Sometimes these maps have been adequate. More, they have elucidated the obscure wanderings of the explorer; helped him; given him landmarks; worked out right. Time after time he puts his finger on some spot—some great hill of vision, some city of the soul—and says with conviction, '*Here* have I been.' (Underhill 124)".

---

© KONINKLIJKE BRILL NV, LEIDEN, 2020 | DOI:10.1163/9789004375826_009

EMBRACING                                                                135

the works of Paul Elmer More. Moreover, Henry thought, based on whom he
was quoting at that moment, that Eliot's own doctrinal beliefs mirrored Inge's
ideas instead of More's whose *The Greek Tradition*[3] carries some similar ideas
to Inge's on this matter (*Letters* VII.761). Eliot, also, defended, somewhat reti-
cently, Inge and Chesterton against Pound in public (*Letters* VII.174). In fact,
Eliot's opinions on the mystics, and the ascetic ideal he derived from them, appear remarkably consonant with his earlier reading even in the face of not only
his secular but even religious friends, like Paul Elmer More. In his eulogy for
More, Eliot indicates that he disapproves of More's dismissal of the early mystics and references "the probable importance of the mystics of the fourteenth
century—of Richard Rolle and Julian of Norwich for instance" (*Prose* V.420).
Thus, Eliot's education in mysticism appears to have been deeply ingrained,
which suggests that these works are still germane for studying the ascetic ideal
that appeared in the *Four Quartets.*

This was not merely a matter of a return to favorite books; the ascetic ideal,
which he had studied, now influenced all aspects of his spiritual life. Eliot, at
this point in his life, had Father Francis Underhill, the cousin of Evelyn, serving
as his confessor, and in the year of Eliot's conversion, Father Underhill published a book entitled *Prayer in Modern Life.*[4] There is no evidence for Eliot
having read this book, and it is not my intention to peek inside the confessional; however, Father Underhill's teaching does support the ascetic ideal. In
*Prayer in Modern Life*, he has a chapter devoted to "Prayer and the Body" subdivided into "The Body as Hindrance" and "The Body as Help" (Father Underhill
118–25). One would expect that Father Underhill would discuss an ascetic view
and then a counter; however, this is not the case. In his discussion of "The Body
as Help," he proposes the value of fasting and that the body is a help because
of the virtues its suffering can imbue to the soul: "There can be no doubt at all
that God uses pain, and that some of the most beautiful and heroic characters in the history of prayer have—like the Captain of their salvation—been
made perfect through suffering" (Father Underhill 122). This is keenly ascetic
phrasing, and Father Underhill's sentiments show the influence of his cousin's
theories on mysticism (Father Underhill 122). Rather than the "healthy-minded
spirituality" of William James and D. H. Lawrence that embraces the body as a
means to spiritual healing, Father Underhill portrays the body as the source of
temptations to be resisted. The body is useful *because* of them; its temptations
are cast as an ascetic mechanism through which holiness flows.

---

3   Cf. "Paul Elmer More" (*Prose* V.419).

4   In both the text and citations, Father Underhill is referenced with his title to distinguish him
    from his more prominent cousin.

"[some] find through temptation the strengthening of their character. They emerge refined and beautified from the ordeal they pass through. For some, temptation of this kind is an unceasing trial; but they get the upper hand and are splendid Christians. Here again, however, the greatest use of this kind of suffering is not merely the production of heroic character. It is not only that men and women by the power they have just gained are a strength to the world they live in and to the people among whom they dwell. The higher purpose of temptation is that it drives people to prayer. [...] The simple Christian will be thankful for any discipline, however hard, which forces him to God.

FATHER UNDERHILL 124–5.

While not a particularly deep nor original thinker, Father Underhill expressed views that seemed to support the ascetic ideal. Why Eliot chose him as a confessor is unclear and outside the scope of this study; however, it seems safe to say that Eliot would have found in Father Underhill spiritual instruction more supportive of any of his own inclinations to discipline. It is also possible that Father Underhill's teaching reinforced and reminded Eliot of his earlier education especially in the orthodox mystical readings of Evelyn Underhill and elsewhere.

No more than understanding an allusion removes the artistry of it, the verse of *Four Quartets* is not emptied by its turn to what Eliot would have considered doctrinal orthodoxy; it shows Eliot's poetic virtuosity that he can reconstitute the stiff, translated words of mediaeval saints and dusty tenets of recondite theologians into living poetry. That Eliot would even attempt to do so, actually, shows his adherence to these orthodox mystical readings. As he read in Inge,

Strictly speaking, visions of divine truth are not communicable. [...] The memory preserves only a pale reflection of them, and language, which was not meant for such purposes, fails lamentably to produce even that pale reflection. Those only can understand the mind of the prophet or saint who can supply what is lacking in his words from their own hearts, renewing from the fire within them, the lustre and the glow, which his descriptions strive ineffectually to render permanent.

INGE *English Mystics* 3–4.

This is quite similar to the definition of mystical illumination that Eliot himself gives in *The Use of Poetry and the Use of Criticism*: "[Mystical illumination] is a vision which may be accompanied by the realization that you will never be able to communicate it to anyone else, or even by the realization that when it

EMBRACING  137

is past you will not be able to recall it yourself" (*Prose* IV.686).[5] Both of these, however, are attenuated echoes of the infamous Epistle to Can Grande, attributed to Dante:

> *Vidit ergo, ut dicit, aliqua "que referre nescit et nequit rediens." Diligenter quippe notandum est quod dicit "nescit et nequit." Nescit quia oblitus, nequit quia, si recordatur et contentum tenet, sermo tamen deficit. Multa namque per intellectum videmus quibus signa vocalia desunt; quod satis Plato insinuat in suis libris per assumptionem metaphorismorum; multa enim per lumen intellectuale vidit que sermone proprio nequivit exprimere.*[6]
> "Epistle to Can Grande" 83–4.

Here is the ascetic ideal in Eliot's *Four Quartets* in a nutshell—as Eliot read in Caldecott, "that Dante, after duly venerating the great Doctors, retreated into the Faith based on Revelation alone" (Caldecott 414). Likewise, Eliot, too, comes to rest in the dogmas of the orthodox Christian mystical tradition and its ascetic ideal. Eliot, then, transforms the fully embraced ascetic ideal into verse. However, his interest in the ascetic ideal is not uniform. Different aspects of it are explored throughout the poems, and it is normally addressed in relatively small sections in each poem. The ascetic ideal, is, after all, only a part of mysticism. In "Burnt Norton," Eliot is not always interested in the ascetic ideal as the focus more on the moment of Illumination and its relation to the timeless. For practicality's sake, the poem will not be considered at length. However, in "East Coker," the ascetic ideal is extensively employed through the mystical τόποι of the cloud of unknowing and the dark night of the soul. Eliot had already explored it in *Murder in the Cathedral,* but his discussion in "East Coker" is far more intricate than the earlier dramatization. In "The Dry Salvages," the ascetic ideal is not as prevalent as a theme, but the connective ability of the λόγος, discussed in Chapters 4 and 5, appears briefly in conjunction with the role of the mysticism for those other than the saints. Finally, in "Little Gidding," the ascetic ideal is posited as a necessary step in its own transcendence.

---

5  Cf. Murray 17.
6  In Toynbee's translation: "He saw, then, as he says, certain things 'which he who returns has neither knowledge nor power to relate'. Now it must be carefully noted that he says 'has neither knowledge nor power'–knowledge he has not, because he has forgotten; power he has not, because even if he remembers, and retains it thereafter, nevertheless speech fails him. For we perceive many things by the intellect for which language has no terms—a fact which Plato indicates plainly enough in his books by his employment of metaphors; for he perceived many things by the light of the intellect which his everyday language was inadequate to express." ("Epistle to Can Grande" 83–4).

138 CHAPTER 7

Out of all of Eliot's poems, "East Coker" is the most extensively involved in the ascetic ideal. Here in "East Coker," Eliot asserts the orthodox and ascetic solution to the harrowing solipsism found in "Gerontion," *The Waste Land*, and "The Hollow Men." Because Eliot is interest in humility throughout the poem, the ascetic ideal is at the forefront, and this idea in particular, which is not only about humility but community. The connection is exemplified in a quotation from William Law, that Eliot read in several of the mystical authors: "to know that the greatest humility, the most absolute resignation of our whole selves to God, is our greatest and highest fitness to receive our greatest and highest purification from the hands of God" (Underhill 242; Inge *English Mystics* 152). The most succinct statement, though, of the connection between asceticism and humility occurs in Inge where he says simply, "the ground of all the virtues is humility" (Inge *Christian Mysticism* 169). Any number of passages in "East Coke," could illustrate this. The best is where Eliot writes,

> Do not let me hear
> Of the wisdom of old men, but rather of their folly,
> Their fear of fear and frenzy, their fear of possession,
> Of belonging to another, or to others, or to God.
> The only wisdom we can hope to acquire
> Is the wisdom of humility: humility is endless.
> > "East Coker" II.43–8.

This is a particularly rich passage as it also highlights the part of the ascetic ideal seen in "Gerontion," *The Waste Land*, and "The Hollow Men." Yet, what Eliot hinted at in those poems is now fully espoused. The tie between this thread in mystical thought is made explicit in Inge's *Personal Idealism and Mysticism* where Eliot had read that:

> The absolute freedom of the Christian man is absolute allegiance to God. His freedom is from the tyranny of partial claims, individual desires, and objects; and it is won by identification with the universal. It is here that humility comes in. Humility is the sense of solidarity and community; the controlling and regulating power of the consciousness that we are not our own, but God's and our neighbor's. Finally, the most practical corollary is love. There are two great commandments on which hinge all the law and the prophets. The first bids love God; the second, love the neighbor as self. These are not separate, and cannot be balanced one against the other. God, self, and neighbor, form an indissoluble Trinity.
> > WALLACE qtd. in INGE *Personal Idealism* 91–2.

EMBRACING                                                                    139

Eliot may not be deliberately echoing this passage; nonetheless, it clearly represents how the ascetic ideal, based in humility, is also an ideal of community—as I have quoted before, "[t]he personal relation between the soul and Christ is not to be denied; but it can only be enjoyed when the person has 'come to himself' as a member of a body. This involves an inward transit from the false isolated self to the larger life of sympathy and love which alone makes us person" (Inge *Christian Mysticism* 51). Thus, humility is the remedy to the folly of fearing to belong to others, fearing that "larger life of sympathy and love."[7] Eliot was, of course, writing "The Idea of a Christian Society" at this same time, and this seems to be the reason he insists offhandedly that the church's "masters of ascetic theology" were a key part of its "relations to the Community of Christians" (*Prose* v.708).

While that is the core of the ascetic ideal in "East Coker," Eliot's discussion of "the darkness of God" in Part III requires exposition. Eliot writes, "I said to my soul, be still, and let the dark come upon you / [w]hich shall be the darkness of God" ("East Coker" III.12–3). This is an elaboration of an idea in "Burnt Norton" where Eliot speaks of "darkness to purify the soul / [e]mptying the sensual with deprivation / [c]leansing the affection from the temporal" ("Burnt Norton" III.7–9). Eliot returns to this concept of the darkness of God and explores it in all its difficulty and complexity. Despite the seemingly abstracted nature of this "night of God," it is, as previously discussed, one firmly rooted in the ascetic ideal. St John of the Cross writes that a desire for spiritual things is necessary or "we should never overcome our natural and sensible satisfactions, nor be able to enter on the night of sense, neither should we have the courage to remain in the darkness, in the denial of every desire" (*The Ascent of Mount Carmel* I.xiv.2).[8] The root of the difficulty this poses is that Eliot seems to be eliding two different conceptions from his mystical readings: The Cloud of Unknowing and the dark night of the soul. While they are often separated by later mystics, the two are ultimately both rooted in the concepts of Pseudo-Dionysius the Areopagite who states that the mystic "must leave behind all things both in the sensible and in the intelligible worlds, till he enters the darkness of nescience which is truly mystical" (Pseudo-Dionysius qtd. in Inge *Christian Mysticism* 109). The primary difficulty with these two is that language used of one is often applied to the other, and occasionally, no effort is made to distinguish them. Generally, though, when the concept of the Cloud of Unknowing is discussed, it focuses on the *locative* aspect of the Darkness of God. By contrast, the Dark Night is mentioned more in terms of how the deprivation

---

7   Cf. Schuchard 188.
8   Eliot first encountered this passage in Underhill 245.

of the divine presence upon the mystic. Nonetheless, the Cloud of Unknowing and the Dark Night needs must be discussed separately, even if Eliot, along with his sources, tends to conflate them. Additionally, I should note that, while the authorities I am quoting are perhaps not the foremost of contemporary ones, I am using the words of the mystical authors that Eliot is known to have read in his early years as they form the basis of *his* knowledge which is the focus of this study.

The central concept of The Cloud of Unknowing is that it is the veil that hides the Divine from direct apprehension. The idea is biblical at its heart; God "made darkness his secret place, His pavilion round about Him with dark water, and thick clouds to cover Him" (2nd Samuel 22:12 qtd. in Inge *Christian Mysticism* 227). The work most dedicated to this concept is *The Cloud of Unknowing,* which Eliot quotes directly in "Little Gidding,"[9] and it states that:

> For at the first time when thou dost it, thou findest but a darkness; and as it were a cloud of unknowing, thou knowest not what, saving that thou feelest in thy will a naked intent unto God. This darkness and this cloud is, howsoever thou dost, betwixt thee and thy God, and letteth thee that thou mayest neither see Him clearly by light of understanding in thy reason, nor feel Him in sweetness of love in thine affection. And therefore shape thee to bide in this darkness as long as thou mayest, evermore crying after Him that thou lovest. For if ever thou shalt feel Him or see Him, as it may be here, it behoveth always to be in this cloud in this darkness.
> The Cloud of Unknowing III[10]

There are significant overlaps with the dark night as to ascend into the Cloud is also to depart from the knowledge of temporal things.[11] The overlap between the mystical state of the darkness of God and timelessness is visible in "East Coker" III and the application has some relevance to "Burnt Norton" as well. Consider the lines that follow:

---

9   Cf. "Little Gidding" v.25.
10  It is unclear what edition Eliot read. I have here and hence quoted from Underhill's.
11  For this, consider Eckhart's discussion, although Eliot had serious reservations about him: "He who penetrates into himself, and so transcends himself, ascends truly to God. He whom I love and desire is above all that is sensible, and all that is intelligible; sense and imagination cannot bring us to Him, but only the desire of a pure heart. This brings us unto the darkness of the mind, whereby we can ascend to the contemplation even of the mystery of the Trinity. Do not think about the world, nor about thy friends, nor about the past, present, or future; but consider thyself to be outside of the world and alone with God, as if thy soul were already separated from the body and had no longer any interest in peace or war, or the state of the world." (Eckhart qtd. in Jones 219).

# EMBRACING

141

> As, in a theatre,
> The lights are extinguished, for the scene to be changed
> With a hollow rumble of wings,[12] with a movement of darkness on darkness,
> And we know that the hills and the trees, the distant panorama
> And the bold imposing facade are all being rolled away—
> Or as, when an underground train, in the tube, stops too long between stations
> And the conversation rises and slowly fades into silence
> And you see behind every face the mental emptiness deepen
> Leaving only the growing terror of nothing to think about;
> Or when, under ether, the mind is conscious but conscious of nothing—
>
> > "East Coker" III.13–22[13]

Here, the detachment from the temporal is reified as the stage-trappings of the world being rolled away. This seems to be something that Eliot associates with not only mystical illumination as seen in "Burnt Norton" but also with the darkness of God. Even St John of the Cross, the greatest proponent of the Dark Night, discusses the Cloud of Unknowing, and he notes that it occurs as

> the soul approaches a great way towards union, in darkness, by means of faith, which is likewise dark, and in this wise faith wondrously illumines it. It is certain that, if the soul should desire to see, it would be in darkness much more quickly, with respect to God, than would one who opens his eyes to look upon the great brightness of the sun.
>
> Wherefore, by blinding itself in its faculties upon this road, the soul will see the light, even as the Saviour says in the Gospel, in this wise: *In judicium veni in hunc mundum: ut qui non vident, videant, et qui vident, caeci fiant.*[14] That is: I am come into this world for judgment; that they which see not may see, and that they which see may become blind. This,

---

12     The reference to the theatre structure is obvious—less so is the association in his readings of wings with the Divine Love as seen in *Phaedrus* §246d–249e or especially in Underhill's reference to Pseudo-Dionysius' discussion of the Seraphim who burning in perfect Love as being "all wings" (Underhill 55).

13     The use of ether in generating mystical states was very much a feature of Eliot's early readings on mysticism, especially in William James. However, it is not a part of the more orthodox readings, and I am leery to ascribe any *specific* interpretive value to it. It is sufficient to note that ether would be associated with the artificial generation of mystical states and so its value as a metaphor for a genuine one certainly seems legitimate.

14     John 9:39.

as it will be supposed, is to be understood of this spiritual road, where the soul that is in darkness, and is blinded as regards all its natural and proper lights, will see supernaturally; and the soul that would depend upon any light of its own will become the blinder and will halt upon the road to union.[15]

> *Ascent of Mount Carmel* II.iv.6–7.

This is one of the clearest portrayals of the Cloud of Unknowing as a locative aspect of the darkness of God. However, this is only half of what Eliot's reading states regarding this—the second is the dark night of the soul.[16]

Because of the interconnection among the *Four Quartets*, the use of the Dark Night as part of the ascetic ideal in "East Coker" is actually the resumption of a thread from "Burnt Norton," which should not be a surprise given the presence of this idea in *Murder in the Cathedral*. The Dark Night is, to summarize, the deprivation of the things of God. It may seem curious to employ the discussion found in *The Ascent of Mount Carmel* instead of *The Dark Night of the Soul* itself; however, it is the former to which Eliot is most indebted for his own ascetic ideal. St John of the Cross's entire commentary on the titular poem survives for *The Ascent of Mount Carmel* whereas it does not for *The Dark Night of the Soul*. Now, in his summary of Book I, St. John of the Cross states that

> For to this end the soul profited by going forth upon a 'dark night'—that is, in the privation of all pleasures and mortification of all desires, after the manner whereof we have spoken. And by its 'house being now at rest' is meant the sensual part, which is the house of all the desires, and is now at rest because they have all been overcome and lulled to sleep. For until the desires are lulled to sleep through the mortification of the sensual nature, and until at last the sensual nature itself is at rest from them, so that they make not war upon the spirit, the soul goes not forth to true liberty and to the fruition of union with its Beloved.
>
> *Ascent of Mount Carmel* I.xv.2.

Underhill, however, expands the concept to include a broader range of states, while still emphasizing the ascetic nature of the dark night. As discussed

---

15 Cf. what Eliot read of Scotus Eriugena in Jones 219.

16 Contra Murray 92–5. His discussion drawing wholly on St John of the Cross and Hay's argumentation seems reductive, ignoring the diverse tradition Eliot is drawing from. This is not to say that St John of the Cross is neither valid nor important to this passage, but it is not a case of straightforward insertion, except in the instance of "East Coker" III.35–46.

# EMBRACING

previously, in her somewhat idiosyncratic schematic, the dark night represents a separate phase of purgation for the mystics before the ultimate vision.

> All these forms of the Dark Night—the "Absence of God," the sense of sin, the dark ecstasy, the loss of the self's old passion, peace, and joy, and its apparent relapse to lower spiritual and mental levels—are considered by the mystics themselves to constitute aspects or parts of one and the same process: the final purification of the will or stronghold of personality, that it may be merged without any reserve "in God where it was first." The function of this episode of the Mystic Way is to cure the soul of the innate tendency to seek and rest in spiritual joys; to confuse Reality with the joy given by the contemplation of Reality. It is the completion of that ordering of disordered loves, that trans-valuation of values, which the Way of Purgation began. The ascending self must leave these childish satisfactions; make its love absolutely disinterested, strong, and courageous, abolish all taint of spiritual gluttony. A total abandonment of the individualistic standpoint, of that trivial and egotistic quest of personal satisfaction which thwarts the great movement of the Flowing Light, is the supreme condition of man's participation in Reality.
>
> UNDERHILL 472–3.

Underhill, here, is creating a definition of the Dark Night that is very much separate from the Cloud of Unknowing, so the Dark Night is a kind of purgation of the soul rather than the senses. This is what Eliot is following in the quotation in "Burnt Norton" where Eliot writes of the darkness of God as "purify[ing] the soul / [e]mptying the sensual with deprivation / [c]leansing the affection from the temporal" ("Burnt Norton" III.7–9).[17] The language employed here is that of ascetic detachment which places this as a feature of the darkness of God.[18] The first statement is a paraphrase of "Empty thy spirit of all created things, and thou wilt walk in the Divine Light, for God resembles no created thing" (St John of the Cross qtd. in Inge *Christian Mysticism* 22). The reference to "cleansing affection" emphasizes that this imagery is purgative. Specifically, the loss of affection in sin is something that Eliot read about; in Inge's discussion of Hylton, the initial step of conversion leaves "the image of the sin" *i.e.* the body "intact in point of feeling. (That is, the commission of sin would still give pleasure but is avoided by a sense of duty)"; however, "through great spiritual pains," it

---

17    Murray's application of St John of the Cross to this passage seems reductive. Cf. Murray 96.

18    Murray notices but does not explore this aspect. Cf. Murray 74, 79.

144                                                                                    CHAPTER 7

is possible to "[put] out the pleasure felt in sin" (Inge *English Mystics* 97). This
is an extension of what St John of the Cross states when he says that "I call this
detachment the night of the soul, for I am not speaking here of the absence
of things—for absence is not detachment if desire remains[19]—but of that detachment which consists in suppressing desire, and avoiding pleasure; it is this
that sets the soul free even though possession may still be retained" (*Ascent of
Mt. Carmel* I.iii.4) These passages by no means exhaust Eliot's readings on the
Darkness of God and its purgatorial powers. Nonetheless, they should suffice
to show that Eliot is operating within the confines of the orthodox mystical
tradition and distilling its essence to poetry.

   Another instance of Eliot embracing the ascetic ideal from his readings in
"East Coker" is the speaker's injunctions against his soul.

> I said to my soul, be still, and wait without hope
> For hope would be hope for the wrong thing; wait without love,
> For love would be love of the wrong thing; there is yet faith
> But the faith and the love and the hope are all in the waiting.
> Wait without thought, for you are not ready for thought:
> So the darkness shall be the light, and the stillness the dancing.
>         "East Coker" III.23–8.

While the command to "be still" is biblical and here most likely a contraction
of the "be still and know that I am God" of Psalm 46:10,[20] the injunctions to
wait without hope, love, and thought seem difficult to interpret. However, this
is an idea also found in St John of the Cross, although, Eliot likely first encountered this in Inge who summarizes "[t]he soul has three faculties—intellect,
memory, and will. The imagination (*fantasia*) is a link between the sensitive
and reasoning powers, and comes between the intellect and the memory. Of
these faculties, "faith (he says) blinds the intellect, hope the memory, love
the will"; he adds, "to all that is not God"; but "God in this life is like night"
(Inge *Christian Mysticism* 226).[21] Now, in this light, this passage is a disavowal

---

19    This passage is highlighted in Underhill 255.
20    Other possible scriptural sources are Exodus 14:4, Psalm 37:7, Nehemiah 8:11, and Zecha-
       riah 2:13.
21    As St John of the cross himself states: The journey of the Soul to the divine union is called
       night for three reasons. The first is derived from the point from which the soul sets out,
       the privation of the desire of all pleasure in all the things of this world, by detachment
       therefrom. This is as night for every desire and sense of man. The second, from the road
       by which it travels; that is faith, for faith is obscure, like night, to the understanding. The
       third, from the goal to which it tends, God, incomprehensible and infinite, Who in this life

EMBRACING                                                                        145

of mystical ambitions as it would place the speaker within only the first of
the three dark nights.[22] St John of the Cross elaborates on how these virtues
function; he states that they "render empty all the powers of the soul; faith
makes the understanding empty and blind; hope takes everything away from
the memory, and charity detaches the will from every pleasure and affection
which are not God. [...] Thus, these virtues bring darkness over the soul, and
empty it of all created things" (*Ascent of Mount Carmel* II.vi.2). If the soul is to
wait without hope and love, then it is not to attempt the road to the complete
union with God but only the initial detachment from the things of this world.
Therefore, Eliot may be suggesting that the night of the senses *i.e.* of ascetic
purgation has occurred which is the necessary condition for Illumination, but
the nights of spirit and memory which, though necessary for the Divine Union,
have not transpired as the hope and love are not to be engaged. This may seem
a strange point of emphasis, but it is fully in line with Underhill's idiosyncratic idea of the mystical poet. For Underhill, the mystically-inclined artist may
journey to the third stage of the mystical journey but is not able to attain, as
Eliot says in "A Song for Simeon," "the ultimate vision" ("A Song for Simeon" 30).
While the emphasis is strongest in Underhill's work, Inge also asserts in his
chapter on nature-mysticism that "Wordsworth was an ascetic of an unfamiliar type" who required "a severe course in moral training" to see the supernal
in nature (Inge *English Mystics* 188, 185). Incidentally, Eliot echoes this idea,
at the time of *Four Quartets*, in his own words: In "Types of English Religious
Verse," Eliot insists that Wordsworth possessed "a wholly undogmatic nature-
mysticism" (*Prose* VI.53). In fact, the very term "nature-mysticism" appears
to be Inge's own coinage—I do not recall seeing it in Eliot's other readings
on mysticism. These references to the mystically-inclined artist, regardless of
whether critics interpret them biographically or not, still show that this portion of "East Coker" is indeed ascetic in character. The implicit conclusion and
result of the ascetic ideal is in the line, "So the darkness shall be the light and
the stillness the dancing" ("East Coker" 129). This idea does have a consistent
basis in the mystical readings, although its paradoxical concision is unique to
Eliot's poetry. The best example of this is quoted by Underhill where the dying
to the things of sense produces the end result that "it seems to [the mystic]
hereafter more joyful, good and pleasant to die than to live, for he finds life in

---

is as night to the soul. We must pass through these three nights if we are to attain to the
divine union with God. (*Ascent of Mount Carmel* I.ii.1).

22   It is possible that the poem also takes Browning's *Paracelsus* as a source where Eliot read
in Inge's *Christian Mysticism* of "the *ascetic* element" in Browning that "thou shalt pain-
fully attain to joy, / [w]hile hope and fear and love shall keep thee man" (Browning qtd. in
Inge *Christian Mysticism* 319).

death and light shining in darkness" (Tauler qtd. in Underhill 262–3).[23] That Eliot declares that there is a light to be found in the darkness of asceticism seems to indicate his embrace of the ascetic ideal as "an earnest increasing of life" (Underhill 243).

Eliot's best known use of mystical literature follows when he closely paraphrases *The Ascent of Mount Carmel* I.xiii.11[24] (*Poems* I.945).

> In order to arrive there,
> To arrive where you are, to get from where you are not,
> You must go by a way wherein there is no ecstasy.
> In order to arrive at what you do not know
> You must go by a way which is the way of ignorance.
> In order to possess what you do not possess
> You must go by the way of dispossession.
> In order to arrive at what you are not
> You must go through the way in which you are not.
> And what you do not know is the only thing you know
> And what you own is what you do not own
> And where you are is where you are not.
>
> "East Coker" 137–48.

Undeniably, this represents his interest in the ascetic ideal; however, it is *not* the bleak statement of Eastern apophasis as it is often portrayed.[25] In her introduction to the relevant passage in St John of the Cross, Underhill states that "[t]he answer to the riddle lies in the ancient paradox of Poverty: that we only enjoy true liberty in respect to such things as we neither possess nor desire" (Underhill 249). The exposition of this will require another foray into the mystical literature, but the heart of it is found in the line that "[i]n order to possess what you do not possess / [y]ou must go by the way of dispossession" which is a succinct way of stating that

> Wicked men "maintain a *meum* and *tuum* between God and themselves," but the good man is able to make a full surrender of himself, "triumphing

---

23 Cf. "we may see only the icy darkness of perpetual negations: but [the mystic], beyond the coincidence of opposites, looks upon the face of Perfect Love" (Underhill 65).

24 In addition to occurring in William James (Cf. *Poems* I.945), Eliot also read it in Underhill 249. On the whole though, I am in agreement with Murray's assessment of this passage and Eliot's source for it (Murray 89–92).

25 Murray's treatment of this problem in St John of the Cross is less convincing (Murray 95–100). Cf. Murray 133.

EMBRACING

147

in nothing more than in his own nothingness, and in the allness of the Divinity. But indeed, this his being nothing is the only way to all things; this his having nothing the truest way of possessing all things"

SMITH qtd. in INGE Christian Mysticism 291[26]

Or, as Underhill summarizes, Holy Poverty is "the selfless use, not the selfish abuse, of lovely and natural things" (Underhill 260). This neatly explains why Eliot employs a flurry of natural images to bridge these two sections of mystical philosophy. The final part of the portion of *The Ascent of Mount Carmel* that Eliot quotes completes his thought: "[i]n detachment the spirit finds quiet and repose, for coveting nothing, nothing wearies it by elation, and nothing oppresses it by dejection, because it stands in the centre of its own humility; for as soon as it covets anything it is immediately fatigued thereby" (*Ascent of Mount Carmel* I.xiii.12).[27] Here is the centering of this seemingly apophatic statement in the virtue of humility that Eliot declares to be "endless" in the poem. "The detachment of the mystic is just a restoration to the liberty in which the soul was made: it is a state of joyous humility in which he cries, 'Naught I am, naught I have, naught I lack'" (Underhill 261). This is yet another place in *Four Quartets* where, centered in the orthodoxy of the Christian mystical tradition, Eliot can be found embracing the ascetic ideal and making it his.[28]

One of the other major loci of asceticism in "East Coker" is in Part IV, which begins:

> The wounded surgeon plies the steel
> That questions the distempered part;
> Beneath the bleeding hands we feel
> The sharp compassion of the healer's art
> Resolving the enigma of the fever chart.

"East Coker" IV.1–5.

Now before discussing the more obvious asceticism deeper within this section, I would first like to consider the seemingly eccentric physician metaphor beyond the sources listed in the *Collected Poems*[29] as it actually has a rather venerable tradition worth examining in an ascetic context. Eliot first came

---

26  Cp. Eliot's "Their fear of possession / [o]f belonging to themselves, to another or God" ("East Coker" II.45–6).

27  Again, Eliot encountered this in Underhill 249.

28  Cf. Schuchard 191.

29  Cf. *Poems* I.946–50.

across this in the fragments of Heraclitus which heightens the the relevance to *Four Quartets*. Eliot read that "[t]he physicians, therefore, says Heraclitus, cutting, cauterizing, and in every way torturing the sick, complain that patients do not pay them fitting reward for thus effecting those benefits—and sufferings" (Heraclitus qtd. in Patrick 98). As seen in G. T. W. Patrick's notes,[30] this idea is expanded upon in Plato's *Gorgias* where the physician is given a moral angle as Eliot, also, read:

> [the rhetorician] should bring to light the iniquity and not conceal it, that so the wrong-doer may suffer and be made whole; and he should even force himself and others not to shrink, but with closed eyes like brave men to let the physician operate with knife or searing iron, not regarding the pain, in the hope of attaining the good and the honorable; let him who has done things worthy of stripes, allow himself to be scourged, if of bonds, to be bound, if of a fine, to be fined, if of exile, to be exiled, if of death, to die, himself being the first to accuse himself and his own relations, and using rhetoric to this end, that his and their unjust actions may be made manifest, and that they themselves may be delivered from injustice, which is the greatest evil.
>
> *Gorgias* §480c–d[31]

That Eliot was aware of the ascetic impulse inherent in the physician metaphor is certain because his own notes on the *Gorgias* from approximately 1914 survive in Harvard, and there he wrote, in the broken style of lecture notes, that

> It is better for the wrongdoer to suffer[—]better to be wicked and fail than to be wicked and prosper—Punishment chastens. The misfortune descending after crime is a benefit. Here Plato turns away from the

---

30    As discussed in Chapter 1, Patrick's edition of Heraclitus is the one recorded in Eliot's notecards.

31    This idea is repeated towards the ending of the dialogue with an almost messianic overtone where Socrates states: "I shall be tried just as a physician would be tried in a court of little boys at the indictment of the cook. What would he reply under such circumstances, if some one were to accuse him, saying, 'O my boys, many evil things has this man done to you: he is the death of you, especially of the younger ones among you, cutting and burning and starving and suffocating you, until you know not what to do; he gives you the bitterest potions, and compels you to hunger and thirst. How unlike the variety of meats and sweets on which I feasted you!' What do you suppose that the physician would be able to reply when he found himself in such a predicament? If he told the truth he could only say, 'All these evil things, my boys, I did for your health,' and then would there not just be a clamor among a jury like that? How they would cry out! (*Gorgias* §521e–522a)."

# EMBRACING

ancient world. An ascetic theory of spiritual good.—theory of penance.[32] The mediaeval world. Exaltation of righteousness—concerns the honor of the universe. St Augustine—Hell is a remedy to cure the world, and even the innocent should be willing to suffer[.] If one man does good[,] the whole world prospers. If one does evil, the whole world is stained. The doctrine of the Atonement.[33]

> "Notes on Philosophy (9)" 45.

Although "East Coker" was written nearly thirty years later, I doubt the later Eliot would have appropriated this physician metaphor for a different purpose than displaying "an ascetic theory of spiritual good" which can only be the ascetic ideal ("Notes on Philosophy (9)" 45). The ascetic casting of the physician, then, makes the immediate transition to an image of purgation in the fourth stanza of "East Coker" IV quite natural:[34]

> The chill ascends from feet to knees,
> The fever sings in mental wires.
> If to be warmed, then I must freeze
> And quake in frigid purgatorial fires
> Of which the flame is roses, and the smoke is briars.
> "East Coker" 164–8.

Now, Eliot here draws on Underhill's descriptions of the Dark Night as a "dark fire of purification" marked by "[i]mpotence, blankness, and solitude" (Underhill 454).[35] It is a period where "not only the transcendent vision [is] withdrawn, but [the mystic's] very desire for, and interest in, that vision should grow cold" (Underhill 467). These various images are condensed by Eliot into the stanza, in which the attendant asceticism is so obvious as to require no general exposition. Nonetheless, there are a few matters which investigation may render more lucid.

---

32  A difficult reading in the manuscript.

33  This final phrase is set off from the others and centered on the page, seemingly for emphasis.

34  Murray's assertion that this passage is indebted to Sor Maria della Antiqua is less convincing (Murray 68–9).

35  As mentioned before, a more biographically-minded critic would find much in Underhill's description of the Dark Night as analogous to how "many seers and artists pay [...] by agonizing periods of impotence and depression for each violent outburst of creative energy" (Underhill 457).

The first is Eliot's phrase "[i]f to be warmed," which, as an anacoluthon, requires some grammatical exposition. Now, the phrase seems to elide the grammatical subject and the copula—presumably, "I am"; however, the real difficulty is in the unusual subject-complement, the passive infinitive "to be warmed," which has the force of a Latin passive periphrastic (and an attendant futurity). This structure is further situated within a conditional clause. Thus, the phrase written in full would be "If I am to be warmed." This indicates a passivity on the part of the speaker, as he renders himself available to being warmed; the warming, however, is independent of his action and might not transpire as indicated by the condition.[36] The passivity of the speaker as rendered by the grammar is analogous to the passage into the mystical Dark Night where it is necessary that "the soul which is reduced to Nothing, ought to dwell therein; without wishing, since she is now but dust, to issue from this state, nor, as before, desiring to live again" (Madame Guyon qtd. in Underhill 479).[37] Underhill's five-step process does forbid the artist from the Dark Night and consequent ultimate vision. However, she does allow an analogous action, noting that

> A total abandonment of the individualistic standpoint, of that trivial and egotistic quest of personal satisfaction [which is the ultimate purpose of the Dark Night and] thwarts the great movement of the Flowing Light, is the supreme condition of man's participation in Reality. This is true not only of the complete participation which is possible to the great mystic, but of those unselfish labors in which the initiates of science or of art become to the Eternal Goodness "what his own hand is to a man."
> Underhill 473.

In this context, the warmth would, of course, be the return of the Divine impulse or creativity—to say which would be reductive—instead of the icy aridity of the Dark Night.

The second phrase of interest is the "flame is roses and smoke is briars."[38] This is also an example of Eliot's compression of orthodox mystical doctrines

---

36    In Eliot's readings, this passivity is particular to mysticism rather than magic which focuses on the active will. Cf. Underhill 83–5.

37    This passage is intriguing in light of what the bones sing in *Ash-Wednesday* II; however, it seems that a strict application would be reductive in that passage.

38    There is the possibility that this image is drawn from Chapter 8 of George MacDonald's *The Princess and the Curdie* which describes how "on a huge hearth a great fire was burning, and the fire was a huge heap of roses, and yet it was fire" in which Curdie must clean his hands (*The Princess and the Curdie* 69). As there is no evidence, to my knowledge, that

EMBRACING 151

into poetry. Of the many connotations of roses, their use as the representation of the divine fullness in Dante[39] is the most relevant. If this is so, there appears to be a very serious paradox in Eliot's argumentation. After all, if the Dark Night is the deprivation of God, then how can the "frigid purgatorial fires" be the Divine Rose? The answer is that Eliot's work is a faithful depiction of the paradox inherent in the conception of the Divine Darkness. St John of the Cross explains in *The Dark Night of the Soul* that

> This dark night is an inflowing of God into the soul, which purges it from its ignorances and imperfections, habitual natural and spiritual, and which is called by contemplatives infused contemplation, or mystical theology. Herein God secretly teaches the soul and instructs it in perfection of love without its doing anything, or understanding of what manner is this infused contemplation. Inasmuch as it is the loving wisdom of God, God produces striking effects in the soul for, by purging and illumining it, He prepares it for the union of love with God. Wherefore the same loving wisdom that purges the blessed spirits and enlightens them is that which here purges the soul and illumines it. [...] A thing of great wonder and pity is it that the soul's weakness and impurity should now be so great that, though the hand of God is of itself so light and gentle, the soul should now feel it to be so heavy and so contrary, though it neither weighs it down nor rests upon it, but only touches it, and that mercifully, since He does this in order to grant the soul favors and not to chastise it.
> *Dark Night of the Soul* II.v.1,7[40]

This is the exact collocation of elements seen in this passage of "East Coker"; a purgation from dwelling within the Divine who is nonetheless felt to be absent. This purgation is then the "sharp compassion of the healer's art" ("East Coker" 152). While this is certainly complex, Eliot's use of this is certainly well within the orthodoxy of the mystical readings, and a further confirmation of how profoundly the mature Eliot has embraced the ascetic ideal articulated in those early readings.

While "The Dry Salvages" is not as involved with ascetic ideals as "East Coker" and "Little Gidding," there are still a few passages of interest, primarily in

---

Eliot read MacDonald and both could easily have derived the image independently from Dante, it seems, on the whole, unlikely, although a complete investigation is beyond the scope of this study. I am, nonetheless, indebted to my colleague John Pazdziora for alerting me to this passage.

39   Cf. *Paradiso* XXX–XXXI.

40   Eliot first encountered this passage and idea in Underhill 477.

the final portion of the poem. A close reading will show that here too Eliot is echoing the ascetic ideal as he found it in the mystical traditions:[41]

> But to apprehend
> The point of intersection of the timeless
> With time, is an occupation for the saint—
> No occupation either, but something given
> And taken, in a lifetime's death in love,
> Ardour and selflessness and self-surrender.
> For most of us, there is only the unattended
> Moment, the moment in and out of time,
> The distraction fit, lost in a shaft of sunlight,
> The wild thyme unseen, or the winter lightning
> Or the waterfall, or music heard so deeply
> That it is not heard at all, but you are the music
> While the music lasts.
> > "The Dry Salvages" v.17–29.

It may seem curious upon initial inspection that a saint would be involved in something esoteric as "the point of intersection of the timeless / [w]ith time"; however, this is simply a rephrasing, in terms already seen within the poem, of Inge's definition of mysticism "as the attempt to realize the presence of the living God in the soul and in nature, or more generally, as *the attempt to realize, in thought and feeling, the immanence of the temporal in the eternal, and of the eternal in the temporal*" [italics his] ("The Dry Salvages" 205–6; Inge *Christian Mysticism* 5). Here, without equivocation, Eliot is restating the orthodox conception of mysticism, although whether he consulted Inge or had so absorbed it as to paraphrase the definition, unintentionally is, for the purposes of my argument here, irrelevant.

The phrase "a lifetime's death in love" as a poetic statement of the ascetic ideal may also have some antecedents in the mystical tradition—and, what is surprising, in F. H. Bradley's *Appearance and Reality*. Eliot first encountered this idea most clearly in Inge's *Personal Idealism and Mysticism* where he read that

---

41    Murray's assertion that "Dry Salvages" represents a significant change in Eliot's thinking on mysticism is unconvincing (Murray 104–7). However, Murray's assertion that mystical Illumination fades with age is consistent with the orthodox mystical readings. Cf. Inge *Christian Mysticism* 218–9.

EMBRACING                                                                  153

Clement of Alexandria tells us that faith, the first stage of our course, and love, the last, "are not taught": there is a spontaneity in them which is lacking in the long day's work. Platonism and Christianity are at one in representing the final consummation as a passing of knowledge into love. The "intellect in love" loses itself in the supreme transit which is its goal and the end of its labors.

> INGE *Personal Idealism* 12–3.

The phrase "intellect in love" is related to one that Eliot used before; in a much less orthodox vein early in his life, he states that "without a labor which is largely a labor of intelligence, we are unable to attain to that stage of vision *amor intellectualis Dei*" (*Prose* II.269).[42] Here knowledge, in contradistinction to both the orthodox mystical authors and the Eliot of *Four Quartets*, is the means to attain revelation.[43] Nonetheless, Eliot did see this idea outside of the mystical literature, even if he did not immediately adopt it; Bradley, in a rather poetic flourish, writes

> Let us pass to another objection against our view. We may be told that the End [the Absolute], because it is that which thought aims at, is therefore itself (mere) thought. This assumes that thought cannot desire a consummation in which it is lost. But does not the river run into the sea and the self lose itself in love?

> BRADLEY 173.

This is, of course, not the only place Eliot saw this concept; Heraclitus states that "[i]t is hard to contend against passion, for whatever it craves, it buys with its life" (Heraclitus qtd. in Patrick 109). Indeed, Eliot himself says something similar in his first essay on Dante where he writes that "the true mystic is not

---

42    The terms are related elsewhere in Inge: "The intellectual life has its mystical state, when the religious philosopher, whose thoughts have long been concentrated upon the deeper problems of existence, endeavouring to find the unity which underlies all diversity, the harmony which reconciles all contradictions, seems to behold what he sought in a blank trance which imposes silence on all the faculties, even the restless discursive intellect, and unites the thinker for a few moments with the primal source of all thought, the ineffable One. Such was the goal of the 'intellect in love' ([νοός] ἐρῶν) of Plotinus, and the *amor intellectualis Dei* of Spinoza" (Inge *English Mystics* 7–8).

43    The best expression of this is from *The Cloud of Unknowing*, where he read "By love may [God] be gotten and holden; but by thought never" (*Cloud of Unknowing* VI). Eliot also read this line in Underhill 57 and Jones 337.

satisfied merely by feeling, he must pretend at least that he *sees*, and the absorption into the divine is only the necessary, if paradoxical, limit of this contemplation" (*Prose* II.233). In terms of the ascetic ideal—which, let me be clear, is only one way of interpreting this passage—this phrase should be read as the death to the self that is necessary for revelation, especially the saints. Eliot read that for the mystic "to learn to suffer and to learn to die; this is the gymnastic of eternity, the noviciate of Immortal life"—but this is always a labor of love for "mystical exercises are exercises of *love* rather than of *thought*" (Underhill 196, Jones 307). The Blessed Henry Suso writes that "[b]y ancient right, love and suffering go together. There is no wooer but he is a sufferer; no lover but he is a martyr" (Suso IV).[44] The appositive, "ardor, selflessness, and self-surrender" confirms this passage may be read ascetically.

The following phrase, "[f]or most of us, there is only" still echoes orthodoxy in that the ultimate vision is inaccessible except to the saint; however, as emphasized in Underhill, Eliot did believe that *something* is accessible to those who are not mystics. After all, "[n]o deeply religious man is without a touch of mysticism," and the "unattended moment" which Eliot proceeds to describe is characteristic of the state of Illumination (Underhill 84).[45] Underhill notes that Illumination "is popularly supposed to be peculiar to the mystic"; however, again, these orthodox readings state otherwise (Underhill 279). As she notes later, "[t]o 'see God in nature,' to attain a radiant consciousness of the 'otherness' of natural things, is the simplest and commonest form of illumination. Most people, under the spell of emotion or beauty, have known flashes of rudimentary vision of this kind" (Underhill 282). It is in this light that Eliot describes, as he did in "East Coker," a series of natural objects, such as "winter lightning," coupled with the description of a "moment in and out of time" ("The Dry Salvages" v.25–7). Now, timelessness as a means of describing Illumination is easily seen in "Burnt Norton." Clearly, this indicates that Eliot is ascribing, within the orthodoxy of the mystical tradition, this illuminative experience to a much broader swathe of the population than just the cloistered saints. He says as much himself in his introduction to the Pensées of Pascal—"but what can only be called mystical experience happens to many men who do not become mystics" (*Prose* IV.340). As Underhill rather poetically notes, "*l'amor che move il sole e le altre stelle* is the motive force of the spirit of man: in the

---

44  Eliot also encountered this passage in Underhill 267.

45  While beyond the pale of this study, Eliot states something similar of his personal experience (Eliot qtd. in *Poems* I.985).

EMBRACING                                                                     155

inventors, the philosophers, and the artists, no less than in the heroes and the saints" (Underhill 56).[46]

The much-discussed description[47] of "music heard so deeply / [t]hat it is not heard at all, but you are the music / [w]hile the music lasts" requires some additional explication ("The Dry Salvages" v.28–9). There are many possible sources for this line, including mere observation; however, this phrase too, as a description, is well-grounded in the mystical tradition. Eliot first encountered the idea in Starbuck's *Psychology of Religion* where in a discussion of sanctification, he states that "a musician may suddenly reach a point at which pleasure in the technique of the art entirely falls away and in some moment of inspiration he becomes the instrument through which the music flows" (Starbuck 385).[48] There are, though, more timely possibilities. Underhill, in her chapter on the Characteristics of Mysticism, engages in a long discussion between music and mystical thought, of which the following lengthy quotation is only a brief excerpt.

> The mystic, too, tries very hard to tell an unwilling world his secret. But in his case, the difficulties are enormously increased. First, there is the huge disparity between his unspeakable experience and the language which will most nearly suggest it. Next, there is the great gulf fixed between his mind and the mind of the world. His audience must be bewitched as well as addressed, caught up to something of his state, before they can be made to understand.[49]
>
> Were he a musician, it is probable that the mystic could give his message to other musicians in the terms of that art, far more accurately than language will allow him to do: for we must remember that there is no excuse but that of convenience for the pre-eminence amongst modes of expression which we accord to words. These correspond so well to the physical plane and its adventures, that we forget that they have but the faintest of relations with transcendental things. Even the artist, before he can make use of them, is bound to re-arrange them in accordance with the laws of rhythm: obeying unconsciously the rule by which all arts "tend to approach the condition of music."

---

46    Underhill quotes *Paradiso* XXXIII:143 in Italian.

47    An abbreviated version of this discussion here is included in *Poems* I.986.

48    I provided this citation to the *Collected Poems* from an earlier draft of this study.

49    Though beyond the scope of this study, the resemblance of this statement to Eliot's assertion that "genuine poetry can communicate before it is understood" has, to my knowledge, never been fully examined (*Prose* III.701).

156  CHAPTER 7

So too the mystic. Mysticism, the most romantic of adventures, from one point of view the art of arts, their source and also their end, finds naturally enough its closest correspondences in the most purely artistic and most deeply significant of all forms of expression. The mystery of music is seldom realized by those who so easily accept its gifts. Yet of all the arts music alone shares with great mystical literature the power of waking in us a response to the life-movement of the universe: brings us— we know not how—news of its exultant passions and its incomparable peace. Beethoven heard the very voice of Reality, and little of it escaped when he translated it for our ears.

UNDERHILL 90–1.

It may not be coincidence that Underhill uses Beethoven as her example, and that Eliot speaks of hearing in Beethoven's A-minor quartet a kind of inhuman joy beyond tremendous suffering—perhaps the illumination that follows purgation (Ackroyd 189). The description of music and mysticism found here is wholly consistent with Eliot's poem.[50] Here too is evidence of Eliot embracing the ascetic ideal in his poetry.

This portion of "The Dry Salvages" also contains one of the more interesting loci of the orthodox mystical tradition.

The hint half guessed, the gift half understood, is Incarnation.
Here the impossible union
Of spheres of existence is actual.

"The Dry Salvages" 219–21.

I will not digress into the importance of the Incarnation in mystical theology; instead, I would like to focus on the reference to uniting spheres of existence.[51] The difficulty of this is that the passage refers to two distinct concepts simultaneously: the first, though probably secondary meaning, being the union of monads of both man and man, and man and God. This was, of course, an unattainable ideal when Eliot discussed it in "Gerontion," *The Waste Land*, and "The Hollow Men," but here it is allowed by the dogma of the Incarnate λόγος. The second may also, in a way that is not intrinsically ascetic, refer to the union of the Divine and human existences in the person of Christ.[52]

---

50  Cf. Murray 21–2.

51  The socio-political possibility that this is derived from Martin Luther's doctrine of the two kingdoms in *The Solid Declaration of Concord* VI is not here explored.

52  To summarize the point succinctly, Inge states, "[h]ence the necessity for the Incarnation. The union of the Divine and human life, to make man again a partaker of the Divine nature, is the only possible salvation for man" (Inge *English Mystics* 163).

EMBRACING                                                                                                    157

In discussing the first meaning, I will not repeat the argumentation of Chapter 4. Instead, showing the union of spheres of existence is both long-desired and orthodox will be enough. Eliot has discussed the idea before during his doctoral dissertation, noting that

> The point of view (or finite center) has for its object one consistent world, and accordingly, no finite center can be self-sufficient, for the life of the soul does not consist of the contemplation of one consistent world but in the painful task of unifying (to a greater or lesser extent) jarring and incompatible ones, and passing, when possible, between two or more discordant viewpoints to a higher which shall somehow include and transmute them.
>
> *Prose* I.362.

Here, the idea of uniting finite centers is shown as a kind of Hegelian dialectic, but Eliot discussed this same concept in terms of individuals more clearly in his earlier student papers. He states that "a finite center is exclusive, in that you cannot go in or out with impunity. You cannot, without completely abandoning your point of view, completely understand that of another. I do not say that a point of view may not be transcended or that two points of view may not melt in to each other; but in this transformation the ingredients have ceased to exist" (*Prose* I.175). These statements by Eliot as a young man are in contradistinction to both what is read in *Four Quartets* and many of the most orthodox Christian authors. As Inge notes,

> So far is it from being true that the self of our immediate consciousness is our true personality, that we can only attain personality, as spiritual and rational beings, by passing beyond the limits which mark us off as separate individuals. Separate individuality, we may say, is the bar which prevents us from realizing our true privileges as persons.
>
> INGE *Christian Mysticism* 51.

As early as his Clark Lectures, Eliot wondered if the notion of the *fusion* of souls expressed in Donne's verse was "strictly orthodox," but he drops the question under the admission that he was "not qualified to express an opinion" (*Prose* II.658). Let me say, though, that what is being expressed in both Inge and in "The Dry Salvages" is not fusion. This may seem counterintuitive, but consider Jones's comment that "[w]e often have such experiences in some degree. All our high moments of beauty, of love, of worship are experiences beyond the subject-object type of consciousness" (Jones 76). This is complete communion, but it is not fusion. While tied to the images of nature and music earlier, this effect of communion with other spheres of existence is generated by the λόγος. Eliot read that, in a philosophical conception descended from the Stoics, "we have communion with each other through our participation in the [λόγος], which remains one and the self-same spirit" (Inge *Personal Idealism* 44). An application of this may not seem germane to *Four Quartets*; however, let me remind of the first, and oft-neglected, quotation from Heraclitus that opens "Burnt Norton": τοῦ λόγου δ' ἐόντος ξυνοῦ—"λόγος is common to all." Underhill elaborates on this in her discussion of Vitalism *i.e.* Bergsonism:

> Union with reality—apprehension of it—will upon this hypothesis be union with life at its most intense point: in its most dynamic aspect. It will be a deliberate harmony set up with the [λόγος] which [Heraclitus] described as "man's most constant companion." Ergo, says the mystic, union with a Personal and Conscious spiritual existence, immanent in the world—one form, one half of the union which I have always sought, since this is clearly life in its highest manifestation. Beauty, Goodness, Splendor, Love, all those shining words which exhilarate the soul, are but the names of aspects or qualities picked out by human intuition as characteristic of this intense and eternal Life in which is the life of men.
> UNDERHILL 35.

In short, the Incarnate Word allows for the otherwise impossible communion between finite centers, and here, as ever, Eliot is resting in the orthodoxy of the mystical tradition by indicating the way in which the soul purified may have communion with others.

While this is a desirable goal, it is one only possible for brief moments, "and the rest / [i]s prayer, observance, discipline, thought and action" ("The Dry Salvages" v.30–1). In other words, that a life of ritual and discipline is typical for the average believer. The connection between discipline and the ascetic ideal has already been made, but the poem further highlights this tie with the wordplay in the final line. Consider,

> We, content at the last
> If our temporal reversion nourish
> (Not too far from the yew-tree)
> The life of significant soil.
> "The Dry Salvages" 234–7.

The phrase "temporal reversion" is, admittedly, confusing to me, but I must take it to refer to the aforementioned timelessness of contemplation—not the

EMBRACING

rewinding of time, but the *un*winding, not reversing time, but undoing the imposition of time, making things Eternal. The asceticism is located in the final two words: "significant soil" as it means both earth but also stain—sin. Thus, the impurities of the self are significant when they are the ground from which spiritual growth occurs.

The ascetic ideal is apparent often in "Little Gidding," but in light of the previous discussions and Chapters 11 and 12 of Murray's work, I will focus on three primary aspects here (Murray 197–255). The first is the ascetic collocation of God and the imagery of fire. The second is a brief close-reading of "Little Gidding IV." The third is a discussion of the ending of "Little Gidding" as the consummation of mystical religion. These will suffice to show how Eliot has made the ascetic ideal in the mystical readings his.

The image of fire as an expression of God is as ancient as Heraclitus.[53] Nonetheless, the image in the mystical readings carries a strong ascetic overtone.[54] This may seem a divergent point from the Pentecostal fire signifying the divine presence; however, the image is biblical in its origins. The divine presence and the purifying fire being the same is most succinctly seen in Thomas à Kempis.[55] While it is difficult to imagine that Eliot would not have read *De Imitatione Christi*, I have here quoted Jones as this was likely the context he first encountered these quotations, and the juxtaposition of these sundry extracts enhances the ascetic tone to the passage:

> "The saints of God [...] ravished above self and drawn out of love of self, plunged wholly into love of Me (Christ): in whom also they rest in fruition. Nothing can turn them back or hold them down, for being full of eternal truth, they burn with the fire of unquenchable love" [...] The saints of God, and all the devoted friends and followers of Christ, regarded not the things that gratified the appetites of the flesh, nor those that were the object of popular esteem and pursuit; but their hope and desire panted for the purity and glory of the celestial kingdom: their whole soul was continually elevated to the eternal and invisible" [...] "Love panteth after its original and native freedom.... Nothing is sweeter than love, nothing stronger, nothing loftier, nothing broader, nothing pleasanter, nothing

---

53    Cf. Underhill 32.

54    It is of minor relevance that the Greek word for fire used in Heraclitus, πῦρ, is nearly homophonic with the English "pure."

55    Cf. Ezekiel 8:1–2. In addition to Eliot's seeming fondness for the book of Ezekiel, this passage is highlighted by J. B. Pratt's *The Psychology of Religion*. Cf. Pratt 142.

fuller or better in heaven or in earth; for love is born of God, and cannot rest save in God from whom it is derived".

THOMAS À KEMPIS qtd. in JONES 328.

This is not the only place in which fire is tied to purgation, of course. In his introduction to St Teresa of Aviles and St John of the Cross, Inge, with his characteristic dislike of Roman Catholicism,[56] asserts that "we must not expect to find in St. Teresa and St. Juan any of the characteristic independence of Mysticism. The inner light which they sought was not an illumination of the intellect in its search for truth, but a consuming fire to burn up all earthly passions and desires" (Inge *Christian Mysticism* 217–8). This characterization of God as fire is not restricted even to the mystical readings as it also appears in Pascal's memorial.[57]

Moreover, Eliot himself used this idea in his poem "Elegy" where God is portrayed "in a rolling ball of fire / pursu[ing] by day my errant feet. / His flames of anger and desire / [a]pproach me with consuming heat" (Elegy 21–5). Obviously, this early poem has some interesting deviations from orthodoxy in *Four Quartets*; the well-known story in Exodus 13:21 has Yahweh going before the Israelites in a pillar of cloud by day and fire by night. The origin of the "rolling ball" may derive from what Eliot read of Theophrastus's description of Anaximander's generation of the Heavens. "[Anaximander] says that something capable of begetting hot and cold out of the eternal was separated off at the origin of this world. From this arose a sphere of flame which fitted close round the air surrounding the earth as the bark round a tree" (Theophrastus qtd. in Burnet 70). Regardless of the curious origin of the images, even as early as this fragment, the image of the Divine as a fire, both loving and wrathful is seen, and it is a common one as Underhill notes, "fire imagery has seemed to many of the mystics a peculiarly exact and suggestive symbol for the transcendent state which they are struggling to describe" (Underhill 503).

The apotheosis of the ascetic ideal in Eliot's work may be in "Little Gidding" IV, which follows in its entirety. It is not strongly derived from any of the mystical readings but instead represents an original, though very orthodox, statement of the ascetic ideal.

> The dove descending breaks the air
> With flame of incandescent terror

---

56   Cf. Inge *Christian Mysticism* xviii–ix.

57   Eliot discusses the memorial for over a paragraph in his introduction to Pascal's *Pensees*; it is firmly delineated as a mystical experience (*Prose* IV.340). For further application of Pascal's Memorial to Eliot, cf. Kendall 301–4.

EMBRACING                                                            161

> Of which the tongues declare
> The one discharge from sin and error.
> The only hope, or else despair
> Lies in the choice of pyre or pyre—
> To be redeemed from fire by fire.
>> "Little Gidding" IV.1–7.

While this section is, at the very least, concerned with the Blitz, it is just as much, if not more, concerned with theological matters. The connection between the two is drawn by Eliot himself. In a letter to Mary Trevelyan dated 24th of June 1944, Eliot, in an apparent flight of morbid fancy when imagining an excuse for Mary to escape an unwanted social engagement, states "[a]s to the Poetry Reading, I have an idea. On Thursday night, or rather early Friday morning, one of these things descended in Russell Square. The office and the flat were blasted: fortunately, both the Fabers and I had retired to the country, he suffering from hay fever, and I from lack of sleep, and still more fortunately, no one was injured" ("Letters to Mary Trevelyan" June 24 1944). Eliot then proceeds for over a page to elaborate on this macabre scenario. This is followed, quite curiously, by a paragraph, apparently at Trevelyan's prompting, where Eliot mentions efforts to move "[his] wife," Vivienne, for safety but says that he can't and only Maurice, her brother, could do so as Eliot has "no official standing in the matter" ("Letters to Mary Trevelyan" June 24 1944). The juxtaposition of this dark imagination with the situation of his difficult marriage is very interesting given the discussion of love in "Little Gidding" IV. Nonetheless, it is the letter's ending, in which Eliot states that "[i]f one is also of a worrying disposition, as I am, one worries about all the possible consequences short of death, even the more trivial ones like how one is to get any clothes, or carry out an important engagement in nothing but a shirt and trousers. But there is something else which I can't get to the bottom of, disgust, horror, physical nausea, the *nightmare* of evil" ("Letters to Mary Trevelyan" June 24 1944). This final comment bubbles up unexpectedly in the letter and shows the theological implications latent in Eliot's consideration of the Blitz. This letter's applicability to "Little Gidding" is seen both in its timeliness and in the echoed wording: the word "descend" is used of both dove[58] and bomb—the latter of which Eliot will not even name directly.

A close-reading of the poem itself will highlight the ascetic ideal. Eliot writes that "the one discharge from sin and error" "lies in the choice of pyre or

---

58    It is possible, though somewhat tangentially, that Eliot has in mind Récéjac's rather flashing phrase that "mystics have been conscious in their minds of 'a dove' of 'flames'" (Récéjac 156).

162                                                                                      CHAPTER 7

pyre / [t]o be redeemed from fire, by fire" ("Little Gidding" IV.4,6–7). These lines work via wordplay. The "discharge" of sin and error can be "release" as in discharged from prison but also discharge as in the emission of festering sore. As such, the penultimate and final line both hinge on the wordplay of fire used as imagery of sin and as an image of purgation. The former is most prominently seen in the Buddha's Fire Sermon; however, it is not unknown in the mystical readings. As Eliot read, "[t]here is no wrath that stands between God and us, but what is awakened in the dark fire of our own fallen nature" (Law qtd. in Inge *English Mystics* 147). The imagery of fire as purification requires no exposition, especially in light of Eliot's fondness for the episode of Arnaut Daniel in *Purgatorio* XXVI. "To be redeemed from fire by fire" is itself only an elegant restatement of "Love submits itself to the fire of wrath that it might become a fire of love," or as Eliot himself says in "The Idea of a Christian Society," "That prospect, [becoming a Christian] involves at least, discipline, inconvenience, and discomfort: but here as hereafter the alternative to hell is purgatory" (Jacob of Böhme qtd. in Inge *English Mystics* 142; *Prose* V.694–5). The appearance of love in this quotation explains its inclusion inclusion in the second stanza.

> Who then devised the torment? Love.
> Love is the unfamiliar Name
> Behind the hands that wove
> The intolerable shirt of flame
> Which human power cannot remove.
> > We only live, only suspire
> > Consumed by either fire or fire.
> > > "Little Gidding" 209–15.

While this stanza may seem bewilderingly contradictory, it is wholly in-line with the mystical tradition. For example, Eliot read of St Catherine of Genoa, "[a]s she, plunged in the divine furnace of purifying love, was united to the Object of her love, and satisfied with all he wrought in her, so she understood it to be with the souls in Purgatory" (St Catherine qtd. in Underhill 226). The allusion to the death of Hercules in the "intolerable shirt of flame" is carefully wrought. After all, it is for love, albeit a jealous one, that Deianira gives him the poisoned shirt of Nessus, and there is a purgatorial aspect to this allusion as well as the fire burns away his mortal side and leaves only that which is divine in him (*Poems* I.1039).[59] Corollary to the previous stanza, there is only the choice of the fire of love and the concomitant purgation from sin or the fire of

---

59      Cf. *Metamorphoses* IX:98–272.

EMBRACING                                                                                       163

wrath and desire. This is a very clear statement of the ascetic ideal found, not only in Dante, but in the mystical readings as well.

Yet, at the end of "Little Gidding," Eliot also explores the end of the ascetic ideal. The relevant portion of the final lines is as follows:

> A condition of complete simplicity
> (Costing not less than everything)
> And all shall be well and
> All manner of things shall be well
> When the tongues of flame are in-folded
> Into the crowned knot of fire
> And the fire and the rose are one.
>> "Little Gidding" v.40–6.

While this is not obviously ascetic, a few final forays into Eliot's mystical readings will show the clear presence of the ascetic ideal. The lines above are, of course, about many things; however, purgation is one of them. The term here "condition of complete simplicity" is the end of the ascetic ideal.[60] As Eliot read in Underhill:

> "The essence of purgation," says Richard of St Victor, "is self-simplification." Nothing can happen until this has proceeded a certain distance: till the involved interests and tangled motives of the self are simplified, and the false complications of temporal life are recognized and cast away.
>> UNDERHILL 246.

Thus, a "condition of complete simplicity" is both the goal and the completion of purgation. The following phrase "[c]osting not less than everything" is simply explained. Underhill states, "[b]y Poverty, the mystic means an utter self-stripping, the casting off of immaterial as well as material wealth, a complete detachment from all finite things" (Underhill 247).

After this, Eliot repeats Julian of Norwich's "All shall be well and all manner of things shall be well." However, here, he departs from the saint with the "when." What is actually happening, I believe, is that Eliot is answering the

---

60    Cf. the following passage by Eliot's professor, J. H. Woods: "Do we not feel that in our harsh and greedy modern life we have lost something which these tireless wandering dreamers [the great mystics] found, and are we not the poorer when they take to their path again and leave us, with our machinery and our possessions and our piled-up furniture, feeling vulgar and needy and wondering through what ages of striving we must pass before we can approach their simplicity?" (Woods *Religious Facts* 99).

164 CHAPTER 7

question of Julian of Norwich by echoing, in a humble fashion, the final vision of Dante. Yet, in all of this, Eliot is also giving the answer of his orthodox mystical readings for what lies beyond asceticism in poetry. The question that Julian of Norwich asks is *how* all shall be well. In her own words,

> And thus signifieth He when He saith: Thou shalt see thyself [that] all manner of things shall be well. As if He said: Take now heed faithfully and trustingly, and at the last end thou shalt verily see it in fulness of joy.
>
> And thus in these same five words aforesaid: I may make all things well, etc., I understand a mighty comfort of all the works of our Lord God that are yet to come. There is a Deed the which the blessed Trinity shall do in the last Day, as to my sight, and when the Deed shall be, and how it shall be done, is unknown of all creatures that are beneath Christ, and shall be till when it is done.
>
> Julian of Norwich XXXII.

Yet, Eliot here provides something of an answer with the conjunction—all shall be well [...] / [w]hen" ("Little Gidding" v.42–4). Though Eliot, as he does elsewhere, declines the ultimate mystical vision; he posits a fulfillment that he does not actually see. At the risk of gross anachronism, consider what he says in his very first essay on Dante: "But the true mystic is not satisfied merely by feeling, he must pretend at least that he *sees*, and the absorption into the divine is only the necessary, if paradoxical, limit of this contemplation" (*Prose* II.233). This is what occurs at the end of "Little Gidding"—as Underhill says, in her chapter on contemplation, "Dante tells us how he pierced, for an instant, the secret of the Empyrean. Already he had enjoyed a symbolic vision of two-fold Reality, as the moving River of Light and the still White Rose. Now these two aspects vanish, and he saw the One" (Underhill 406). However, what Dante, the true mystic, sees, Eliot the mystically-inclined artist is left to posit dogmatically. In the poem, he does not claim a vision of this, but rather asserts that all shall be well *when* the fire and the rose are one.

According to Eliot's mystical readings, the fire and the rose in "Little Gidding" are equivalent to the final beatific vision of Dante. Just a few lines before the previous quotation, Underhill states that

> Certain rare mystics seem to be able to describe to us a Beatific Vision experienced here and now: a knowledge by contact of the flaming heart of Reality, which includes in one great whole the planes of Being and Becoming, the simultaneous and the Successive, the Eternal Father, and His manifestation in the "energetic Word"
>
> UNDERHILL 340.

EMBRACING 165

Obviously, she intends Dante's Rose to be the Eternal Father, and the Fire to be the λόγος.[61] Eliot seems to concur when he states that it is "the tongues of flame in-folded / [i]nto the crowned knot of fire" ("Little Gidding" v.44–6). Now, the tongues of flame seem to be primarily a reference to Acts 2:3[62] and as such, the collected church folds into the Divine λόγος, which might seem highly heterodox, and yet, it is what Julian of Norwich means when she says:

> Wherefore He would have us understand that the noblest thing that ever He made is mankind: and the fullest Substance and the highest Virtue is the blessed Soul of Christ. And furthermore He would have us understand that His dearworthy Soul [of Manhood] was preciously knit to Him in the making [by Him of Manhood's Substantial Nature] which knot is so subtle and so mighty that (it)—[man's soul]—is oned into God: in which oneing it is made endlessly holy. Furthermore He would have us know that all the souls that shall be saved in Heaven without end, are knit and oned in this oneing and made holy in this holiness.
>
> Julian of Norwich LIII.

This certainly within the orthodox mystical tradition as well as the philosophical one. As Eliot read in the introduction to Patrick's edition of Heraclitus, "[a]gainst the unity of Xenophanes, a unity opposed to the manifold, Heraclitus grasped the idea of a unity which included the manifold within itself" (Patrick 27). Note Julian's wording "in which oneing it is made endlessly holy." This is the end of the ascetic ideal that Eliot is portraying, of purification when the souls of the devout are rapt into communion with the flux, the divine fire of the λόγος, and the Ever-Becoming merges with the Eternal—the fire and the rose are one.

It is also the unification of the various themes seen throughout the long history of the ascetic ideal in Eliot's work: the desire for communion with others and with God manifested as Inge suggested in the λόγος, the need for purity, and detachment from the world and time.[63] No other consummation would do, according to his mystical readings. Consider Underhill's comment that

> "'[t]o know the hidden unity in the Eternal Being'—know it with an invulnerable certainty, in the all-embracing act of consciousness with which we are aware of those we truly love—is to live life at its fullest the

---

61    The connection between the Becoming, the Flux, the Heraclitean Fire, and the Son is fully delineated in Underhill 32–4.

62    Given the context, *Inferno* XXVI and XXVII seem less likely.

63    Cf. Inge *Personal Idealism* 44.

Illuminated life, enjoying 'all creatures in God and God in all creatures'[64] [...] [the soul] hears the crying aloud of that 'Word which is through all things everlastingly.' It participates, actively and open-eyed in the mighty journey of the Son towards the Father's heart: and seeing with purged sight all things and creatures as they are in that transcendent order, detects in them too that striving of Creation to return to its centre which is the secret of the Universe"

UNDERHILL 309–10.

Underhill has little interest in society or the possibility of the connection to others, but she nonetheless, expresses the same sentiment of restoration in and through the λόγος as the other orthodox mystical authors. However, it is Jones, who expresses the sentiment most succinctly, writing:

The great prayer of John 17 drops figures and utters the naked truth of a Divine-human fellowship—a union of spiritual beings with a spiritual Head,
    "Two distincts, division none,
    Number there in love is slain."[65]
We are here beyond the competitive basis of self-seeking individuals. The law is now each for other "all mine are thine, and thine are mine." The very condition and basis of such a self-denying fellowship is incorporation in the Divine Life: "I in them, thou in me, that they may be made perfect in one." This is the Divine event towards which all true mystical Christianity moves.

JONES 19.

Here, as ever in *Four Quartets*, Eliot is in the center of the orthodoxy of Christian mysticism as he knew it. Yet, even in a discussion of the ultimate fulfillment, the ascetic ideal is present: Underhill mentions the need for "purged sight" and Jones "a self-denying fellowship." And so it is with Eliot. A condition of complete simplicity comes before a discussion of the final fulfillment.

It seems that, in Eliot's case, the biblical proverb "train up a child in the way he should go: and when he is old, he will not depart from it" was true (Proverbs 22:6). He carried the ascetic ideal with him through parody and rebellion,

---

64     This is a quotation from Meister Eckhart that Underhill had previously highlighted during the chapter on purgation when discussing the virtues of detachment. Cf. Underhill 248.

65     Jones is slightly and most likely intentionally misquoting "The Phoenix and the Turtle" 27–8.

through faithless longing, to affirmation, and finally to hope in its promise. Eliot never claimed a place among the mystics; he did not assert that the ultimate vision, though perhaps desired, was his. At the end of "Little Gidding", he posits what the mystic hopes to see. Yet, the poetry shows a continual engagement with the need for purification in preparation for perfection in oneing with the λόγος, the end of his ascetic ideal.

CONCLUSION

# Summing

Let me conclude by, apart from the manifold technicality, telling the story of Eliot's ascetic ideal. Eliot's early encounters with the ascetic ideal began a lifetime of interplay and reflection upon self-denial, purgation, and self-surrender. In 1909, he began a study of mysticism, likely, in George Santayana's seminar, and thereafter showed the influence of this education. Yet, his interaction with the ascetic ideal and his background in mysticism was not a simple thing. Still, his early cynicism was slowly transformed to an embrace.

In the earliest period of his work, the poems written before his marriage in 1915, Eliot interrogates and parodies the ascetic ideal. Unsurprisingly, this is the period with the most direct, verbatim quotations from the mystical readings yet the least concerned with doctrines. Many of the authors quoted, such as Max Nordau, would not be lasting influences. In "The Love Song of J. Alfred Prufrock" particularly, Eliot seems to have used characterizations found in his readings to synthesize the behavior of Prufrock perched on a moment of crisis. Characters likes St. Sebastian and St. Narcissus are morbid inversions of saints who fail to achieve the ideal of purgation set out in Eliot's education. St. Sebastian performs his mortifications with an improper object, a woman instead of God, and St. Narcissus displays only self-love instead of the love of God. Each of these portraits of failure are informed by Eliot's education in mysticism and suggest a deliberate inversion of the ascetic ideal.

Eliot's interest in the ascetic ideal returned slowly following his doctoral study, but in 1916, he explored it along two distinct lines, a public vein through his prose and a private through his poetry. These two lines only merged after his conversion to Anglo-Catholicism. During his early work as a critic, Eliot began to formulate aesthetic positions rooted in the ascetic ideal. This may have been suggested by Underhill and Inge, both of whom include poets and other creative artists as quasi-mystics and discuss their need for purgation. While it is not difficult to connect impersonality to self-denial, even the idea of Tradition is often cast as a form of asceticism: artists must conform to a law outside of themselves. These two ideas are quickly integrated into Eliot's ongoing participation in the cultural war of Classicism versus Romanticism where his dislike of the latter is often couched in terms that suggest a lack of discipline and an overt emotionality begging for self-denial. As Eliot approaches his conversion, Royalism and an interest in Anglo-Catholicism are also absorbed into this complex of intellectual conservatism rooted in his ascetic ideal.

© KONINKLIJKE BRILL NV, LEIDEN, 2020 | DOI:10.1163/9789004375826_010

SUMMING 169

At the same time, a more personal integration of the ascetic ideal is occurring primarily through his poetry. In particular, Eliot is fascinated by the promise that, at the end of purification, there could be a mystical communion of souls. By 1919, his interest in mysticism began to recur as the influence of the skeptical philosophy of F. H. Bradley waned. References to the mystical authors and verbal echoes to the texts studied at Harvard begin to reappear somewhat frequently in the poetry written in this time period. While the poems still feature portraits of ascetic failure, there is a deeper engagement with the concepts in the mystical readings, and Eliot repeats many of these ideas as his own in his 1926 Clark Lectures. The ascetic ideal portrayed here focuses on the expansion of the self, an idea which also appears behind Eliot's interest in Tradition. As he read in the mystical authors, real communion with either the Absolute or other beings is only possible through the divine λόγος, but that purification was required for this to be actualized. Yet, at this skeptical time in his life, his poems, "Gerontion," *The Waste Land*, and "The Hollow Men," all show the dissolution of this ideal. There is a failure of purification evident in the lingering sense of sin, there is a deliberate omission of the λόγος in the poems, and the result is solipsistic isolation. Yet, there is nothing programmatic about the way that Eliot employs this particularly abstruse aspect of the ascetic ideal; the three themes occur largely separately in "Gerontion" but are almost wholly fused in "The Hollow Men."

When Eliot turned his attention to drama, he took an interest in the formal structure in the plays of Aristophanes, derived from his reading of F. M. Cornford's *Origin of Attic Comedy*. One of the core theses of Cornford's book is that Attic Old Comedy centers on a battle between concepts with society in the balance; the victorious principle effects the rejuvenation of the protagonist who is carried off in glory. While the application of Cornford to *Sweeney Agonistes* is a matter of critical consensus, a detailed investigation implies that the ascetic ideal, found in the epigraph to St John of the Cross, may be the principle for which Eliot argues, although the incomplete nature of the play stifles detailed interpretations. However, in his first complete play, *Murder in the Cathedral*, Eliot also appears to have employed an Aristophanic structure. As in *Sweeney Agonistes*, the ascetic ideal, submission to the divine, is the principle that Eliot puts forward. Thomas's primary struggle is against not only worldly temptations but self-will, which writers such as Underhill connected with the dark night of the soul. Eliot's early plays show clear evidence of his interest in asceticism.

Finally, in particularly the latter three *Quartets*, Eliot expresses, not in a play but in his own words, the ascetic ideal within the "orthodox" tradition of Christian mysticism, particularly as represented by Underhill who had become a personal friend. Unsurprisingly, there are very few instances of verbal echoes of his mystical education at this time, but Eliot comes to assert the doctrines he had read as his own. His usages of St John of the Cross and Julian of Norwich are in line with the way that he first encountered them in the mystical readings in his youth. Ultimately, the theodicy at the end of "Little Gidding" repeats in poetry the ideal of the mystical tradition: that at the end of purification, Jesus' prayer in John 17, that "[that all believers] may be one as we are one—I in them and you in me—so that they may be brought to complete unity," would be fulfilled (John 17:22–3).

# Bibliography

## Published Works by T. S. Eliot

*After Strange Gods*. London: Faber and Faber, 1934.

*The Annotated Waste Land, with Eliot's Contemporary Prose*. Ed. Lawrence S. Rainey. New Haven, Conn: Yale UP, 2006.

*Christianity and Culture*. New York: Harcourt, Brace, and World, 1949.

*Collected Poems: 1909–1962*. London: Harcourt Brace & Company, 1963.

*The Collected Prose of T. S. Eliot*. Ed. Ronald Schuchard and Jewel Spears Brooker. Vol. I. Baltimore: Johns Hopkins UP. 2014.

*The Collected Prose of T. S. Eliot*. Ed. Ronald Schuchard and Anthony Cuda. Vol. II. Baltimore: Johns Hopkins UP. 2014.

*The Collected Prose of T. S. Eliot*. Ed. Ronald Schuchard, Francis Dickey, and Jennifer Formicelli. Vol. III. Baltimore: Johns Hopkins UP. 2015.

*The Collected Prose of T. S. Eliot*. Ed. Ronald Schuchard and Jason Harding. Vol. IV. Baltimore: Johns Hopkins UP. 2015.

*The Collected Prose of T. S. Eliot*. Ed. Ronald Schuchard, Iman Javadi, and Jayme Stayer. Vol. V. Baltimore: Johns Hopkins UP. 2015.

*The Collected Prose of T. S. Eliot*. Ed. Ronald Schuchard and David Chinitz. Vol. VI. Baltimore: Johns Hopkins UP. 2017.

*The Collected Prose of T. S. Eliot*. Ed. Ronald Schuchard and Iman Javadi. Vol. VII. Baltimore: Johns Hopkins UP. 2018.

*The Criterion*. Vol. II. London: Faber and Faber, 1966.

*Inventions of the March Hare: Poems 1909–1917*. Ed. Christopher Ricks. New York: Harvest Books, 1998.

Introduction. *Pascal's Pensees*. By Blaise Pascal. Ed. W. F. Trotter. New York: Dutton, 1958.

*Knowledge and Experience in the Philosophy of F. H. Bradley*. London: Faber and Faber, 1964.

*The Letters of T. S. Eliot*. Ed. Valerie Eliot and John Haffenden. Vol. I. London: Faber and Faber. 2009.

*The Letters of T. S. Eliot*. Ed. Valerie Eliot and John Haffenden. Vol. II. London: Faber and Faber. 2009.

*The Letters of T. S. Eliot*. Ed. Valerie Eliot and John Haffenden. Vol. III. London: Faber and Faber. 2012.

*The Letters of T. S. Eliot*. Ed. Valerie Eliot and John Haffenden. Vol. IV. London: Faber and Faber. 2013.

*The Letters of T. S. Eliot*. Ed. Valerie Eliot and John Haffenden. Vol. V. London: Faber and Faber. 2014.

172

BIBLIOGRAPHY

*The Letters of T. S. Eliot.* Ed. Valerie Eliot and John Haffenden. Vol. VI. London: Faber and Faber. 2015.

*The Letters of T. S. Eliot.* Ed. Valerie Eliot and John Haffenden. Vol. VII. London: Faber and Faber. 2017.

*The Poems of T. S. Eliot.* Ed. Christopher Ricks and Jim McCue. Vol. I. Baltimore: Johns Hopkins UP, 2015.

*The Poems of T. S. Eliot.* Ed. Christopher Ricks and Jim McCue. Vol. II. Baltimore: Johns Hopkins UP, 2015.

*Murder in the Cathedral.* New York: Harcourt, 1963. Rpt.

*On Poetry and Poets.* London: Faber and Faber, 1969.

*Poems Written in Early Youth.* London: Faber and Faber, 1967.

*The Sacred Wood.* London: Faber and Faber, 1997.

*Selected Prose of T. S. Eliot.* Ed. Frank Kermode. New York: Harcourt Brace Jovanovich, 1975.

*To Criticize the Critic and Other Writings.* New York: Ocatagon, 1980.

*The Use of Poetry and the Use of Criticism.* 2nd ed. London: Faber and Faber, 1944.

*The Varieties of Metaphysical Poetry.* Ed. Ronald Schuchard. London: Faber and Faber, 1993.

*The Waste Land: A Facsimile.* Ed. Valerie Eliot. New York: Harcourt Brace Jovanovich, 1971.


## Unpublished Works by T. S. Eliot

"[Aristotle: Definition of Metaphysics]." Additional Papers (MS Am 1691.14 30). Houghton Library, Harvard University.

"[Causality]." Additional Papers (MS Am 1691.14 18). Houghton Library, Harvard University.

"The Bible as Scripture and Literature" (MS Am 1691 26). Houghton Library, Harvard University.

"[Εἶδος]." Additional Papers (MS Am 1691.14 20). Houghton Library, Harvard University.

"[Ethics]." Additional Papers (MS Am 1691.14 32). Houghton Library, Harvard University.

"[Ethics of Green and Sidgwick]." Additional Papers (MS Am 1691.14 32). Houghton Library, Harvard University.

"Letters to Eleanor Hinkley." Correspondence, 1910–1970 (MS Am 2244). Houghton Library, Harvard University.

"Letters to Mary Trevelyan." Correspondence, 1940–1956 (MS Am 1691.2). Houghton Library, Harvard University.

BIBLIOGRAPHY 173

"[Matter and Form]." Additional Papers (MS Am 1691.14 30). Houghton Library, Harvard University.

"Notecards." (MS Am 1691 129). Houghton Library, Harvard University.

"[Notes on a text]." Additional Papers (MS Am 1691.14 10). Houghton Library, Harvard University.

"[Notes on Aristotle]." Additional Papers (MS Am 1691.14 16). Houghton Library, Harvard University.

"[Notes on Aristotle]." Additional Papers (MS Am 1691.14 17). Houghton Library, Harvard University.

"[Notes on Eastern philosophy]" Additional Papers (MS Am 1691.14 12). Houghton Library, Harvard University.

"[Notes on] Fine arts 20b." Additional Papers (MS Am 1691.14 7). Houghton Library, Harvard University.

"[Notes on Italy]." (MS Am 1691 131). Houghton Library, Harvard University.

"[Notes on lectures of Henri Bergson.]" (MS Am 1691 130). Houghton Library, Harvard University.

"[Notes on logic]." Additional Papers (MS Am 1691.14 11). Houghton Library, Harvard University.

"[Notes on logic]." Additional Papers (MS Am 1691.14 13). Houghton Library, Harvard University.

"[Notes on logic]." Additional Papers (MS Am 1691.14 15). Houghton Library, Harvard University.

"[Notes on] Philosophy 10." Additional Papers (MS Am 1691.14 9). Houghton Library, Harvard University.

"Object and Point of View." Additional Papers (MS Am 1691.14 26). Houghton Library, Harvard University.

"[On Change]." Additional Papers (MS Am 1691.14 19). Houghton Library, Harvard University.

"[On Definition]." Additional Papers (MS Am 1691.14 25). Houghton Library, Harvard University.

"[On Matter]." Additional Papers (MS Am 1691.14 28). Houghton Library, Harvard University.

"[On Objects]." Additional Papers (MS Am 1691.14 21). Houghton Library, Harvard University.

"[On Objects]." Additional Papers (MS Am 1691.14 23). Houghton Library, Harvard University.

"[On Objects]." Additional Papers (MS Am 1691.14 24). Houghton Library, Harvard University.

"A Paper on Bergson" (MS Am 1691 132). Houghton Library, Harvard University.

"Physiology of organs of skin." Additional Papers (MS Am 1691.14 8). Houghton Library, Harvard University.

"The Validity of Artificial Distinctions." Additional Papers (MS Am 1691.14 27). Houghton Library, Harvard University.

Eliot, Charlotte C. [Poetry] (67). T. S. Eliot Collection (MS Am 2560). Houghton Library, Harvard University.


## Other Works

Akroyd, Peter. *T. S. Eliot: A Life*. New York: Simon and Schuster, 1984.

Alighieri, Dante. *Divina Commedia*. Ed. Giorgio Petrocchi. Milan: Mondadori, 1966–7. *The Princeton Dante Project*. Princeton University. Web.

Alighieri, Dante. "Epistle to Can Grande." *Epistola*. Ed. Ermenegildo Pistelli. Florence: *Societa' Dantesca Italiana*, 1960. Trans. Paget Toynbee. *Princeton Dante Project*. Princeton University, 1998. Web.

Alighieri, Dante. *Inferno*. Trans. Robert Hollander and Jean Hollander. Doubleday/Anchor, 2000. *Princeton Dante Project*. Princeton University. Web.

Alighieri, Dante. *Paradiso*. Trans. Robert Hollander and Jean Hollander. Doubleday/ Anchor, 2007. *Princeton Dante Project*. Princeton University. Web.

Alighieri, Dante. *Purgatorio*. Trans. Robert Hollander and Jean Hollander. Doubleday/ Anchor, 2003. *Princeton Dante Project*. Princeton University. Web.

Alighieri, Dante. *The Inferno of Dante: a New Verse Translation*. Trans. Robert Pinsky. Ed. Nicole Pinsky. New York: Noonday, 1997.

Alighieri, Dante. *The Paradiso*. Trans. John Ciardi. New York: Signet Classic, 2001.

Alighieri, Dante. *The Purgatorio*. Trans. John Ciardi. New York: Signet Classic, 2001.

Andrewes, Lancelot. *Seventeen Sermons on the Nativity*. London: Griffith, Farran, Okeden, and Welsh, 1850.

Aristophanes. *Aristophanes I: Acharnians, Knights*. Trans. Jeffrey Henderson. Cambridge, MA: Harvard UP, 1998. Loeb Classical Library.

Aristophanes. *Aristophanes II: Clouds, Wasps, Peace*. Trans. Jeffrey Henderson. Cambridge, MA: Harvard UP, 1998. Loeb Classical Library.

Aristophanes. *Aristophanes III: Birds, Lysistrata, Women at the Thesmophoria*. Trans. Jeffrey Henderson. Cambridge, MA: Harvard UP, 2000. Loeb Classical Library.

Aristophanes. *Aristophanes IV: Frogs, Assemblywomen, Wealth*. Trans. Jeffrey Henderson. Cambridge, MA: Harvard UP, 2002. Loeb Classical Library.

Aristophanes. *Aristophanes V: Fragments*. Trans. Jeffrey Henderson. Cambridge, MA: Harvard UP, 2007. Loeb Classical Library.

Augustinus, Aurelius. *St Augustine's Confessions*. Trans. William Watts. Vol. II. Cambridge (Mass.): Harvard UP, 1988.

# BIBLIOGRAPHY

Badenhausen, Richard. *T. S. Eliot and the Art of Collaboration*. Cambridge: CUP, 2004.

Bergsten, Staffan. *Time and Eternity: A Study in the Structure and Symbolism of T. S. Eliot's Four Quartets*. Stockholm: Scandinavian University, 1960.

Bradley, F. H. *Appearance and Reality*. 2nd ed. London: Swan Sonnenschein, 1897.

Brooker, Jewel Spears. *Mastery and Escape: T. S. Eliot and the Dialectic of Modernism*. Amherst: University of Massachusetts, 1994.

Browne, E. Martin. *The Making of T. S. Eliot's Plays*. Cambridge: CUP, 1969.

Bultmann, Rudolf Karl. *The Gospel of John: A Commentary*. Trans. Rupert William, Noel Hoare, and John Kenneth Riches. Oxford: B. Blackwell, 1971.

Burnet, John. *Early Greek Philosophy*. 2nd ed. London: Adam and Charles Black, 1908.

Bush, Ronald. *T. S. Eliot: A Study in Character and Style*. New York: OUP, 1983.

Buttram, Christine. "*Sweeney Agonistes*: A Sensational Snarl." *A Companion to T. S. Eliot*. Ed. David Chinitz. Chichester: Wiley Blackwell, 2014.

Caldecott, A. A. *The Philosophy of Religion*. London: Methuen, 1901.

Childs, Donald J. *From Philosophy to Poetry*. London: Athlone, 2001.

Childs, Donald J. *Modernism and Eugenics: Woolf, Eliot, Yeats, and the Culture of Degeneration*. Cambridge, UK: Cambridge UP, 2001.

Childs, Donald J. *T. S. Eliot: Mystic, Son, and Lover*. New York: St. Martin's P, 1997.

Chinitz, David. *T. S. Eliot and the Cultural Divide*. Chicago: Chicago UP, 2003.

Coleridge, Samuel Taylor. *The Major Works*. Ed. H. J. Jackson. Oxford Worlds Classics. Oxford: OUP, 2008.

Comley, Nancy R. "From Narcissus To Tiresias: T. S. Eliot's Use Of Metamorphosis." Modern Language Review 74.2 (1979): 281–86.

Cooper, John Xiros. *T. S. Eliot and the Politics of Voice: The Argument of The Waste Land*. Ann Arbor, Mich.: UMI Research, 1987.

Cornford, Francis. *The Origin of Attic Comedy*. London: Edwin Arnold, 1914.

Crawford, Robert. *The Savage and the City in the Work of T. S. Eliot*. New York: OUP, 1987.

Cutten, George B. *The Psychological Phenomena of Christianity*. New York: Charles Scribner's Sons, 1908. Rpt. Nabu Public Domain.

Däumer, Elisabeth, and Shyamal Bagchee, eds. *The International Reception of T. S. Eliot*. London: Continuum, 2007.

Donoghue, Denis. *Words Alone: The Poet, T. S. Eliot*. New Haven: Yale UP, 2000.

Dübner, Frederich. *Scholia Graeca in Aristophanem: Cum Prolegomenis Grammaticorum, Varietate Lectionis Optimorum Codicum Integra, Ceterorum Selecta, Annotatione Criticorum Item Selecta*. Paris: Firmin-Didot, 1855. *Archive.org*. University of Toronto, 27 Feb. 2009. Web.

Ellmann, Maud. *Poetics of Impersonality: T. S. Eliot and Ezra Pound*. Brighton, Sussex: Harvester, 1987.

Ferguson, Raquel Halty. *Laforgue Y Lugones: Dos Poetas De La Luna*. London: Tamesis, 1980.

Frazer, James George. *The Golden Bough*. Ed. Robert Fraser. Oxford: OUP, 1994.

Frye, Northrop. *T. S. Eliot*. London: Oliver and Boyd, 1968.

Gardner, Helen. *The Art of T. S. Eliot*. London: Cresset, 1949.

George, A. G. *T. S. Eliot: His Mind and Art*. London: Asia House, 1962.

Gish, Nancy K. *Time in the Poetry of T. S. Eliot*. London: Macmillan, 1981.

Gomperz, Theodor. "Empedocles." *Greek Thinkers*. Trans. Laurie Magnus. Vol. I. London: John Murray, 1901.

Gordon, Lyndall. *Eliot's Early Years*. Oxford: OUP, 1977.

Gordon, Lyndall. *T. S. Eliot: an Imperfect Life*. New York: W. W. Norton, 1998.

Gray, Piers. *T. S. Eliot's Intellectual and Poetic Development, 1909–1922*. Brighton, Sussex: Harvester, Humanities, 1982.

Grove, Robin. "Pereira and after: the cures of Eliot's theater." *The Cambridge Companion to T. S. Eliot*. Ed. A. D. Moody. Cambridge: CUP. 2005 Rpt.

Habib, M. A. R. *The Early T. S. Eliot and Western Philosophy*. New York: Cambridge UP, 1999.

Harding, Jason, *The Criterion: Cultural Politics and Periodical Networks in Inter-war Britain*. Oxford: OUP, 2002.

Harding, Jason. Ed. *T. S. Eliot in Context*. Cambridge, UK: CUP, 2011.

Hargrove, Nancy Duvall. *T. S. Eliot's Parisian Year*. Gainesville: Florida UP, 2009.

Hay, Eloise Knapp. *T. S. Eliot's Negative Way*. Cambridge, Mass: Harvard UP, 1982.

Holmes, Anne. *Jules LaForgue and Poetic Innovation*. Oxford: Clarendon, 1993.

Inge, William R. *Christian Mysticism*. London: Methuen, 1899.

Inge, William R. *Personal Idealism and Mysticism*. London: Longmans Green, 1907. The Paddock Lectures. Rpt. Kessinger.

Inge, William R. *The Philosophy of Plotinus*. Vol. I. London: Longmans, Green, and, 1919.

Inge, William R. *Studies of English Mystics*. London: John Murray, 1907.

Jain, Manju. *T. S. Eliot and American Philosophy*. Cambridge: CUP, 1992.

James, Henry. *The Ambassadors*. Oxford: Oxford World Classics, 2008.

James, William. *The Varieties of Religious Experience*. 2nd Ed. Rpt. New York: Longmans, Green, and, 1919.

Jevons, Frank B. *An Introduction to the History of Religion*. London: Methuen, 1896.

Jones, Rufus M. *Studies in Mystical Religion*. 1st ed. Rpt. London: Macmillan, 1919.

Julian of Norwich. *Julian of Norwich: Showings*. Trans. Edmund Colledge and James Walsh. New York: Paulist, 1978.

Kearns, Cleo McNelly. *T. S. Eliot and Indic Traditions*. Cambridge [Cambridgeshire]: Cambridge UP, 1987.

Kendall, Tim. "'Joy, Fire, Joy': Blaise Pascal's 'memorial' and the Visionary Explorations of T. S. Eliot, Aldous Huxley, and William Golding." *Literature and Theology* 11.3 (1997): 299–312.

# BIBLIOGRAPHY

Kenner, Hugh. *The Invisible Poet* (*University Paperbacks*). New York: Routledge, 1965.

Kim, Dal-Yong. *Puritan Sensibility in T. S. Eliot's Poetry*. Grand Rapids: Peter Lang, 1994.

Kirk, Russell. *Eliot and His Age*. 2nd ed. Washington: Isi, 2008.

Laforgue, Jules. *Poems of Jules Laforgue*. Trans. Peter Dale. London: Anvil Poetry, 2001.

Liddell, Henry George, and Robert Scott, comps. *A Greek-English Lexicon*. Ed. Henry Stuart Jones and E. A. Barber. Oxford: Clarendon, 1977.

Lotze, Hermann. *Outlines of the Philosophy of Religion*. Trans. George T. Ladd. Boston: Ginn, Heath, &, 1885.

MacDiarmid, Laurie J. *T. S. Eliot's Civilized Savage: Religious Eroticism and Poetics*. New York: Routledge, 2003.

MacDonald, George. *The Princess and the Curdie*. London: Blackie and Son, 1888.

Malamud, Randy. "Eliot's 1930s Plays." *A Companion to T. S. Eliot*. Ed. David Chinitz. Chichester: Wiley Blackwell, 2014.

Malm, M. W. "Checks and Balances: Functions of Mysticism in T. S. Eliot's Prose." *Zeitschrift fur Anglistik und Amerikanistik* 51.1–2 (2003): 113–22.

Manganiello, Dominic. *T. S. Eliot and Dante*. New York: St. Martin's, 1989.

Marett, R. R. *The Threshold of Religion*. 2nd ed. London: Methuen, 1914.

Mayer, John T. *T. S. Eliot's Silent Voices*. New York: OUP, 1989.

McCaslin, Susan. "Vision and Revision in Four Quartets: T. S. Eliot and Julian of Norwich." *Mystics Quarterly* 12.4 (1986): 171–78.

Medcalf, Stephen. "Points of View, Objects, and Half-Objects." *T. S. Eliot and Our Turning World*. Ed. Jewel S. Brooker. New York: St. Martin's, 2001. 63–79.

Menand, Louis. *Discovering Modernism: T. S. Eliot and His Context*. London: OUP, 1987.

Moody, A. D. *Tracing T. S. Eliot's Spirit: Essays on his Poetry and Thought*. Cambridge: CUP, 1996.

Moody, A. D. *T. S. Eliot: Poet*. Cambridge: CUP, 1979.

Murray, Paul. *T. S. Eliot and Mysticism: the Secret History of* Four Quartets. MacMillan: Basingstoke, 1991.

Neff, Rebeccah. "'New Mysticism' in the Writings of May Sinclair and T. S. Eliot." *Twentieth Century Literature* 26.1 (1980): 82–108.

Nordau, Max. *Degeneration*. 5th ed. London: William Heineman, 1895.

Patrick, G. T. W., trans. *The Fragments of the Work of Heraclitus On Nature*. Boston: N. Murray, 1889.

Peter, John. "*Murder in the Cathedral*." *T. S. Eliot*. Ed. Hugh Kenner. Englewood Cliffs: Prentice Hall, 1962.

Plato. *The Dialogues of Plato*. Trans. Benjamin Jowett. Vol. I. New York: Random House, 1937.

Plato. *The Dialogues of Plato*. Trans. Benjamin Jowett. Vol. II. New York: Random House, 1937.

Poulan, August. *The Graces of Interior Prayer*. Trans. Daniel Considine. Kessinger, 2010.

Pratt, James B. *The Psychology of Religious Belief*. New York: Macmillan, 1907. Rpt. BiblioLife.

Raine, Craig. *T. S. Eliot*. London: OUP, 2006.

Rainey, Lawrence S. *Revisiting* The Waste Land. New Haven, Conn: Yale UP, 2005.

Récéjac, E. *Essay on the Bases of the Mystic Knowledge*. Trans. Sara Carr Upton. New York: Charles Scribner's Sons, 1899. Rpt. Kessinger.

Reckford, Kenneth. "Recognizing Venus (II): Dido, Aeneas, and Mr. Eliot." *Arion* 3rd 3.2/3 (1996): 43–80. *JStor*. Web.

Reeves, Gareth. *T. S. Eliot: A Virgilian Poet*. New York: St. Martin's P, 1989.

Richards, E. Randolph. "John: Signs of the Restoration." Ed. C. Marvin Pate. *The Story of Israel: A Biblical Theology*. Downers Grove, IL: InterVarsity, 2004. 153–76.

Ricks, Christopher B. *Decisions and Revisions in T. S. Eliot*. London: British Library, Faber & Faber, 2003.

Robertson, O. Palmer. *The Books of Nahum, Habakkuk, and Zephaniah*. Grand Rapids, MI: W. B. Eerdmans, 1990. The New International Commentary on the Old Testament.

Rose, Jaqueline. "Hamlet—The Mona Lisa of Literature." *T. S. Eliot*. Ed. Harriet Davidson. New York: Longman, 1998. 181–96.

Santayana, George. *Three Philosophical Poets*. Boston: Harvard, 1910.

Schneider, Elisabeth Wintersteen. *T. S. Eliot: The Pattern in the Carpet*. Berkeley: University of California, 1975.

Schuchard, Ronald. *Eliot's Dark Angel: Intersections of Life and Art*. New York: OUP, 1999.

Scofield, Martin. *T. S. Eliot: The Poems*. Cambridge: CUP, 1988.

Sewell, Elizabeth. "Lewis Carroll and T. S. Eliot as Nonsense Poets." *T. S. Eliot*. Ed. Hugh Kenner. Englewood Cliffs: Prentice-Hall, 1961.

Shakespeare, William. *Hamlet*. Ed. Ann Thompson and Neil Taylor. Arden Shakespeare. 3rd Ed. Revised. Bloomsbury.

Skaff, William. *The Philosophy of T. S. Eliot*. Philadelphia: University of Pennsylvania, 1986.

Smidt, Kristian. *Poetry and Belief in the Work of T. S. Eliot*. 2nd ed. London: Routledge and Kegan Paul, 1961.

Smith, Carol H. *T. S. Eliot's Dramatic Theory and Practice*. New York: Gordian, 1977.

Smith, Grover Cleveland. *T. S. Eliot and the Use of Memory*. Lewisburg: Bucknell UP, 1996.

Southam, B. C. *A Guide to the Selected Poems of T. S. Eliot*. San Diego: Harcourt Brace, 1996.

Spicq, Ceslas. "Hypostasis." *Theological Lexicon of the New Testament*. Trans. James D. Ernest. Vol. III. Peabody, MA: Hendrickson, 1994.

BIBLIOGRAPHY

179

Spurr, Barry. *"Anglo-Catholic in Religion": T. S. Eliot and Christianity*. Cambridge: Lutterworth, 2010.

Srivastava, Narsingh. *The Poetry of T. S. Eliot*. New Delhi: Sterling, 1991.

Starbuck, Edwin D. *The Psychology of Religion*. London: Walter Scott, 1899.

Sultan, Stanley. *Eliot, Joyce, and Company*. New York: OUP, USA, 1990.

Suso, Henry. *The Life of Blessed Henry Suso by Himself*. Trans. Thomas F. Knox. Ed. W. R. Inge. 2nd ed. London: Methuen, 1913. Rpt. Kessinger 2009.

Svarny, Erik. *The Men of 1914: T. S. Eliot and Early Modernism*. Chicago: Open UP, 1989.

Symons, Arthur. *The Symbolist Movement in Literature*. 2nd ed. London: Constable, 1911.

Terrien, Samuel. "The Pantomime Cat: T. S. Eliot and Hebrew-Christian Dynamics." *Theology Today* 44.4 (1988): 450–61.

Underhill, Evelyn. *The Cloud of Unknowing*. Mineola, NY: Dover Publications, 2003.

Underhill, Evelyn. *Mysticism*. Third ed. London: Methuen, 1912.

Underhill, Francis. *Prayer in Modern Life*. London, A. R. Mowbray, 1929. Rpt. Kessinger.

Virgil. *Vergil's Aeneid and Fourth ("Messianic") Eclogue in the Dryden Translation*. Trans. John Dryden. Ed. Howard Clarke. University Park: Pennsylvania State UP, 1989.

von Arnim, Hans, ed. *Stoicorum Veterum Fragmenta*. Vol. I. Stuttgart: Stuttgart UP, 1905.

von Hochheim, Eckhart. *Meister Eckhart*. Trans. Raymond B. Blakney. 2nd ed.. New York: Harper & Brothers, 1941.

Ward, David. "The Pain of Purgatory." *T. S. Eliot's Murder in the Cathedral*. Ed. Harold Bloom. New York: Chelsea House, 1988.

Williamson, George. *A Reader's Guide to T. S. Eliot*. New York: The Noonday P, 1953.

Wilson, Frank. *Six Essays on the Development of T. S. Eliot*. London: Fortune, 1948.

Wolosky, Shira. *Language Mysticism: The Negative Way of Language in Eliot, Beckett, and Celan*. Stanford, CA: Stanford UP, 1995.

Woods, James H. *Practice and Science of Religion*. New York: Longmans, Green, and Co, 1906.

Woods, James H. *The Value of Religious Facts: a Study of Some Aspects of the Science of Religion*. New York: E. P. Dutton, 1899.

Wright, Doris. "Metaphysics through Paradox in T. S. Eliot's Four Quartets." *Philosophy & Rhetoric* 23.1 (1990): 63–9.

# Index

## Works by T. S. Eliot

"An American Critic"   2, 40, 41, 49, 50, 60
"Andrew Marvell"   67
*Ariel*   4–5
"Artists and Men of Genius"   44
*Ash-Wednesday*   4, 33, 150
"Appearances, Appearances"   18, 39, 62

"Baudelaire"   95
"The Beating of a Drum"   119
"Ben Jonson"   114–115
"Beyle & Balzac"   66
"The Bible as Scripture and Literature"   159
"Burnt Norton"   133, 134, 137, 139–143, 154, 158

"Commentary – April 1924"   49–50
"Commentary – July 1924"   69
"*Conscience and Christ*"   48–49
"Contemporanea"   53

"Dante (1920)"   109, 153–154, 164
"Dante (1929)"   65, 109, 112
"The Death of St Narcissus"   3, 20, 27–29, 32, 36–39, 97, 168
"The Dry Salvages"   1, 64, 137, 151–159
"Durkheim (I)"   2, 48, 49, 115

"East Coker"   6, 106, 137–151, 154
"Eeldrop and Appleplex"   30
"*Elements of Folk Psychology*"   44
"Euripides and Professor Murray"   115
"F. H. Bradley"   63–64

"[Finite Centres and Points of View]"   70, 73, 157
"The Function of Criticism"   39, 41, 54–59, 66
"The Function of a Literary Review"   45–46

"Gerontion"   4, 16, 38, 61, 68, 70, 73, 80, 81, 83, 86, 87, 89–98, 104, 106, 108, 112, 138, 156, 169

"*Group Theories of Religion* (I)"   52, 115
"*Group Theories of Religion* (II)"   52, 54, 115

"Hamlet"   22
"The Hippopotamus"   28
"The Hollow Men"   4, 61, 68, 70, 73, 82, 83, 86, 94, 95, 97, 106, 108–113, 119, 121, 138, 156, 169
*Knowledge and Experience*   157
*The Idea of a Christian Society*   139, 162
"The Idea of a Literary Review"   46–47
"In Memory of Henry James"   43, 46
"Mr. Eliot's Sunday Morning Service"   86–89
"The Interpretation of Primitive Ritual"   115

"Lancelot Andrewes"   44, 47, 60
"Leibniz's Monads and Bradley's Finite Centres"   62–63, 69–70
"The Lessons of Baudelaire"   54
"The Letters of J. B. Yeats"   51
"Little Gidding"   137, 140, 151, 159–167, 169, 170
"The Love Song of J. Alfred Prufrock"   3, 18, 20–27, 65, 168
"The Love Song of St Sebastian"   3, 20, 22–36, 38, 39, 97, 168
"Lune de Miel"   1, 107
"Mr. Read and Mr. Fernandez"   41, 47–48
"The Modern Dilemma"   1, 12

*Murder in the Cathedral*   5, 113–115, 121–133, 137, 142, 169
"A Note on the American Critic"   45
"On a Translation of Euripides"   45
"Paul Elmer More"   135
"*The Pensees of Pascal*"   154, 160
"The Perfect Critic"   153
    "Phillip Massinger"   115
"The Preacher as Artist"   52
"A Prediction in Regard to Three English Authors"   115
"Preface to *For Lancelot Andrewes*"   40
"Professional, or..."   53

INDEX

181

"Reflections on Contemporary
    Poetry (II)"   42
*"Reflections on Violence"*   54–55
"Relativity of Moral Judgment"   98
"Religion and Science (I)"   56
"Religion and Science (II)"   54
"Religion without Humanism"   2

"Sermon Preached in Magdalene
    College"   64
"Silence"   18
"A Song for Simeon"   145
"Studies in Contemporary Criticism (I)"
    53
*Sweeney Agonistes*   5, 73, 76, 113–121, 130, 133,
    169

*To Criticize the Critic*   63
"Tradition and the Individual Talent"   41–44,
    50–57
"Turgenev"   43
"Types of English Religious Verse"   145
*The Use of Poetry and The Use of
    Criticism*   137

*"Ultimate Belief"*   43
*"Ulysses*, Order, & Myth"   46, 115
Unpublished Course Notes   13, 17, 18, 33, 37,
    65, 69, 74, 77–79, 81, 82, 83, 87–89, 91,
    148–9

*Varieties of Metaphysical Poetry* (The Clark
    Lectures 1926)   11, 49, 74, 79–83, 91,
    109, 110

"War Paint and Feathers"   52
*The Waste Land*   1, 4, 7, 14, 23, 29, 39, 61,
    66–68, 70, 71, 73, 81, 83, 86, 94, 95,
    97–108, 112, 115, 138, 156, 169

## Other Authors and Works

Alighieri, Dante   14, 33, 65, 80–81, 92,
    95, 98, 99, 109, 110–112, 137, 151, 153,
    163, 164
Aristophanes   5, 113–118, 120–121, 123–126,
    128–133, 169
Aristotle   43, 57, 62, 65, 79, 82, 83

Andrewes, Lancelot   44, 47, 60, 86, 89–90,
    92, 95, 103
St Augustine   84, 90, 98, 99, 103, 107, 149

Baudelaire, Charles   5, 54, 95, 97
Badenhausen, Richard   131
Bergson, Henri   82, 115, 158
Bradley, F. H. (*Appearance and Reality*)   3,
    61–68, 70, 90, 91, 153, 169
Brooker, Jewel Spears   21, 43
Browne, E. Martin   122, 124, 128, 129
Browning, Robert   14, 78, 82, 145
Bultmann, Rudolf Karl   82
Burnet, John   16–18, 37–39, 87, 88, 105, 160
Bush, Ronald   20, 26, 93
Buttram, Christine   114, 115, 118, 120–127

Caldecott, A. A.   13, 17, 62, 64, 137
St Catherine of Genoa   127, 162
Childs, Donald   6, 12, 17, 23, 27, 28, 37, 62, 104
Chinitz, David   114–115
Comley, Nancy   37
Cornford, F. M. (*Origin of Attic Comedy*)   5,
    113–126, 128–133, 169
Crawford, Robert   16, 25, 37, 38, 114, 120
Cutten, G. B.   15, 28–30, 41, 49, 75, 78, 106

Donne, John   44, 47, 74, 79, 80, 81
Donoghue, Denis   20, 22–23

Ellmann, Maud   20, 23, 24, 26–28, 37, 38, 55
Euripides   114–115, 120, 123

Gomperz, Theodore   16–18, 37
Gordon, Lyndall   12, 16–18, 27, 30, 38

Habib, M. A. R.   22, 25
Harding, Jason   15, 69
Hargrove, Nancy   24, 25, 28
Hay, Eloise   5, 6, 16, 17, 20, 28, 37, 38, 142
Heraclitus   16, 37, 71, 82, 88, 148, 153, 158, 159,
    165

Inge, W. R. (in his person or in general)   5,
    13–15, 30, 33, 44, 67–69, 73, 77, 78, 82,
    134, 135, 168
    *Christian Mysticism*   4, 13, 14, 17, 29–33,
    38, 63, 69, 71–73, 75, 78, 80, 83, 84, 88,
    90, 91, 96, 99, 102, 103, 106, 107, 134,
    138–140, 143–147, 152, 157, 160

182 INDEX

Inge, W. R. (cont.)
  *Studies in English Mystics*   14, 29, 38, 41,
    73, 78, 91, 103, 136, 138, 143–145, 153, 156,
    162
  *Personal Idealism and Mysticism*   14, 37,
    41, 42, 70, 71, 75, 82, 84, 87, 88, 96, 100,
    138, 152, 153, 158, 165
  *Philosophy of Plotinus*   78

Jain, Manju   17
James, Henry (*The Ambassadors*)
    43, 118
James, William (*Varieties of Religious
    Experience*)   15, 17, 26, 30–32, 41, 106,
    135, 141
Jevons, F. B.   15, 17
St John of the Cross   91, 96, 110, 120, 126, 133,
    134, 139, 141–146, 157, 160, 169
Jones, Rufus (*Studies in Mystical
    Religion*)   13–15, 17, 29–34, 38, 39, 75,
    82, 91, 93, 101, 134, 140, 145, 153, 154, 157,
    159, 160, 166
Julian of Norwich   14, 98, 100, 135, 163–165,
    170

Kearns, Cleo   3, 103–4
Kenner, Hugh   20, 121

Laforgue, Jules   3, 22–26, 71
Lowell, James Russell   102–103
Lawrence, D. H.   7, 11, 91, 135

MacDiarmid, Laurie   16, 25, 27, 28, 35, 38
MacDonald, George   150–151
Malamud, Randy   132
Manganiello, Dominic   20, 25, 108
Marett, R. R.   16, 102
Moody, A. D.   25
Murray, Paul   6, 18, 137, 142, 143, 146, 149, 152,
    156, 159

Nordau, Max (*Degeneration*)   15–17, 20,
    23–25, 29, 30, 168

Plato   72, 74–81, 96, 110, 137, 148
Plotinus (*Enneads*)   29, 77–78, 81–82, 87–89,
    91, 153
Poulan, August   59, 78, 91, 96, 98, 110
Pound, Ezra   88, 105, 114, 135
Pratt, J. B.   16, 99, 102, 159
Rainey, Lawrence   27, 35, 97

Récéjac, E.   15, 29, 75, 98, 161
Richard of St Victor   2, 163
Ricks, Christopher   94, 99
Russell, Bertrand   11, 35, 69, 74

Santayana, George   16–18, 81, 95, 102
Schuchard, Ronald   18, 40, 42, 114, 119, 139,
    147
Smith, Carol   115
Smith, Grover   20, 22, 33, 34
Skaff, William   8, 12, 17, 18
Starbuck, E. D.   15, 21–23, 29, 49, 155
Sultan, Stanley   25, 124
Suso, Henry   26–27, 20–34, 36, 99, 154

St Teresa of Aviles   82, 160

Underhill, Evelyn (in her person or in gen-
    eral)   5, 11, 14, 29, 66, 67, 72, 76, 95, 127,
    134–136, 145, 168, 169
  *Mysticism*   2, 4, 5, 11–14, 16–18, 29, 30, 32,
    33, 41, 43, 45, 46, 50, 52, 55–57, 59, 64,
    66, 75, 82, 83, 91, 95, 97–99, 108, 110,
    126–128, 130, 133, 134, 138, 139, 144–147,
    149–151, 153–156, 158–160, 162–166
Underhill, Father Francis   14, 135, 136

Van Hochheim, Eckhart   15, 38, 59, 91, 99,
    146, 166
Virgil (*Aeneid*)   27, 65

Wagner, Richard   24, 98, 105
Wolosky, Shira   6
Woods, J. H.   1, 2, 15, 163
Wordsworth, William   14, 41, 56, 145

Printed in the United States
By Bookmasters